AUSTRALIAN CULTURAL STUDIES
Series editors: John Tulloch and Terry Threadgold

Communication and Cultural Literacy

An Introduction

Tony Schirato and Susan Yell

ALLEN & UNWIN

To Bill, Helen and Patricia

First published in 1996

Allen & Unwin Pty Ltd
9 Atchison Street, St Leonards, NSW 2065 Australia

Phone: (61 2) 9901 4088
Fax: (61 2) 9906 2218
E-mail: 100252.103@compuserv.com

National Library of Australia
Cataloguing-in-Publication entry:

Schirato, Anthony.
    Communication and cultural literacy: an introduction.

    Bibliography.
    Includes index.
    ISBN 1 86448 040 8.

    1. Communication. 2. Communication and culture.
    3. Communication—Social aspects. I. Yell, Susan. II. Title.
    (Series: Australian cultural studies).

302.2

Set in 11/12 pt Adobe Garamond by DOCUPRO, Sydney
Printed by SRM Production Services Sdn Bhd, Malaysia

10 9 8 7 6 5 4 3 2 1

3/97
LR/LEND/001

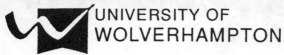 UNIVERSITY OF
WOLVERHAMPTON

Wolverhampton Learning Centre

St. Peter's Square
Wolverhampton   WV1 1RH

Wolverhampton (01902) 322305

Telephone Renewals: 01902 321333
**This item may be recalled at any time. Keeping it after it has
been recalled or beyond the date stamped may result in a fine.**
See tariff of fines displayed at the counter.

- 6 DEC 1997

- 9 OCT 2003

- 2 APR 1998

0 3 NOV 2006

2 5 FEB 2000

- 7 MAR 2000

1 2 JAN 2001

CONTENTS

ACKNOWLEDGMENTS

This book arose out of our need to develop material for use in teaching a first year subject in communication and cultural studies. To a large extent, the approach we have taken in this text has been directed by the responses to and feedback about the unit which our students gave us.

Professor David Birch and Professor Terry Threadgold gave us useful feedback on early drafts of the book. Pat Goon provided illustrations which are valuable supplements to the written text. Dr Wally Woods, Dean of Arts at Central Queensland University, provided support and encouragement, as did many of our colleagues within the faculty.

We gratefully acknowledge the support of Central Queensland University for making a period of study leave available to Susan Yell while she was working on this project.

Finally, we would like to thank Elizabeth Weiss, Jo Jarrah and Elizabeth Feizkhah at Allen & Unwin for their sound advice and exemplary professionalism.

Tony Schirato and Susan Yell
Central Queensland University
September 1995

SERIES EDITOR'S FOREWORD

Unlike the earlier books published in this series this book, *Communication and Cultural Literacy*, is an introductory text, one that attempts to signpost a field of enquiry, and to provide some basic tools and understandings for negotiating that field. In this the book is to be distinguished from the recent spate of cultural studies readers. It provides an introduction to the field in a way that those readers do not, an introduction of a kind that has not really been attempted since John Fiske's *Introduction to Communication Studies* (Methuen 1982) and Gunther Kress (ed.) *Communication and Culture* (NSW University Press 1988). Like those books this one does focus on communication as an essential part of cultural studies. Like the recent readers it also inevitably constructs its own version of cultural studies, one that includes an earlier Australian tradition of social semiotics, and places an important focus on textual studies. This book is an excellent introduction to a number of the theories and debates that inform current arguments in the field and it has the very considerable advantage of introducing them in ways that will be manageable for beginning students.

There was a time when we argued that cultural studies was about the displacement of an aesthetic, and largely literary, definition of culture by a broader, anthropological definition, a time when the struggle was for the recognition of the very existence of other cultural domains than those which had been encompassed by 'high' culture. But recent arguments (Goodall 1995; Frow 1995) have shown that the 'culture' which displaced high cultural definitions in mainstream cultural studies was Raymond Williams' version—and that it was flawed as the basis for an undertaking that would call itself 'cultural' studies. Goodall and Frow arrive at this conclusion in different ways but they both agree that the time for Williams' polemical argument for an undifferentiated culture has passed. Frow's very recent book provides a painstaking account of what might be involved in a more useful account of 'culture' for cultural studies by exploring and critiqueing the work of Pierre Bourdieu, Michel de Certeau, Laclau and Mouffe and a number of other Marxist and post-Marxist theorists. One of his conclusions is that current definitions and perceptions of the 'high' and the 'popular' are so problematic that we need to learn to construct them in quite different ways.

Like Goodall, Frow insists that 'high' culture is no longer the dominant form, but 'rather a *pocket* within commodity culture' (p.86) and, like Goodall, Frow argues that the 'high', because of its ability to appropriate the 'popular', is an essential part of what cultural studies must learn to understand. For Frow, this is because:

> Its (i.e., high culture's) primary relationship is not to the ruling class but to the intelligentsia, and to the education system which is the locus of their power and the generative point for most high-cultural practices. And like 'popular' culture, it can incorporate any number of quite heterogeneous aesthetic texts—from Jean Renoir to John Waters, from Palestrina to fusion rock, from Racine to Kathy Acker. (p.86–7)

Frow is quite explicit about the way in which we need to reconstruct these relationships between high and popular culture in cultural studies. The first essential is that 'the analysis of cultural texts must be set in relation to the institutionalised regimes of value that sustain them' (p.87). The second is to turn our attention away from 'that mythical popular subject immediate to observation' (p.87) and to focus on the relation of two kinds of practice—'a "first-order" practice of everyday culture, and the "second-order" practice of analysis of it conducted by a reader endowed with considerable cultural capital' (p.87).

If Frow's and Goodall's work has recently questioned the constitution of this apparently most basic of cultural studies' understandings of itself, Meaghan Morris and Stephen Muecke in their recent editorial in the first issue of *The UTS Review* have raised further questions about the packaging and selling of cultural studies, about false popular perceptions of the ubiquity of cultural studies in the Humanities and about the participation of cultural studies in what has become 'an expansion of interdisciplinary projects . . . barely thinkable thirty years ago' (p.2). These are questions we cannot ignore when it comes to those very issues of cultural value John Frow so carefully and productively puts on the cultural studies agenda. What do we teach our students in first year if we claim we are introducing them xii COMMUNICATION AND CULTURAL LITERACY

to 'cultural studies'? What are the intellectual interests at stake in such decisions, and what difficult questions do these pose for 'pedagogic strategy, political activity and the organisation of cultural institutions' (Frow 1995, p.159)? These are questions to which *Communication and Cultural Literacy* provides some answers.

Much that has been written of late about what is and is not cultural studies could benefit from some of Frow's careful analysis of intellectual 'interests' and from a better attempt to understand and account for, in both Frow's and Elspeth Probyn's (1993) senses, the positions from which we speak. In the McKenzie Wark report on the UTS editorial in *The Australian* Higher Education Review (Wednesday October 26, 1995, p.38) the sensibly articulated positions of Morris and Muecke are transformed in a media representation which is intertextually connected to that other media genre which periodically constructs the connections between English departments and the evils of foreign theory—a genre Morris and Muecke refer to when they speak of 'tirades about those jargon-ridden works of French theory' (p.1). In the *Australian* version of Morris and Muecke English departments are at it again—this time 'dressing themselves up as a marketing exercise' while 'the real action is elsewhere'. The anxiety about theory is expressed again later in: 'It would be a very bad moment indeed for cultural studies to become too theoretical or too caught up in the mundane task of rescuing English departments from oblivion'.

The agendas of this review are specifically anti-disciplinary, rather than interdisciplinary. They could do with some careful historical and textual analysis of the kind to which *Communication and Cultural Literacy* provides an introduction. Historically, of course, there are very good reasons for this concern with cultural studies in English Departments—the many different histories of cultural studies in the various cultural studies readers published of late all attest to these. But there are other reasons why this might be a particularly relevant place for cultural studies to take root (if not to masquerade and pretend to be what it is not). Frow is quite right to point out that one model for teaching how to move between incommensurable regimes is and always has been the study of literary texts from different historical periods, as a way of mediating interpretive frameworks. Frow argues only that this might be an 'established and regularised methodology' which indicates one possible way of teaching an openness to cultural difference. Morris and Muecke speak of 'work at the boundaries between literary and theoretical genres' as 'vitally connected to cultural studies' (p.3). Goodall is concerned with the importance of not ignoring or disparaging the 'high' in the rush to embrace the 'popular' and the specific, arguing that: 'a "Cultural Studies" which feels it is able to ignore high art, Culture with a capital C, even if only temporarily and for strategic reasons, seems to me to be a fatally compromised project' (p.172).

Perhaps most relevant to *Communication and Cultural Literacy* is the anti-English attitude to cultural studies expressed in the review, an attitude associated with another tendency, the tendency to want to remove the study of 'texts' from cultural studies, as if that, too, were too close to English. This is not at all the way Morris and Muecke see things. They argue strongly for the importance of 'history, textual analysis and social research' as part of cultural studies, recognising that there is a tendency to want to acquire one's 'cultural studies' credentials by demonstrating that one can talk about the 'popular' in abstract ways at the expense of the advantages of knowing how to look at the textual and the non-textual in their critical intersections. In this difference between Wark and Morris and Muecke one has to comment that John Frow is absolutely right about the intellectual 'interests', fears and desires which shape the current cultural studies canons and border skirmishes. These are differences, differences in reading formation and in positioning and context, that beginning students need to learn how to read and they are critical in the current constitution of cultural studies.

Here I will quote from Morgan, speaking from the social theory position in 1993, again against theory, with his plaintive cry that cultural studies is 'now more like philosophy than an exercise in semiotics' (p.13), his comparison of Meaghan Morris and McKenzie Wark as members of the 'French high intellectual tradition' and thus not 'proper' exponents of cultural studies, and his hankering for the 'more empirically grounded scholarship of British Cultural Studies' (p.13). He sets up a series of oppositions between empirical practice and theory, and between theory and semiotics/textual analysis, and clearly prefers (unreconstructed) ethnography to 'essays and studies of representations'.

I will not dwell here on the interesting incompatibility between his readings and those of Muecke and Morris. What I do want to do is to return for a moment to Frow and to his careful account of xlv COMMUNICATION AND CULTURAL LITERACY

ethnography and sociology within cultural studies, where he points to the conservative political implications of ethnomethodology's historical refusal of a metadiscourse, a position which 'makes it impossible to critique everyday processes' (p.136), and to the complexity of ethnography's own recent rewriting of itself in relation to its complicity with colonial domination (p.161). Both points bespeak the need for textual studies, semiotics and critical theory in any attempt, in an interdisciplinary enterprise like cultural studies, to bring together empirical and other disciplines whose regimes of knowledge are or were incommensurable. The textual, the discursive, the political and the theoretical are indispensable to interdisciplinarity. It is only rewritten, theorised versions of ethnography, sociology and anthropology and history which can begin to work in tandem in the field of cultural studies. There actually is a need, even in these theoretical debates and conjunctions, to remember what Bernstein said sociology had forgotten, that people speak, and as the linguist Michael Halliday (1978) put it: that people speak, 'not in solitude, but to one another' and that this is central to understanding 'how the innermost patterns of language and culture are transmitted through the countless microsemiotic processes of social interaction' (p.92).

This, it seems to me, is the way to make a connection between Frow's conclusions about what cultural studies is, or should be, and this book and its claims to introduce students to the complexity of some of the issues around cultural studies which I have been exploring. This is a book about communication as cultural process and about cultural literacy, the ability to read and write the everyday culture one inhabits and to know and have the resources to deal with the fact that that process requires negotiation and struggle. It is a book which engages with the question of just what cultural capital one needs to be able to engage in these debates, and which accepts that there is a need in the tertiary training of those who will become members of what Frow calls 'the knowledge industries', to 'read' at two levels—the everyday and the mediated. That is, it accepts the need for metalanguage and it accepts the need to be able to be self-reflexive about the self who does that reading and the positions that self takes up within particular reading formations. It is also a book which does not ignore the question of value.

Goodall quotes Jim McGuigan as saying that 'the study of culture is nothing if it is not about values' and that 'if we cannot say that the *Sun* has told lies on behalf of oppressive power we are in trouble' (p.273). This book is not in that kind of trouble. The reading strategies and methodologies it develops and makes accessible to students are strategies for understanding the complexities of the relationships between communication and cultural processes. It provides ways of contextualising the analysis of cultural texts in relation to the institutions and practices that sustain and organise them and it does this in ways that would allow precisely the re-thinking of the relations between the high and the popular in cultural studies that recent work demands.

It is also a book which is truly interdisciplinary, recognising the need for certain kinds of basic literacies, derived from many different disciplinary locations and theoretical positions, and acknowledging the need to theorise subjectivity and otherness and to provide access to theories about these things even in the introductory stages of a cultural studies curriculum. The authors range widely in their choice of textual examples. The themes and issues these examples raise always engage with global issues of subjectivity, gender, race and ethnicity, with issues of ideology and intertextuality, and with issues of value. The book provides an introduction to communication in cultural studies as 'an international and comparative practice' (Morris and Muecke p.2), and it faces squarely the need to teach about language, written text structures, and the values attached to different textual performances in different contexts, as part of that practice. The book does this in the process of teaching that communication is much more complex than language or verbal text itself, always addressing a range of mediums and focusing finally on the visual. That ordering of events, it seems to me, is important. Students entering tertiary study today are often more visually than verbally literate. Cultural studies cannot afford to ignore that if it wants seriously to engage with the need to provide for access to the kind of cultural capital which most of those currently theorising cultural studies already have.

Communication and Cultural Literacy problematises the idea of communication from its very first chapter, critiqueing the process model of communication with a number of telling examples. Pierre Bourdieu and the crucial notion of the habitus are introduced early and the NASA example which follows immediately confronts the reader with the problems of communication, context, value and interest that are always involved in policy decisions. Woven into the rest of the chapter in accessible and useful ways are issues of race, gender and ideology, and questions about the reading of critical theory and the possibility of different readerships. Chapter 2, which follows up on this with an introduction to Saussurean semiology, also contains an inbuilt critique, juxtaposing the Saussurean model with Volosinov and illustrating the difference with contentious issues around gender and race and two well chosen media texts on the theme of the discovery of Australia. Competing values and interests and different reading practices are constantly foregrounded.

Chapters 3, 4 and 5 are the chapters most influenced by the work of Australian social semiotics. Chapter 3 introduces the Hallidayan framework of field, tenor and mode to talk about the immediate context of textual production, providing a useful way of beginning to talk about what Frow calls incommensurable regimes of truth and value. Chapter 4 puts back into cultural studies some badly needed basic information about speech and writing, dialect, creoles and pidgins. These linguistic matters are nicely linked to Bernstein's notion of coding orientations and Bourdieu's habitus, so that the value of different kinds of linguistic and textual capital in different contextual markets is able to lead into a discussion of Bakhtin on dialogism. This chapter connects with Chapter 6 on written genres where there is a very useful discussion of lexical density and nominalisation in relation to questions of value and genre. Chapter 5 talks about intertextuality in the form of codes, narratives, genres and discourses as a way of thinking the relationship between contexts and texts. The textual examples here range from Vegemite jars to advertisements in which images of same (genres) are embedded, to media representations of Aboriginality and femininity in the persons of Pat O'Shane and Evonne Cawley. Chapter 7 returns to the wider question of cultural practice on which Chapter 5 is predicated and now seriously engages with the work of Pierre Bourdieu, dealing with the issues of subjectivity and objectivity, the habitus and the concepts of cultural field and cultural capital.

Chapters 8, 9 and 10 then circle back to pick up and discuss specifically three major issues that are implicit in most of the rest of the book—ideology, subjectivity and the making and reading of visual representations. Chapter 8 is particularly welcome in its discussion of the question of ideology as constructed by a number of prominent Marxist scholars—and indeed in its explicit discussion of Marxism as an issue in the theories and frameworks that inform cultural studies. Here this book makes real and important connections with John Frow's recent book. The chapter provides an important critical vocabulary and a clear sense of the notion of ideology as naturalised reading process, something of course which supports the argument of the book as a whole for the need for cultural literacy as cultural capital.

Chapter 9 addresses in detail the issues of subjectivity and sexual identity that are never far from the surface in this book. Again the discussion of a number of central informing theoretical positions provides a valuable critical vocabulary and a set of metalanguages as cultural capital. These include psychoanalysis (Freud and Lacan), Foucault on sexuality and the body and Judith Butler on the gender hierarchy in western cultures and the performed nature of gender genres and narratives.

Chapter 10 concludes the book with a 'making strange' of the visual, which, in the context of the rest of the book, can now be seen to be highly structured, constructed, intertextual and ideological as well as critically related to the questions of subjectivity and the performance of the gendered body addressed in the previous chapter. Given the naturalness of visual representation in our cultures, and the far greater access to it that most of our first year cultural studies students have than to the verbal and the textual, this seems to me to be an excellent way to conclude.

Communication and Cultural Literacy does not build disciplinary or anti-disciplinary fences within the interdisciplinary space of cultural studies. It allows semiotics, textual studies and philosophy, social and critical theory to talk to one another and shows how useful it might be to let them. It makes it clear throughout that men and women *do* cultural studies and that men and women, of all kinds, need to be addressed *by* cultural studies. That, it seems to me, is an important place to begin. Beyond that beginning, an introduction to the field which reaffirms the importance of communication and cultural literacy in cultural studies is what this book seeks to provide. It will be extremely valuable as a text wherever issues of cultural value, communication, cultural capital and cultural literacy are on the teaching agenda, and it offers, in accessible and challenging ways, the tools that are needed to understand and to engage with current debates.

Terry Threadgold

References

John Frow 1995 *Cultural Studies and Cultural Value*. Clarendon Press, Oxford.

Peter Goodall 1995 *High Culture, Popular Culture: The Long Debate*. Allen & Unwin, Sydney.

M.A.K. Halliday 1978 *Language as Social Semiotic: The Social Interpretation of Language and Meaning*. Arnold, London.

George Morgan 1993 'More Frenching: report from the 1993 Australian Cultural Studies Conference' *Arena* February–March 1994, pp.13–14.

Meaghan Morris and Stephen Muecke 'Editorial' in *The UTS Review* vol.1, no.1, 1995, pp.1–4.

Elspeth Probyn 1993 *Sexing the Self: Gendered Positions in Cultural Studies* Routledge, London and New York.

PREFACE

Communication and Cultural Literacy aims to provide readers with a set of perspectives, approaches and analytical techniques for understanding the range of practices which are labelled 'communication'. We understand communication as the practice of producing and negotiating meanings, a practice which always takes place under specific social, cultural and political conditions. If we take communication to be a set of situated practices, we need to adopt approaches to studying these which do not idealise communication. It follows that there are a number of choices we as authors have made about what to include in this book.

What this book is not: it is not a historical account of the development of either communication studies or cultural studies. It does not claim to or attempt to provide an account of current research in these fields. Nor is it a book about 'effective communication' or a 'how to . . . (write reports, make public speeches)' book. Useful as that kind of book is, our purpose here is to present the study of communication in a way that moves beyond the immediately pragmatic to equip readers with the means to reflect on and analyse a broad range of communication practices. That is, this book aims to develop the reader's critical understanding of communication in terms of:

- what is happening
- how it is happening, and
- what the consequences are of particular communicative acts and specific types of communicative practices.

We see this goal as pragmatic in the wider sense of equipping readers with flexible literacies which will be transposable from one context to another. Literacy, then, is a key term: this book aims to render visible (as opposed to transparent and naturalised) the forms of literacy which all members of a culture use in negotiating their daily lives. In doing so, it aims to help readers develop their own communicative and cultural literacies.

Both cultural studies and communication studies are traditionally interdisciplinary areas. In order to address the questions posed above, we call upon a range of theoretical approaches. We move between a number of theoretical positions and disciplinary areas, including cultural theory, semiotics (both 'classical' and 'social'), linguistics, media studies, psychoanalysis and Marxism.

The approaches we have selected, however, are linked by a commitment to the notion of communication as a contextualised practice. While we provide a brief introduction to basic concepts of classical structuralist semiotics, particularly the sign, we move on from this paradigm fairly quickly, because of its limitations in dealing with contexts. (Instead of the sign, we will treat the basic units of meaning making as texts or, more broadly, practices.) Social semiotics and related linguistic approaches are introduced for their usefulness in linking the analysis of texts to social contexts. Bourdieu provides a set of concepts for understanding practice and literacies in terms both of specific situations and of more general cultural systems. Marxist and neo-Marxist work on the relation between communication and ideology provides ways of understanding how specific communication practices are valued and deployed for political means (that is, for social groups to obtain or maintain power). Cultural theory derived from psychoanalysis enables us to make the important link between meaning-making practices and the ways in which people are assigned cultural identities, identities which have cultural values and ideological effects. These are the theoretical strands which inform this work.

The book focuses on three areas of communication practice which could be considered 'primary' systems of communication: spoken, written and visual communication. These are mediums of communication which are arguably central to most cultures, and integral to more complex technological mediums and systems. Spoken, written and visual genres, as well as a wide range of texts and genres which combine these, are used to introduce and exemplify theoretical concepts and modes of analysis. Examples range from popular culture texts (films, magazines, TV shows) to examples from everyday practice.

How to read this book: chapters are organised into a sequence so that later chapters build on concepts explained in earlier chapters.

Generally speaking, chapters move between introducing and contextualising sets of concepts (Chapters 1, 2, 3, 5, 7, 8, 9) to discussing
specific practices, genres and mediums (Chapter 4 on speech, Chapter
6 on writing, Chapter 10 on visual mediums). However, it is possible
to read the chapters in a different sequence, by using the Glossary
where necessary to supplement your understanding of new concepts.

1

COMMUNICATION AND CULTURE

This chapter addresses the complex and interdependent relationship between communication and culture, particularly in terms of the different ways in which these two concepts influence one another. We argue that meanings are not to be found or understood exclusively in terms of acts of communication, but are produced within specific cultural contexts. Moreover:

- communication can be understood as the practice of producing meanings
- communication practices refer to the ways in which systems of meaning are negotiated by participants in a culture, and
- culture can be understood as the totality of communication practices and systems of meaning.

In this chapter we will also introduce the concept of **cultural literacy**. Cultural literacy can be defined as both a knowledge of meaning systems and an ability to negotiate those systems within different cultural contexts. We argue that it is virtually impossible to describe and analyse what is happening in any communication context or practice without using the concept of cultural literacy.

In approaching communication as a cultural practice requiring various forms of cultural literacy, this text is strongly influenced by the work of Pierre Bourdieu. Bourdieu's ideas are particularly useful to our understanding of communication because of his suggestion that practice, or what people actually do, is both constrained by, and develops as a response to, the rules and conventions of a culture.

One way to understand the relation between culture and practice is through Bourdieu's metaphor of the journey and the map (Bourdieu 1990). Cultures are both the maps of a place (the rules and conventions) and the journeys that take place there (actual practices). Cultural literacy can be understood, then, as a 'feel' for negotiating those cultural rules and systems—for 'making your way' through a

Pierre Bourdieu is a French sociologist and cultural theorist who has written extensively on the relationship between cultural structures and practices. His earliest works were anthropological studies of Algerian people and culture, and include *The Algerians* and *Outline of a Theory of Practice*. He wrote important texts on the way education systems help reproduce certain cultural values and practices (such as *Reproduction in Education, Society and Culture*, with Jean-Claude Passeron), but his most influential work has dealt with the relationship between **cultural fields, capital** and power. These texts include *Distinction, The Logic of Practice, Language and Symbolic Power, In Other Words* and *The Field of Cultural Production*.

culture. And practice can be understood as the **performance** of cultural literacy.

Every communication practice (speaking to one another, wearing certain types of clothing) constitutes an additional part of those cultural maps. Communication and culture are not, then, separate entities or areas. Each is produced through a dynamic relationship with the other.

An example of the relationship between communication, context and cultural literacy can be found in the example of the way the *Challenger* disaster (the explosion of the US space shuttle *Challenger* in 1986 over Cape Canaveral, and the death of the seven astronauts, including a number of civilians, on board) has been interpreted and explained. One technical communication textbook said, for instance: 'The *Challenger* was not an engineering disaster; it was a communication disaster . . . [which shows that] good communication—especially for technically trained people—is essential' (Pattow 1993:11).

Now according to this (probably reasonably representative) account, the *Challenger* disaster occurred, not simply because there were engineering problems (the O-rings didn't set in place) but because the engineers involved couldn't adequately communicate the problem to management groups of both the company involved (Thiokol) and NASA. What is interesting about the account given in the textbook, however, is that it makes clear that the engineers did make several attempts, the night before the disaster, to alert management to the danger. The textbook assumed, because engineers were communicating to management, that the problem was a 'failure of communication'. In a sense they were right, but not in the way they think.

The textbook account of the disaster mentions a variety of contexts that could be brought to bear on why *Challenger* blew up:

- there had been engineering problems with NASA launches going back eight years
- both Thiokol and NASA were anxious to prove their capabilities and competence, which were under question, and
- this launch was important to the US space program, which had been dogged by postponements and technical failures.

There may also have been other political contexts, such as the prestige that politicians and the government wished to gain from a successful launch. The textbook mentions most of these factors, but in the end ditches them all in favour of the 'failure of communication' line.

Let's consider an alternative version—one which takes these contexts into account. Thiokol and NASA management knew about the potential danger, but they were under pressure to launch the shuttle anyway. When Thiokol and NASA engineers tried to convince management to postpone, they ran into a stone wall (as one engineer described it: 'Arnie actually got up from . . . the table, and . . . put a quarter pad down . . . in front of the management folks, and tried to sketch out . . . what his concern was . . . and when he realized he wasn't getting through, he just stopped' (Pattow 1993:8). Management obviously didn't have the same agenda as the engineers.

The engineers communicated effectively in a technical sense, but what they lacked was a wider cultural literacy. For the engineers to convince management to postpone the flight, they would have had to take a different tack and concentrate not on technical problems, but on the possible ramifications of those technical problems, and how these might tie in with the agendas and interests of management. The engineers could have made the point, for instance, that a postponement might be a considerable setback (for NASA, Thiokol, the President), but that decision makers should also consider the consequences of the shuttle blowing up in front of a huge television audience, with the prestige of NASA, Thiokol and the President on the line (which is exactly what happened).

Had the engineers had that wider cultural literacy, they would have known that any attempt to sway management would need to involve treating the launch not as a technical problem but as a PR exercise. We may have cultural maps (rules and conventions) in front of us, but what happens in practice is often informed, and even determined, by agendas that aren't up front, and sometimes can never be publicly articulated. The ability to negotiate between the rules of a culture and what happens in practice is what we have called cultural literacy.

THE PROCESS MODEL OF COMMUNICATION

Gunther Kress, writing in *Communication and Culture* (Kress 1988), points out that when the term communication was first used regularly—in the nineteenth century, in Europe—it mainly referred to the physical means of communication, such as roads, railways and shipping. It was only in the later part of the nineteenth century, with the development of other means of passing information, that communication came to refer to the print media, and later still to radio, film, television, video and computers.

Kress argues that although the old-fashioned notion of communication as a 'thing' was gradually replaced by the notion of communication practices, processes and mediums, this 'thingness', this notion of communication being based on the model of, say, goods being transported by barge or train, persisted in contemporary process models. In other words, communication practices are still largely understood, in process theories, the media, and everyday culture, in terms of the model of Sender–Message–Receiver.

From this perspective, communication is very much like the postal service. First, something is made or composed (written, spoken, signalled), then it is addressed, mailed and delivered (I speak, write or gesture to somebody), and finally the 'thing' is received and taken into possession (the message is read, decoded, accepted by somebody).

At the beginning of this chapter we argued that three points were essential to any understanding and analysis of communication practices. These were:

- the relationship between communication and culture
- the notion that meaning and practice are context specific, and
- cultural literacy.

All three of these points are absent from the process school model of communication, which is mainly used in texts that describe, theorise and teach communication practices in business, scientific and technical contexts.

The process model is largely derived from various American theories of communication that were developed in order to improve and explain communication practices within large organisations such as corporations. These various theories of communication were taken up in a diluted form and passed into everyday and, importantly, media culture. As a result they became the contemporary 'commonsense' idea of communication. We won't be dealing with the specific developments of this approach; an excellent (contextualised) account can be found in Mattelart's *Mapping World Communication* (1994).

We can illustrate the limitations of this model through reference to an example that often appears in process model texts: drawings or cartoons of two figures with 'bubbles' that contain their thoughts or messages (see Figure 1). The cartoon suggests that communication has been effective when both bubbles contain exactly the same content. In this cartoon, for instance, the symbols in the bubble sent by the person on the left correspond to those in the bubble belonging to the person on the right.

It is interesting to examine this commonly used style of cartoon and ask:

- what does it presume about communication, and
- what does it not take into account?

The first point that needs to be made is that in this example, and in the process model generally, communication is almost completely decontextualised. In other words, most background or relevant information, most contextualising detail, is left out. In process models of communication, such details are considered largely irrelevant.

Let's consider the cartoon in some detail. It suggests that the same message went from one brain to another, and was understood—received—exactly as was intended. This seems plausible enough,

FIGURE 1 The process model of communication

ILLUSTRATION BY PAT GOON

because the two characters look the same and presumably think along similar lines.

These two cartoon figures are in some ways marked as different, however, insofar as one is sending, and the other is receiving, a message. How do we know this is what is happening? Well, we can't say for sure, but if we employ very basic and general western cultural literacy, we could say that the body language being employed by the two figures directs us to that interpretation. For instance:

- Reading from left to right (as we usually do in western culture), one figure 'comes before' the other.
- The first figure is standing 'at ease' and holding out a hand, presumably 'communicating' something to the second, who stands at attention, listening.
- The mouth of the first figure is open (we presume this signals 'speaking'), while the mouth of the second is closed (this signals 'silence').
- The first figure's head is tilted so that the gaze is directed above

the head of the second figure, whose gaze is fixed, straight ahead (to check this claim, draw a straight line from the line of where the tips of their respective noses are pointed).

- Finally, and most convincingly, the first figure's bubble seems to be emanating from a mouth, while the second figure's bubble comes from the head.

There is a very useful term that comes out of linguistics—binary—which refers to the way meaning is produced through a relationship between two different concepts. Binaries will be discussed in more detail in Chapter 2. It is sufficent to point out that the two concepts that constitute a binary:

- are normally read as a hierarchy, and
- only make sense, only come to mean, in terms of one *not being the other*.

An example of a binary is man/woman. Conventionally, the term 'man' can be understood, and comes to mean and have value, because it is *not* 'woman', among other things ('man' could also be understood, of course, as 'not boy', or 'not youth'). In western cultures the man/woman binary has usually been constituted as a natural hierarchy that values men over women; that is to say, the values of the two terms, and the relation between them, have historically been ideologised. There is a detailed description of the notion of ideology in Chapter 8.

Let us return to our cartoon and try to describe and analyse the binaries we can identify there. With the left-hand figure, the following first terms of certain binaries might apply:

- manager or boss
- active
- in control
- knowing
- casual.

The right-hand figure could be read in terms of the other aspect of each binary:

- subordinate
- passive
- being controlled

- relatively uninformed, and
- formal and attentive.

These binaries seem to characterise the relationship between the two figures in terms of difference; and yet the details which signal those binaries are hardly prominent in the cartoon. On the contrary, the cartoon in some ways does its best to 'play down' difference. Notice, for instance, the absence of distinguishing features in either figure. Their bodily features (hair style, shape of head, height, weight) are almost exactly the same, as are their clothes. We could reasonably assume that the two figures share backgrounds, cultural literacies and agendas, and think along the same lines. And yet as we noted earlier, this cartoon also makes use of what we could call **markers** (or **signs**) of difference. It 'tells the story' of a boss effectively communicating orders or information to an attentive, comprehending and docile subordinate.

COMMUNICATION AND DIFFERENCE

The cartoon needs to both mark and de-emphasise difference if it is to work. Why? Because there are differences and hierarchies in all organisations. On the other hand, if those differences are made too prominent, or are given too much emphasis, then the process theory of communication, which argues that messages are sent and received by people who are more or less the same, wouldn't really make sense.

What if we were to place greater emphasis on the markers of difference in this cartoon? What if we were to use the notion of difference as our departure point, and read a number of possibilities of illiteracy, disagreement, dissatisfaction, jealousy, resentment, cross-purposes, and competing or mutually exclusive agendas into the figures in the cartoon? In other words, what if we starting thinking about the almost infinite number of contexts that could be brought to bear on reading this cartoon, or the numerous cultural contexts that these two people don't have in common?

This is not to say that people don't understand what is being said to them, or that people don't communicate effectively. What it means is that markers of communication (words and gestures, for instance) will be read and evaluated differently by different people, depending on the cultural contexts they bring to any communication practice, and on the specific contexts in which that practice takes place.

Let us read the cartoon in terms of possible work relationships between the two figures. First of all, they are not on an equal footing: one of them is probably more powerful than the other, at least in this work context. One gives orders, the other receives them. One evaluates the other's responses and work, and is in a position to recommend whether that worker keeps a job or is fired or promoted. There is a power relation between the two which largely determines what they can say to one another and how they treat one another.

This power relation is not, of course, fixed. In certain work areas (technical work, for instance) the subordinate may become the more experienced, competent, and knowing of the two. In a non-work context, say at a squash club, the subordinate, who might be an A-grade squash player, will have much more status and prestige than the boss, who might be a D grader. Again, this will work to redefine the power relations between them, which may remain fluid across different contexts.

Let us take a more specific example of how different contexts determine what happens in communication practices. The cartoon might suggest that the two people are more or less the same, but generally people differ from one another in terms of:

- gender
- sexual preference
- age
- religion
- occupation
- wealth
- political affiliations
- entertainment interests
- social values
- ethnicity
- educational qualifications
- cross-cultural experiences.

Let us pick up on one apparently small point of difference—age—and see where it could take us.

Let us presume that the boss is 50 and the subordinate is twenty years old. The 'message' in the boss's bubble is 'We need someone to clean out the toilets. Go and do it now, and have it finished in 30 minutes. And don't play that stupid loud music—it will stop everybody else in the place from concentrating on their work.' Now, according to the process theory of communication, that is what appears, without qualification, in the subordinate's bubble. However, while the subordinate might hear everything that was said, 'what was said' won't mean the same to both persons.

For the boss, the orders that were given were fair and reasonable. For the subordinate, however, the orders are an insult. The subordinate didn't take on this job (as an apprentice, say) to clean toilets. In western culture cleaning public toilets is low-status work, normally reserved for unskilled workers. Moreover, it is a dirty, smelly and (usually) unpleasant job that is unlikely to do anything but lower a person's sense of worth or self-esteem.

Our twenty-year-old knows this. Through his familiarity with various texts (films, television shows, novels), he is aware cleaning toilets is demeaning. This reaction is produced, of course, out of a particular set of cultural values and literacies specific to this twenty-year-old. On the other hand, the boss, our 50-year-old, has worked at a variety of jobs, including cleaning toilets. The boss does not understand that cleaning the toilets might seem demeaning to the apprentice. Cleaning toilets is, for the boss, a sign of your versatility, a sign you are down to earth, a sign that you obey instructions and therefore in all likelihood are a good and valuable worker.

There might be various other points of contention which stop the boss's message from making its way, with its meaning intact, to the subordinate's bubble. The boss walks in and sees the twenty-year-old apparently idle. The boss 'knows' twenty-year-olds are lazy and easily distracted, 'knows' they 'don't like hard work', and have 'no respect for authority'. From this context, the boss cannot see anything in a twenty-year-old but disrespect and a disinclination to work. The twenty-year-old, on the other hand, hears the boss's words with a mixture of annoyance and practical objections. He is 'in the middle of an important job, and can't leave it at the moment'. Anyway, 'cleaning the toilets takes more than half an hour, and where are the cleaning materials and equipment?'

We could choose any number of examples of different contexts for our cartoon which would demonstrate, very convincingly, that what appears in one bubble need not automatically appear in the other, no matter how clearly or concisely the message might be communicated. And we haven't even moved into the potentially more difficult and contentious area of cross-cultural communication. The process model of communication only makes sense, then, as long as the differences we have referred to are more or less edited out of its diagrams and theories.

BAUDRILLARD AND CONTEXTS

We have been arguing that the various meanings and communication practices within a culture are produced because different contexts are brought to bear to frame signs and events differently. We take the position that meaning is always context specific; or, as Jacques Derrida might phrase it, 'there is nothing outside the (con)text' (Derrida 1988). We mentioned, however, that the process model of communication has passed into everyday use and acceptance, and dominates the way meaning making and communication are understood in important cultural institutions, such as the media.

Let's look at an example of how these two conflicting positions were played out when the print media reported on a visit to Australia by the French 'postmodernist' Jean Baudrillard.

Figure 2 shows one article, taken from the *Australian*, which was particularly sceptical of Baudrillard's Gulf War statement:

What Baudrillard argues in his article on the Gulf War is that much of what happened—the military movements, the air strikes—didn't make much sense in terms of military strategy. Rather than these activities being directed towards specific military goals—destroying the enemy, reclaiming territory—Baudrillard argues that much of what went on in the Gulf War was intended to create the scenario, the event, the theatre of war. That is, various military activities were performed in order to produce the illusion of a conventional war narrative or story.

In considering Baudrillard's argument, it is worthwhile mentioning two other contexts, or **intertexts**, that might help us understand his claim that the Gulf War was largely produced for western audiences by the American military and media acting in concert. First, since the liberation/fall of Saigon, there has been a claim circulating that the Vietnam War was lost 'back home'; that is to say, it was lost because the images and reports that were sent back to western

Jean Baudrillard is a French cultural theorist who has achieved considerable fame and perhaps even greater notoriety. Baudrillard's earlier works (such as *The Mirror of Production* and *For a Critique of the Political Economy of the Sign*) provided extremely important critiques and developments of Marxist versions of the relation between political economy and socio-cultural contexts. From the publication of *Simulations* Baudrillard's work began to emphasise the ways in which (post)modern culture and technology erase reality and replace it with simulations, with what he chose to call the 'hyperreal'. Baudrillard has increasingly come to be seen—even within postmodernist circles—as a maverick, and his work a scandal. His perhaps intentionally provocative remarks about contemporary (non)reality (such as 'the Gulf War never happened') have made him a favourite target for writers critical of poststructuralist and postmodernist theories of meaning.

audiences did not correspond to the official explanations and stories put out by the Pentagon. Official narratives were imposed upon material sent from Vietnam, but gradually alternative readings of that material emerged which challenged the notion that the Vietnam War 'made sense'. Viewed from this context, Baudrillard's claim that the Gulf War 'didn't happen' could be read as an argument that much of the activity that took place in the Gulf was aimed not at winning the war in the desert (that was more or less assured) but at winning a war of conflicting stories and meanings. Paul Patton makes this point very well in his introduction to a text containing Baudrillard's essays on the Gulf War:

> It was not the first time that images of war had appeared on TV screens, but it was the first time that they were relayed 'live' from the battlefront. It was not the first occasion on which the military censored what could be reported, but it did involve a new level of military control of reportage and images. Military planners had clearly learnt a great deal since Vietnam: procedures for controlling the media were developed and tested in the Falklands, Grenada and Panama. As a result, what we saw was for the most part a 'clean' war, with lots of pictures of weaponry . . . and relatively few images of human casualties, none from the allied forces. In the words of one commentator, for the first time, 'the power

FIGURE 2 'Philosopher's art escapes the duty of reality'

The French Government and its protege, rogue philosopher Monsieur Jean Baudrillard, could hardly take official offence when Australian Customs impounded his photographic exhibition, pending payment of duty, after rejecting it as art—under his philosophy, the photos may not even exist.

In fact, under M. Baudrillard's radical 'hyper-reality' philosophy, we're all victims of cultural orgasm and mass-media hype and the Customs service itself along with this newspaper—and you who think you're really reading it—may not exist.

So it has to be said a 'hyper-real' international incident was averted after last-minute federal/State ministerial intervention secured the release of the 50 photographs only hours before the exhibition was due to open in Brisbane.

The man and his photographs are real enough for Brisbane's Institute of Modern Art to be outraged that Customs does not deem any photographs as art.

These events, if they ever took place, began when Brisbane's Griffith University and the institute convinced the acclaimed French theorist and philosopher-turned-artist to bring his photographs to Australia, with the sponsorship of the French Ministry for Foreign Affairs.

M. Baudrillard duly turned up in Brisbane last month with 50 photographs, for an Australian tour, which will include a two-day symposium on his philosophies in Brisbane this weekend.

Nevertheless, his entire Brisbane exhibition, titled The Ecstasy of Photography, was deemed merely photographs and not art by Customs in Brisbane, and demanded excise duty of almost $16,000.

In desperation the Institute of Modern Art turned to Queensland's Minister for the Arts, Mr Wells, who in turn contacted the federal Minister for Customs, Senator Schacht.

A 'facilitation' was reached under which the photographs were released after the institute lodged a surety of almost $16,000, essentially guaranteeing the exhibition was art, was here for public display and would not be sold in Australia.

M. Baudrillard—who wrote a book denying the Gulf War happened and believes mankind has burnt itself out since the cultural orgy of the 60s—was more philosophical.

'Maybe it's no art, not at all. Maybe it's not art in the sense that they are not aesthetic objects,' a bemused M. Baudrillard said modestly.

M. Baudrillard took up photography—after being given a camera five years ago—even though he believed art and just about everything else is dead.

As Griffith University's Dr Nicholas Zurbrugg, who is researching M. Baudrillard's legacy for the 90s, said: 'The man who said art was dead then became (a photographic) artist, but when his art got to Australia the Customs said "Your art isn't art". Perhaps they've read him.'

to create a crisis merges with the power to direct the movie about it
. . . Desert Storm was the first major global media crisis orchestration
that made instant history.'

PATTON IN BAUDRILLARD 1995:3

The second context that might help us frame Baudrillard's statement is the United Nations 'invasion' of Somalia in 1994. When
American troops poured on to Somalian beaches, they were met, not
by the enemy, but by hordes of journalists and photographers who
'shot them' with their cameras. The dramatic night-time landing had
no military significance in any conventional sense—the Somalian
troops were elsewhere, and the Americans could have paddled in on
surfboards in the middle of the day and still achieved the same result.
The invasion was almost pure performance, designed to produce a
'result' . . . back home.

For Matt Robbins, Baudrillard's claim that the Gulf War 'didn't
happen' could be framed in terms of only one context—here was an
ivory-tower philosopher talking nonsense. Robbins knew that during
the Gulf War bombs were dropped, people were killed, and battles
won and lost. Robbins contextualised Baudrillard's position not as a
comment on or analysis of what had happened in the Gulf but as
pure philosophy.

From his context, Robbins understood Baudrillard to be suggesting that there was no physical reality to the Gulf War—no blood or
bodies or battles. He fails to think through the possibility that
Baudrillard's comments could be contextualised differently, thus locat-
ing himself firmly within the process model of communication. As
we have seen, however, what Baudrillard could have been suggesting
was that the events in the Gulf were about the creation of a coherent
war narrative. This is not the same as saying 'nothing happened'.
Rather, it might be suggesting that events—physicality and materiality—have no natural meaning. The Gulf War, for Baudrillard, could
be read as a conflict not about national boundaries but about meanings—and their contexts. That such conflicts of meaning cause blood
to be spilled demonstrates just how serious a matter meaning is.

A second example, in this article, of how meaning is both context
specific and tied up with the notion of cultural literacy is to be found
in the way in which Robbins approaches the question of whether or
not Baudrillard's photographs are 'art'. Baudrillard suggests that they
are 'not art in the sense that they are not aesthetic objects', a position

the customs officials seem to have agreed with, since we are told they do 'not deem any photographs as art' (Baudrillard 1995:6). The customs officials probably evaluated Baudrillard's photographs in terms of a perspective which allows certain objects (paintings, statues) to be designated as art, but disallows this claim when confronted with more everyday objects (photographs, video stills, t-shirts).

When Baudrillard writes that 'art doesn't exist', he could be suggesting that the distinction between one set of objects (say, paintings) and another (photographs) based on the notion of aesthetic value (this is valuable, this isn't) is impossible to maintain because there is no natural or disinterested basis for this distinction. A number of objects, genres and mediums (for example Aboriginal rock paintings, jazz music, film) which weren't previously considered art are now objects of study in schools and universities, exhibited in galleries and museums, and marketed and sold as aesthetic objects.

It could be argued that the context in which an object is placed or located determines whether or not it is evaluated as art. There is an episode of *Doctor Who* in which the Doctor's spaceship, the Tardis, lands in the French art gallery the Louvre. When the Doctor (Tom Baker) and his companion eventually return to the Tardis they find an art critic (played by John Cleese) standing in front of the spaceship and explaining to his companion why it is a wonderful piece of art. Its status as art is produced by its (physical) context: it is an object in the Louvre, and it doesn't have any obvious function (it isn't a toilet or a cafe), so therefore it must be an aesthetic object. Of course if the art critic's cultural literacy had extended to the *Doctor Who* series, this would have introduced another context and changed the way the Tardis was read.

Attempts to hide or edit out contexts, and the notion of difference, can probably best be understood in terms of the notion of ideology. We can suggest here, in a preliminary way, that ideology is a practice whereby a particular group within a culture attempts to naturalise its own meanings, and to pass those meanings, ideas or perspectives off as universally accepted and as commonsense. Ideology will be dealt with in detail in Chapter 8.

The main point that we have been making in this section is that meanings and communication practices are always informed by, and produced out of, different contexts. What we want to do now is to look more closely at the notion of context, most particularly in terms of the relationship between communication, literacy and practice.

CONTEXTS AND CULTURAL LITERACIES

We have suggested that communication practices are always produced, read and negotiated in terms of specific contexts, but what is a context? We have made the point that communication and meanings are not 'things'. What about contexts?

It is often assumed that contexts are stable sets of circumstances. Contexts are often understood as being a simple amalgam of cultural features such as:

• meaning systems (fashion codes, professional codes, body language codes or religious codes, for instance)
• material conditions (say, urban or rural), and
• participants or members (based on categories such as class, gender, age and race).

From here, it is easy to presume that any specific combination of those different cultural features (that is to say, a context) can be used to read and explain communication practices. There are at least two problems with this presumption:

• first, the perception as to what constitutes a particular context is not likely to be shared by everyone, and
• second, the meaning of those communication practices will change across persons, places and time.

Consider the following example. In the US in 1992, Professor Anita Hill claimed that she had been sexually harrassed by Judge Clarence Thomas, who was at the time President Bush's nominee to the US Supreme Court. Hill and Thomas were questioned—interrogated is perhaps the better word—by (male) members of the Senate as part of the process of establishing if Thomas was fit to sit on the Supreme Court. Thomas reacted to this questioning by becoming emotional, and claimed that he was undergoing a 'high-tech lynching'. Hill remained cool and impassive, and handled questions in a competent and professional—and not emotional—manner.

The male senators believed Thomas, not Hill; and the Hill—

Thomas affair, as it came to be known, was contextualised as a huge failure for the American feminist movement. Numerous feminists mulled over what had happened and why. There was a strong suggestion that Hill had failed to 'perform' as a victim—which allowed the men who questioned her to dismiss her as cold and calculating. Hill's communication practices were deemed ineffective by many because they didn't convince her immediate audience—American male senators.

In subsequent political elections in the United States, the number of women standing for office rose dramatically; more importantly, the number of voters willing to elect women rose equally dramatically. In the wake of those results, feminists and other interested parties began to reassess the Hill–Thomas affair; rather than being seen as a failure for American feminism, it was reasoned that the senators' disdainful treatment of Hill and her accusations had aroused strong feelings among women throughout the country. Feminists and political commentators were forced to recontextualise the affair: it became a significant moment in the advancement, rather than the failure, of American feminism.

Contexts can only appear as stable, then, if we read others:

- as being exactly like ourself (sharing our literacies, meanings, agendas, values), or
- as unimportant or valueless (as stupid, naive, childish, barbaric, uncivilised).

What does this do, then, to the notion of communication contexts? How can we say that communication practices must be understood in terms of specific cultural contexts if there is no such thing as a completely stable context?

There are at least two ways in which we can talk about stable contexts:

- First, we could point out that in some contexts (the army, for instance) communication genres and interpersonal relations are very clearly delineated and regulated (the most frequent speech genres used, for instance, are likely to be 'commands' and 'compliance'). This doesn't really allow much room for negotiation (it is unlikely that a private would tell a captain that s/he didn't feel comfortable standing at attention).

- Second, it is important to note that even in reasonably flexible **cultural fields** we often act as if contexts were stable. We have already referred to the notion of ideology and to the ways in which certain ideas, stories and meanings come to be naturalised—even when our experiences are quite different from what we are told is real and natural.

While tutoring a group made up evenly of Aboriginal and non-Aboriginal students, a lecturer drew their attention to a newspaper article which referred to Australia as a 'white' nation. When the students were asked if there were any points in this article that they did not agree with, none of them challenged the statement, even though it effectively excluded half the class from membership of Australian society.

A further context from which to read this response would be to note that the lecturer was white, and an authority figure, and that the Aboriginal students' silence could be understood in terms of a reluctance to express controversial opinions in relation to racism. That is, for the students the classroom could have been a 'rigid' context rather than a 'flexible' one.

A second example of how ideology stabilises contexts can be seen in the way certain events—Churchill's speech about the British never surrendering to Hitler, or the Eureka Stockade revolt—are mythologised and pass 'beyond contestation'. In 1990 a group of Australian veterans of the ANZAC landing at Gallipoli went back to Turkey, accompanied by politicians and journalists, to commemorate the battle fought there in the First World War. Australian journalists reported these events in terms of particular **genres** (reminiscences, celebrations, appreciations) and **discourses** (again mainly military, but also patriotic) which very much constrained the readings viewers had available to them. That is to say, these events—and the battle they commemorated—were naturalised; 'we' were commemorating a heroic and significant moment in Australian history.

The problem with this version of events was that it was natural only as far as most Australians were concerned. When curious Turkish journalists filed their stories they wrote about Australians coming to apologise for their invasion of Turkish soil. Australian journalists reacted with shock and horror. How could anyone 'misread' these events? The Gallipoli landing constituted almost a sacred narrative within Australian culture, but in Turkey the landing was part of a very different story.

How is it that contexts remain open to different readings and practices if cultural rules and ideologies work to stabilise them? One of the defining characteristics of cultural literacy is an ability to recognise the rules that apply in a context, and to negotiate them. Let's consider some examples of these literacies at work.

A lawyer in a courtroom is prosecuting a rape case. At the same time the lawyer is dealing with a judge who thinks that raping a prostitute is not as serious a crime as raping an 'ordinary' person. The lawyer might wish to tell the judge that he is a mysogynist, a bigot, a fool and 50 years out of date in his thinking. The speech genre to be employed is, say, 'criticism'—but how is this to be done? It might be unwise, at least in this context, to use 'feminist' terms (misogyny, patriarchy, sexism) for two reasons:

- First, the institution of the law courts more or less demands that professional members adhere to a certain type of language, what we might call legal **discourse**.
- Equally important, however, is the possibility that the judge will either not understand what is being said or, worse, will treat such comments as insulting, or as symptoms of scandalous politicising of the law, and react negatively.

To point out that the judge's attitudes are dangerously out of date by making use of appropriate legal discourse (references to recent precedents, for instance), or to put that same proposition respectfully to the jury (and hence bypass the judge) would be to demonstrate considerable literacy.

Players are supposed to abide by the official rules of a game, but in practice it is often a person's ability to move outside legitimate rules and moves that makes a difference. Consider the following example: Two people are playing a game of chess, which the first is about to win. The second 'accidentally' knocks the table, the pieces are overturned, and the game ends as a draw. Or this example: Two people are playing chess, and the first is about to win. That person looks up, considers her opponent and says, in a disinterested and matter-of-fact way: 'Your leg's a bit close to the table leg. Watch you don't bump it.' The two players laugh.

The rules of chess are straightforward enough, but there are all kinds of other rules—'unofficial rules'—that come into play and can be used in order to win, or to avoid losing, a game. In the first example the losing player makes a move that is not in the rule book—and gets a draw; after all, it would be 'bad form' to accuse your opponent of cheating. In the second example the winning player foresees such a move and blocks it by pointing out the possibility of just such an 'accident'.

Official rules obviously constrain the kinds of moves that can be made in any game—or communication practice, which is largely the same thing—but at the same time players can take advantage of those constraints. The rules of chess, and of every other cultural activity, from football to politics to polite conversation to sexual relations to tax returns, more or less presume that people will respect the 'spirit' of those laws or rules—which leaves a great deal of scope for all kinds of 'illegitimacies'.

Consider this example: Two friends were teaching in Papua New Guinea many years ago, and were asked to invite a young student, who was soon to visit Australia on a cultural exchange program, to dinner. The school principal wanted the student to learn western table manners, and they were supposed to tutor her in these cultural conventions and 'rules'. What they explained, however, was not so much the rules of dining, but how the student could use those rules to her own benefit.

As the dinner proceeded, they explained to the student that when there was only one piece of potato or cake left on a plate, the student should ask, in as disinterested a voice as possible, if anybody wanted the last piece. The rules of etiquette more or less disallowed answers in the affirmative, which meant that the student could then say: 'Well, if nobody wants it, I may as well have it.' The student ate very well in Australia.

These two apparently different notions of cultural rules and conventions—as constraints, and as opportunities—are addressed very acutely in the works of the French cultural theorist and sociologist Pierre Bourdieu. His work will be discussed again, in some detail, in Chapter 7.

SUMMARY

In this chapter we have argued that:

- communication practices are always informed by and produced within cultural contexts, and
- this is contrary to the process model of communication, which tends to edit out contexts and cultural differences.

We further argue that cultural practices, and the contexts that produce and constrain them, are closely connected to the notion of cultural literacy, which can be understood as both:

- a familiarity with the rules and conventions of a culture, and
- a feel for negotiating those rules and conventions.

FURTHER READING

Baudrillard, J. 1983 *Simulations* trans. P. Foss, P. Patton and P. Beitchman, Semiotext(e), New York

Kress, G. (ed.) 1988 *Communication and Culture: An Introduction* University of New South Wales Press, Kensington

Mattelart, A. 1994 *Mapping World Communication: War, Progress, Culture* trans. S. Emanuel and J. Cohen, University of Minnesota Press, Minneapolis

Virilio, P. 1991 *The Lost Dimension* trans. D. Moshenberg, Semiotext(e), New York

2
SIGNS AND MEANING

This chapter addresses the relationship between signs and meanings. More specifically, we argue that:

- meanings are not just 'out there' waiting to be identified or discovered, but are read into signs, and
- this process of reading signs and making meanings is not arbitrary, but is what we call an **ideological** process.

In the previous chapter we introduced the notion that meaning was context dependent; in other words, we attempted to identify:

- how factors such as cultural literacy help determine the kinds of meanings available to different individuals and groups within a culture, and
- the ramifications of introducing such factors into theories of communication.

We pointed out that thinking about and analysing communication using notions such as context and cultural literacy means there are many things we can't take for granted. For example:

- meanings don't pass unproblematically from the brain of a sender to that of a receiver
- contexts are never identical for, or completely shared by, participants, and
- communication cannot be completely controlled by the intention of the sender.

This does not mean, of course, that people don't claim to know what things truly mean. On the contrary, people frequently claim that everyone agrees, say, about what a word means, and behave as if that meaning is natural or beyond question. For many people (mostly men), the word woman, or a pictorial representation of a woman, seems to have certain innate meanings; in western cultures these have often been associated with notions such as frailty, emotionality, promiscuity, irrationality and domesticity. The fact that these supposedly innate and natural meanings are at least potentially contradictory (the notion of woman as 'damned whores and God's police', for example) has not always been commented upon (or at least, usually not by men).

For a different but related example, let us take the word 'violence'. Does the display of violence on television 'do a violence' to children? One man stands threateningly over another, one person swears at another, a novelist writes about a religion in a way that believers interpret as disrespectful and disparaging: are these acts of violence? It is very difficult to get people to agree to, or to give specific examples of, the 'cut-off' point at which violence begins. Again, the problem is that over time, and even within a culture at the same time, people will not always 'see' the same thing.

There are two points that we are introducing, and dealing with, here:

- words do not function as labels that can be unproblematically attached to things or acts or experiences, and
- despite this, people do use words to label things and acts or experiences. However, what those words 'really' mean is usually a matter of negotiation, disagreement or conflict.

There is a 'commonsense' notion that things have an obvious and natural attachment to words; it was also common sense, at different times in history, to burn witches, predict the future by analysing sheep's entrails, and not to sail too far from land for fear of sailing off the edge of the world.

People, or at least most people, stopped worrying about sailing off the edge of the world after the Copernican revolution, which established that the earth was not the centre of the universe, was not flat, and revolved around the sun. It would be stretching things to talk about a similar kind of revolution with regard to the 'meaning of meaning', but something very important did happen in the early part of the twentieth century which challenged the way meaning had been understood as the authentic reflection, in language, of a thing or of the world.

A 'SCIENCE OF SIGNS': SAUSSURE

What happened was the development of new theories about meaning, called **semiology** (or the science of signs). These theories are now usually referred to as semiotics, and were initially proposed by the Swiss linguist Ferdinand de Saussure (Saussure 1989).

The key to Saussure's revolutionary view of language was the notion that meaning is **relational** rather than **substantive**. What this means is that there is no innate meaning attached to a language's terms, only differences. All meaning, then, is produced through 'language systems' based on a notion of difference rather than identity. Let's consider this in more detail.

Saussure was primarily interested in what he called the linguistic sign, which he divided into three aspects:

* signifier
* signified, and
* sign.

What did he understand by these terms?

* The signifier is the physical form of the sign, for example the written word or the spoken sound (the word 'elephant', for example).
* The signified is the concept that is 'evoked' (the idea of elephant-ness).
* The sign is the combination of the signifier and the signified.

A particular mark or sound 'means' something, according to Saussure, only because an **arbitrary** relation has been established (and institutionalised) between itself and something else. This is borne out by the fact that different cultures have different words for the same thing or concept. Saussure points out that the French use the word 'boeuf', the Germans use 'Ochs', and the English use 'ox' to refer to more or less the same thing (Saussure, quoted in Innis 1985:37)— although a Hereford is not the same as a Charolais or a Friesian. The meaning of each sign does not come from the thing referred to, but from the relation between the sign (boeuf, Ochs, ox) and the sign system (the French, German or English language).

This is true not only across languages but within cultures as well. Differences within cultures (for example, differences of race, class,

Ferdinand de Saussure made a revolutionary contribution to the study of language and meaning in the lectures he gave to students at the University of Geneva in the first decade of the twentieth century. These lectures were recorded by his students and published under the title *Cours de Linguistique Générale*, or *Course in General Linguistics*. Saussure's insight that meaning was produced through the relation between different terms in a language influenced major theorists in the fields of structuralism and semiotics.

profession, gender and age) ensure that different groups produce different meanings from one another. The Nazi swastika, which was part of a Hindu sign system, meant little outside India until after Hitler. Generally it has a very negative value these days, although it does have a positive value for some groups (Ku Klux Klan, white supremacists).

Let's look at the question of how a semiotic system works to produce the 'meaningful' linkage between, say words and things; a question Saussure addressed as an inquiry into the nature of the linguistic sign. Saussure firstly insisted that a 'linguistic sign is not a link between a thing and a name, but between a concept and a sound pattern' (Saussure 1989:66). He used the term signified to refer to the concept, and the term signifier to refer to the sound pattern (or other material form).

For Saussure, the sign is the product of an arbitrary relationship between the signifier and the signified. For example, the signifier 'tree' (or 'arbre' in French), and the concept of a tree, when taken together constitute a sign.

This relationship of a signifier to a signified, which produces the sign, is worked out within the language systems which users have to deal with in their everyday communication practices. According to Saussure, there was always a complete linguistic system available which more or less determined what kinds of things people could do with language. Further, since the relationship between signifiers and signifieds was arbitrary—that is to say, not natural or logical—those relationships tended not to change, precisely because this self-contained relational system could not be 'reasoned' with.

Saussure's theories turn conventional notions of language and meaning upside down. Taking this insight further, structuralists and semioticians argued that semiotic systems were not produced by, or in response to, 'the world' (as a reflection or labelling of what was 'outside there'). Instead they edited out the world, and at the same time "produced' the world, as and through a series of self-contained systemic relationships. The word 'tree' was not produced by the green leafy thing; on the contrary, the green leafy thing came to be understood, to be seen, and to mean in terms of semiotic systems.

Saussure's work has been extremely useful and influential, but is not without its problems. The three most obvious difficulties concern the issues of the signified, intentionality and the arbitrariness of meaning:

- First, the signified: how, we might ask, is the signified different from the signifier? The answer is . . . that it isn't! The word 'elephant' is a signifier, but the concept it evokes (elephantness) is just another signifier (a picture in our mind, or the idea of a large animal that is supposedly scared of mice, or the smell associated with elephants. These are all new signifiers). Every time we use a sign, it gets translated into another sign. At no stage do we get the 'real' elephant, or a concept of elephantness that isn't produced through a sign system. Saussure more or less overlooked this point.

- The problem of intentionality partly follows from Saussure's failure to pay proper attention to the question of the signified. The Italian semiotician Umberto Eco (perhaps best known as the author of *The Name of the Rose*) makes the following point:

  > Saussure did not define the signified any too clearly, leaving it half way between a mental image, a concept and a psychological reality; but he did clearly stress the fact that . . . signs 'express' ideas and . . . such ideas must be mental events that concern a human mind. Thus the sign is implicitly regarded as a communication device taking place between two human beings intentionally aiming to communicate or to express something.
  >
  > ECO 1979:14–15

Saussure presumed that every sign had to be 'put together' and sent by someone, and he strongly, if implicitly, emphasised the role of the sign sender. It is easy to see, however, that there are plenty of signs that are not intended. If you put on the only clean shirt you have, without caring what is on the front of it, you are not intending to act as a walking sign. This does not stop people from reading you in terms of your shirt ('Save the Gastric Brooding Frog', 'Kurt Lives', 'I am an idiot'). Further, we read the moon, the sunset, a lake as signs, and yet nobody produced those signs to communicate to other people.

Eco (1979) suggests that the American theorist C.S. Peirce overcomes this problem of intentionality in Saussure's semiotics by defining a sign as 'something which stands to somebody for something in some respect or capacity' (Peirce quoted in Hawkes 1977:126). This explicitly allows communication to be thought of as both intentional and unintentional, and is able to account for the ways in which meanings are read into the natural world.

• The third problem we had with Saussure's work was tied up with the issue of the arbitrariness of meaning. We previously made the point that the linkage between words and things or acts was not natural; there was nothing essentially elephantish about the word 'elephant'. But there is a second, related point that must also be taken into account; although the use of words to designate or describe things or acts is arbitrary, it is also **motivated**. What this means is that the ways in which words are used and deployed, and the meanings they come to suggest, do not, on the whole, occur accidentally. Rather, meaning is always political. We could say, following the lead of the German philosopher Nietzsche, that the production of meaning is always, first and foremost, a sign of power (Nietzsche 1956).

Let's work our way through these points in more detail. Saussure's theory of the sign does not entirely stand up to close scrutiny, mainly because of problems with the distinction he employs between signifiers and signifieds (or, more specifically, between sound image and concept). We can agree that a signifier—the word 'woman', or the word 'man', for instance—only comes to mean through its relation to other signifiers (what are known as **binaries**) in a semiotic system. The signifier 'man', for instance, can be understood as 'not woman', or 'not boy'. What about the concept, however, that supposedly goes with it? If I were to speak or write the word 'man', there is no single concept, or single thing, not even a particular biology, which corresponds exactly to that signifier. As an example, let us consider Figures 3 and 4.

Figure 3 shows a youngish man who these days would probably be referred to or described (at least by some people) as a 'hunk'. But is a hunk a 'real man'? If the criteria for maleness are exhausted by this representation, then most of the biological specimens that tick the 'male' box on forms aren't 'real' men. Do most men have muscle-bound bodies, jaws seemingly hewn out of rock, and tight, taut stomachs? Not really. And yet most audiences would identify non-hunkish men as . . . men. They appear to have all the bits and pieces, in the right places, shapes and sizes, to qualify as men. But now consider Figure 4: is this a man?

Consider the response we got when we showed a first-year university class these images. We showed an overhead projection of the first photograph and asked 'Is this a man?' The responses ranged from sniggers to 'oohs' and 'aahs' and whistles. We then showed the second photograph and asked the same question. Almost as one, the audience burst out laughing.

What this demonstrated was that not all men are men; or again, that what counts as maleness changes depending on the relations between different signifiers, and the context of those relations. Had we shown a series of photographs of older, working-class men, to a group of older men (or women), then inserted the second photograph and asked, 'Is this a man?', it is unlikely that anyone would have laughed.

The point we are trying to make here is that there are no natural concepts that automatically and naturally 'attach' themselves to signifiers. If someone says the word 'man', all people do not read this signifier the same way. What they do, in fact, is respond to the first signifier by producing another signifier, or series of signifiers. These signifiers are not necessarily shared by other people, and are different from the first signifier.

Meanings might be produced within semiotic systems, but why are different meanings produced? Semiotic systems do not, of course, produce and reproduce themselves. The influential role of Saussure's theories, and in particular the crucial distinction he makes between *langue* (the language system) and *parole* (actual speech), however, caused many later theorists to emphasise the study of the rules of semiotic structures, as opposed to the study of semiotic practices.

Saussure knew that semiotic practices were a mess, hard to make sense of, and difficult to categorise or systematise. Semiotic structures,

FIGURE 3 'Is this a man?'

FIGURE 4 'Is this a man?'

ANDREW WILLIAMS,
COURTESY OF NEWS LTD

BILL KETTERINGHAM, COURTESY OF BILL
BACHMAN/GUIDE BOOK COMPANY

on the other hand, lent themselves to a neat, controlled scientific approach. As Saussure wrote:

> The linguist must take the study of linguistic structure as his primary concern, and relate all other manifestations of language to it. Indeed . . . linguistic structure seems to be the one thing that is independently definable and provides something our minds can satisfactorily grasp.
>
> SAUSSURE 1989:9

Saussure drew an analogy between language and semiotic systems and practices, on the one hand, and the rules of the game of chess and chess moves, on the other. The rules of chess, like the rules and categories of semiotic systems, are always complete and internally logical. Of course both chess rules and semiotic systems undergo changes, and can be studied **diachronically**, that is, across history. Diachronic changes tended to be viewed by Saussure and other like-minded linguists, however, as irrational forces 'distorting the logical purity of the language system' (Volosinov 1986:61).

Let us recap for a moment. Saussure's work and theories were extremely influential, and produced a kind of linguistic revolution, because they changed the way that people came to understand how meaning was produced:

- Instead of seeing language and semiotic systems as containers into which the natural meanings of the world were poured, Saussure made the point that meaning was relational; that is to say, meaning was produced, and the world was read, understood and seen, in terms of how signifiers were related to each other within semiotic systems. Further,
- Each semiotic system was an abstract entity which was complete and self-logical at any moment, and it was the rules and logics of those systems (*langue*), rather than the changes that took place within them across time, or individual semiotic practices (*parole*), that was the proper concern of linguistics and semiology.

We have already noted one effect of this Saussurean approach, which is that you end up writing about meaning and meaning making as if you were dealing with an autonomous and anonymous semiotic machine which arranged rules, categories and meanings in a neutral and dispassionate way. There are a number of problems with this approach, the most obvious of which is that the production of meaning always involves, at some level, questions of power and politics.

Saussure was not particularly interested in how or why the signifier 'woman' could come to be understood as part of a binary such as woman/human, nor would he have been interested in the way in which that same signifier tended to be associated with 'negative' valuations (not reasonable, not intelligent, not responsible). Because of Saussure's preference for the study of *langue* over *parole*, he would simply have rejected the questions we posed above as unscientific, illegitimate, or pointless. And this is not even to begin to take into account the equally crucial question of how the material effects of reality and the world are filtered or produced through semiotic systems.

VOLOSINOV AND HIS CRITIQUE OF SAUSSURE

Saussure's theories of semiotics overturned the notion that language simply reflected reality in a natural and unmediated form. But if this was the case—if semiotic systems determined the way we saw the world—then it is not difficult to understand that the control of how and what meanings were produced was an extremely important political question. It is at this point that we need to turn our attention to the critique of Saussurean linguistics provided by V.N. Volosinov.

Volosinov was a Marxist linguist with a very different approach from Saussure's. His main criticism of Saussure's theories was that they constituted languages as idealised, abstract machines which edited out questions of language practice. In other words, Saussure's models were very much like the clean, smoothly running, perfect hospital in the British comedy series *Yes, Prime Minister* which only ran effectively because it refused to take in patients.

Volosinov turned some of Saussure's major insights against him in order to demonstrate that there was no such thing as an autonomous language system, except perhaps in the mind of the occasional deluded Swiss linguist. If, as Saussure suggested, all meaning was relational, then the notion of *langue*, or a **synchronic** (that is to say, unchanging) semiotic system, did not correspond to any reality, but produced a reality. More to the point, the notion of *langue* and synchronicity could only be understood in terms of what they were not in a semiotic system—in this case *parole* and diachronicity.

Volosinov made just this point, but in a very practical way. How, he asked, could there be such a thing as a perfect, autonomous semiotic system? Since that system was constantly in use, and therefore constantly changing, it was never the same as itself. Moreover, as we discovered in the previous chapter, the production of meaning—the way people read things—is in no way strictly portable or pre-ordained. Volosinov had three important contributions to make on this point:

- 'What is important for the speaker about a linguistic form is not that it is a stable and always self-equivalent signal, but that it is an always changeable and adaptable sign' (1986:68).
- 'Words are always filled with content and meaning drawn from behaviour and ideology' (1986:70).

V. N. Volosinov was a Russian linguist who wrote within what has come to be called the Bakhtin School. This school was made up of a group of writers, mainly active in the 1920s and 1930s, who wrote on a wide variety of areas including linguistics, literature and folk culture. Although the school wrote out of what could be called a Marxist perspective, the Stalinist context in which its members worked was intolerant of anything that diverged from strict official doctrines. As a result the school's members were persecuted, and the exact authorship of their texts, including Volosinov's *Marxism and the Philosophy of Language*, is in dispute. This text which has been ascribed to Volosinov remains, however, the first, and perhaps the best, attempt to understand language practices in terms of specific socioeconomic contexts.

- 'The meaning of a word is determined entirely by its context. In fact, there are as many meanings of a word as there are contexts of its usage' (1986:79).

Let's look at these three propositions and see how they help us to move out of the 'structure without mess, practices or people' that was the legacy of Saussurean linguistics. In other words, how does Volosinov help us to address the gender politics, say, of the history of the signifier 'woman'?

The three propositions we took from Volosinov can be summarised as:

- signs are adaptable and changeable
- words—signifiers—have a history of meanings
- the meanings that are read into signifiers, the meanings that are activated from a variety of potential meanings, depend on the specific context.

Now, this is a long way from Saussure's 'hospital without patients'. Volosinov implicitly accepts Saussure's proposition that meaning is produced through semiotic systems, but rather than seeing this as a natural and neutral process, Volosinov insists that the meanings are always the result of ideological struggles. That is to say, different groups in a culture—groups predicated on notions of, say, class, race, ethnicity, gender, age, profession or religion—work to try and ensure that 'their' meanings are accepted. Because signs are, in Volosinov's terms, adaptable, carry a history of meanings, and can be used in different ways in different contexts, the production of meaning is always open, always a struggle.

The signifier 'woman' has been the site of a number of ideological battles, of course, particularly during the past 30 years. In some ways we could say that the various feminist movements that have fought against sexism and patriarchy have been fighting not only for equal pay or social equality, but even more fundamentally to reclaim and renegotiate what is meant by the signifier 'woman'.

Why is the meaning of a word as important as changing material conditions? Because, as Saussure pointed out, reality, the world, and material conditions are not given, but rather are produced as meaningful through signs. What this means is that there is an important relationship between the dominant value or meaning of the signifier 'woman' and the way women are treated in a culture. If 'woman' is associated with emotionality, lack of reason, unprofessionalism and domesticity, then it is very difficult to change the material conditions in which women find themselves, difficult to help women gain access to different areas of a culture (government, professions, the public sphere) which supposedly require qualities such as reason and professionalism, and difficult to get a culture to revalue those tasks traditionally performed by women (domestic duties, for instance). This is because, as the (circular and patriarchal) logic would have it, those tasks are performed by women, women are emotional and lack reason, therefore those tasks are not valuable.

THE POLITICS OF MEANINGS

We have concentrated, until now, almost exclusively on the question of meaning in a gender context, but the link between meaning and politics can be demonstrated by referring to any number of issues. Consider the feature article shown in Figure 5, concerning the question of whether Australia was settled or invaded by Europeans, which appeared recently in the *Australian*.

The background to the story was that primary school social studies syllabuses in some Australian states were now referring to a European 'invasion' of Australia, whereas previously they had referred

FIGURE 5   'A history of invasion ignores more balanced school of thought'

[1]Was Australia 'invaded' by Europeans, or was it 'settled'? There is no clear answer to this question, since any sensible discussion of the issues involves looking at the complex history of Australia since 1788 and indeed before that, and comparing it with the history of invasions and settlements in other countries.

[2]That is, it is a serious historical question to which there will never be a clear answer. But the recent row over the proposed new primary school syllabus in NSW which proposes to adopt a vocabulary which is not entirely categorical as to what happened in our history is not at all about history. It is about the struggle to own our history.

[3]Partly it is the indoctrination of little children in a view of what we, and they, are doing here and what they should think about it. This is the essence of the ferocious attack on the quite reasonable modifications of the syllabus which the Minister for Education has required of the Board of Studies.

[4]There is a generation of historians and school teachers who now act like the worst of trade unions, and who insist that their 'hard won gains' of the last 25 years should now be defended down to the last comma and the last dogma.

[5]The generation of Australian historians of the 1970s and 80s spent much of its time determinedly rewriting the history of Australia and especially the history of European-Aboriginal relations in Australia, from the point of view of the kindergarten Marxism which gained influence in the universities in those decades. Colonialism, imperialism, exploitation, genocide, invasion, conquest are all key words in this view.

[6]The up and coming historians, and the teachers, journalists and others who popularised their views, have now become the establishment of Australian history (along with the advocates of women's studies, gay studies, and so on) and they are vociferously defending the orthodoxy which they have managed to disseminate widely. Any historian who disagrees with them is either relegated to the sidelines, or, like Geoffrey Blainey, subjected to a sustained campaign of abuse and denigration.

[7]The new establishment is now concerned to insist that the very partial and biased view of Australian history which they have foisted on the educational system should be treated as the unquestioned and unqualified truth. They have espoused the Orwellian thesis: Who controls the present controls the past, and who controls the past controls the future.

[8]It is a system of thought control which, by forbidding the use of vocabulary which suggests that there are alternative views, prevents (it is hoped) the formulation of different programs or interpretations.

[9]Did Europeans invade Australia? Yes, in the sense that they arrived and occupied land. Did they consider it an invasion? No, not really, since they assumed that they

had the right to take what seemed to them a largely unoccupied and unused country, to care for it, and to take account of the welfare of its 'savage' occupants.

[10]The British settlers-invaders were far less brutal in their approach to the whole process than were most other groups, anywhere in the world. They considered themselves settlers, and the British government on numerous occasions gave instructions as to the protection of the welfare of the Aboriginal inhabitants, and even respect for their land rights.

[11]It was later generations of settlers and native-born Australians, in particular, who often enough under the slogans of national independence and even republicanism rejected the civilising influence of the Westminster administration and engaged in sometimes brutal policies towards the Aborigines.

[12]Possibly the worst offenders were the religions, who believed that they were saving the souls of the Aborigines by destroying their culture and traditions. Were the missionaries invaders?

[13]And of course the pre-1788 history of Australia was a history of successive waves of immigration by the precursors of present-day Aborigines, of internecine warfare over hunting lands, of violent conflict and the disappearance of many tribes or bands.

[14]Who invaded Australia first? Even the smallpox epidemic which seems to have killed many of the pre-1788 population seems more likely to have come from trading contact with Asia than from the Europeans.

[15]Invasion or no invasion, the history of the European presence in Australia has been one just as much of settlement, of cultivation, of investment and of the building of an infrastructure of government, industry and urbanisation. The impact of this on the Aboriginal population was in many cases harmful; in many cases beneficial.

[16]It is clear that the Aboriginal cultures, no more than the indigenes of the Americas, could not come to terms with the impact on them of European civilisation and religion: the Europeans usually had not the faintest idea of what they were dealing with, any more than did the indigenes. But again the history of Australia is not nearly so bloody or so brutal as that of the Americas, particularly those parts of the Americas which were faced with Spanish, Portuguese, and French imperialism.

[17]There is absolutely no doubt that one European power or another would have invaded, annexed, occupied, settled—choose your terminology—Australia if the British had not staked their claim first. La Perouse nearly made it first; had it not been for the French Revolution France might in any case have displaced the tiny British enclave; any other of the various hungry imperial powers of the 19th century would have moved in given a chance.

[18]The simple truth is that, given the alternatives of the times, the Aborigines were extremely lucky that it was the relatively gentle Brit-

ish (relatively—the Irish thought otherwise) who got here first.

[19]Now, of course, it is difficult to teach a sophisticated and balanced account of what happened in our history without taking into account the European impact on the indigenes, since many things which were done in its course by the Europeans to the Aborigines were, and are in retrospect, horrifying. But this is not the whole of Australian history, as many of the Aborigines themselves are perfectly aware.

[20]Many of the things which were done to the Aborigines were not about genocide or racism, as is now so frequently pretended, but were the social policy orthodoxies of their day. The removal of children from single mothers and their institutionalisation was a cruelty inflicted on whites, in quantitative terms, much more than on blacks.

[21]The notion that Australian history should be taught, to little children in schools and colleges, as the history of an invasion is the product of a political propagandistic version of history. Our history does not belong to an undistinguished syllabus committee of pedants but to the community as a whole.

THE AUSTRALIAN. McGUINNESS 1994:15

to a 'settlement'. This change was disputed by some state governments, which attempted to restore the reference to a settlement. The article comments on this dispute as to the naming and meaning of this particular period of Australian history; we have included it here because it both discusses and aggressively participates in the politics of naming and meaning. In short, what this article offers is an extraordinarily interesting example of the print media as the site of what we might call 'the contestation and production of meaning'.

On one level the author of the article, P.P. McGuinness, seems to be putting forward the suggestion that meaning is indeed contingent and tied up with politics, and not reducible to simple truths or easy answers. He asks the question about invasion/settlement, and states, in his first paragraph, 'There is no clear answer to this question.' His **discourse** clearly locates meaning and the writing of history within the domain of politics. There are references to the 'struggle to own our history' (paragraph 2) and the Orwellian notion that 'Who controls the present controls the past' (paragraph 7), both of which tie in with Volosinov's suggestion that meaning is always produced through agonistics, through conflict; and towards the end of the article he acknowledges the difficulty of teaching a 'sophisticated and balanced account of what happened in our history' (paragraph 19).

These references to the political nature of meaning making are largely overwhelmed and replaced, however, by a reasonably common ideological ploy, which replaces 'all meaning is political' with the notion that meanings or positions I agree with are somehow disinterested and beyond politics, while the views of those I disagree with are politicised. So while the article seems committed to the position of undecidability ('There is no clear answer to this question'), at the same time it makes clear that there is a clear, disinterested answer, or series of answers (the author's) and a politicised answer (the 'invasion' position).

How does the author move from undecidability and complexity to clear answers? First, he sets the stage for valuing one position over another by appealing to categories and criteria which are supposedly neutral; examples of this are the categories of, and criteria for, a 'sensible discussion' (paragraph 1) and 'the simple truth' (paragraph 18). A sensible discussion is supposedly what is happening in this article, and after that 'discussion', we will be able to identify 'the simple truth'.

We referred earlier in this chapter to the notion of binaries; in other words, each term in a signifying system is related to another term, and meaning is produced through identifying what that term is not; 'good', for instance, is not 'bad'. If this article constitutes a 'sensible discussion', what other terms are deployed to constitute binaries here? A sensible discussion would presumably not involve 'indoctrination' (paragraph 3), 'ferocious attacks on . . . reasonable modifications' (paragraph 3), 'dogma' (paragraph 4), 'vociferously defending . . . orthodoxy' (paragraph 6), 'abuse and denigration' (paragraph 6), a 'partial and biased view' (paragraph 7) and 'a political propagandist version of history' (paragraph 21). In this way, the article takes the first step towards replacing the notion that meaning is political with the notion that 'I am sensible, and the other is political'.

That, of course, is only the first step in the production of this overdetermined binary 'sensible/political'. The second step is to denigrate the term political, and those who hold 'political' views; in other words, the author's 'sensible discussion', having castigated the 'invasion' camp for their 'abuse and denigration', quickly moves to denigration. 'There is a generation of historians and school teachers,' he writes, 'who now act like the worst of trade unions' (paragraph 4), who have rewritten history 'from the point of view of . . . kindergarten Marxism' (paragraph 5); they constitute 'an undistinguished syllabus committee of pedants' (paragraph 21). 'Trade unions', 'Marxism' and 'syllabus committee' are all used pejoratively here; just to make sure this is understood, however, these terms are accompanied by less equivocal terms of 'abuse' ('worst of', 'kindergarten', 'undistinguished', 'pedants').

The author's 'sensible discussion' is supposedly based on taking into account the complexities and undecidability of history (What constitutes an invasion? Would things have been worse if another country had settled/invaded Australia?). The 'invasion' camp does not take this into account, he argues, because they are politically motivated. This sensitivity about complexities should presumably extend to the author's analysis of the 'invasion' group. However, they are casually explained as 'the products of kindergarten Marxism' who have 'become the establishment of Australian history (along with the advocates of women's studies, gay studies, and so on)' (paragraph 6). The 'invasion' group are located on the other side of a 'sensible discussion' because they are abusive and have no sensitivity for complexities; this position is expressed in an extremely abusive manner.

The first part of the struggle over meaning in this article revolves, then, around establishing the binary sensible/political, with the author occupying the positive side, and 'invasionists' the negative side. The author has opened the way for the acceptance of his version of events by discrediting his opponents, and emphasising how different he is from them, even if, in the process, he practises what he vilifies. The second step is to tell 'the simple truth' about settlement/invasion. This means denying, or at least questioning, the validity of the Aboriginal claim that their people were the victims of European violence.

If you recall, we pointed out, towards the beginning of this chapter, that the word 'violence' was one of the most important and contested of signifiers; the right to decide what constitutes violence is, of course, a very powerful weapon. The author is aware of this point, and he moves to question the charge of European violence:

> Did Europeans invade Australia? Yes, in the sense that they arrived and occupied land. Did they consider it an invasion? No, not really, since they assumed that they had the right to take what seemed to them a

largely unoccupied and unused country, to care for it, and to take account of the welfare of its 'savage' occupants (paragraph 9).

What strategies of argumentation are being employed here? The question of settlement/invasion seems to be reduced to a simple relativism:

- yes, the British more or less did invade, but no they didn't because they didn't know anyone was here, and
- anyway, the people who were here were savage, and
- the British only wanted to care for the land and those savage people (who weren't really there).

This reduction relies on two ploys:

- First, any notion of violence is more or less removed from the idea of 'invasion'. There is no reference to mass slaughter, rape or depopulation; the British simply 'arrived and occupied land'.
- Second, it wasn't an invasion because the British acted on the best of intentions: the country was unoccupied, and they felt duty bound to help out those people who didn't occupy it.

Leaving aside the obvious contradiction in the second rationale, we can focus on two crucial moves in this paragraph which repeat the tendency to depoliticise and naturalise those meanings which the author is trying to promote:

- first, if there was an invasion, it wasn't such a bad thing, since it is produced here as bloodless (the British 'arrived and occupied'), and
- perhaps more important, the failure of the British to 'see' that the country was occupied, and their assumption of the burden of taking care of the 'savages', are made to seem innocent and depoliticised.

The author doesn't wish to address the notion, for instance, that failing to treat other groups as human, or assuming that a group needs taking care of, is predicated on a violence, in this case racist violence. The relativistic argument that is presented here (as sensible, as the simple truth) is that there is nothing political or violent about designating other peoples as inhuman or inferior.

There was nothing particularly violent about the British settlement/invasion of Australia, so the argument goes. If there were problems, they were mostly due to the failure of Aboriginal peoples in coming 'to terms with the impact on them of European civilisation and religion' (paragraph 16). Notice the important shift in meaning here: we are dealing not with British violence but with the 'failure' of Aboriginal cultures and societies. Indeed, it was 'extremely lucky' for the Aboriginal peoples that they were 'invaded' by the British; after all, 'the history of Australia is not nearly so bloody or so brutal as that of the Americas, particularly those parts of the Americas which were faced with Spanish, Portuguese, and French imperialism' (paragraph 16).

Finally, the author admits, after carefully editing out or de-emphasising the violence done to Aboriginal peoples, that 'many things which were done . . . by the Europeans to the Aborigines were, and are in retrospect, horrifying' (paragraph 19). But this admission turns out to be another form of relativisation, another version of 'if you think this is bad, you should see South America'. The crucial phrase here is 'in retrospect'. From the privileged, and presumably more civilised, position we now occupy we can agree that mass slaughter was not a good thing, but at the time perceptions—at least the perceptions of the whites, which is all that matters here—were quite different. What happened was not 'genocide or racism', but rather 'the social policy orthodoxies of their day' (paragraph 20).

What is at stake in this article, more than any other issue, is the meaning of the signifier 'violence', and the legitimacy of deciding what constitutes violence and what doesn't. The article quickly denigrates its opponents, and their meanings, by aligning them with the negative side of various binaries (sensible/political, reasonable/dogmatic). But this only disqualifies 'kindergarten Marxists': what about Aboriginal meanings? The second half of the article deals with this, ironically enough, by reproducing the kind of cultural myopia that allowed the British to declare Australia *terra nullius* (or uninhabited) in the first place.

Aboriginal peoples would hardly be likely to accept this meaning of British violence; they could point out, for instance, that it wasn't the social orthodoxy of Aboriginal peoples. Nor would many Jewish or Gypsy or Slavic peoples, or homosexuals or communists who were persecuted during the Nazi period, nod sagely and say, 'Ah, yes, those German social policy orthodoxies of the day'.

Likely Aboriginal perspectives and meanings are completely

absent from this article, as are the arguments of the historians who favour the 'invasion' line. And yet this article bills itself as 'a more balanced school of thought' (headline), as a 'sensible discussion', and as 'the simple truth'. What we have here is a site in the print media which purports to be 'discussing' meanings but which ensures, through various strategies, that only one set of meanings will appear to be 'balanced', 'sensible' and 'truthful'.

What this 'balanced' view crucially neglects, however, is the point that, if the use of the signifier 'invasion' constitutes a form of dogmatism and indoctrination, then the use of 'settlement' over the previous 80 years or so must be seen in exactly the same way. That the author only directs his article against the 'new' meaning means that he is supporting, and in a sense naturalising, the imposition of one meaning over another while at the same time 'discussing' the evils of the imposition of meanings.

SUMMARY

This newspaper article is only one of a number of sites within a culture where the conflict over meanings—what Volosinov called the conflict of ideologies—is played out. Like the various discussions of meaning and gender, these conflicts produce realities rather than mirroring them; that a simple wording change in a primary school syllabus should produce such intense debate confirms, in a variety of ways, the importance and usefulness of the theories of meaning put forward by Saussure, Peirce and Volosinov. Why? Because all the main points and theories of semiotics that we touched upon in this chapter are being practised in this article:

- Meanings are relational. That is, meanings are produced through the relations between signs (examples are binaries such as sensible/political or discussion/indoctrination). Signs do not possess meanings in and of themselves.
- The interpretation of a signifier is always made through another signifier. Note the way the author interprets signifiers such as Marxist, trade unions and feminists pejoratively.
- The production of meaning is an area of ideological contestation (The First Fleet: settlement or invasion?).

What this article demonstrates, against and despite itself, is the openness of meaning, on the one hand, and, on the other, that attempts to close down or naturalise meaning are always political practices and are always ideological.

FURTHER READING

Bourdieu, P. 1991 *Language and Symbolic Power* ed. and introduced by J.B. Thompson, trans. G. Raymond and M. Adamson, Polity Press, Cambridge

Derrida, J. 1976 *Of Grammatology* trans. G. Spivak, Johns Hopkins University Press, Baltimore

Innis, R. (ed.) 1985 *Semiotics: an Introductory Anthology* Indiana University Press, Bloomington

Volosinov, V.N. 1986 *Marxism and the Philosophy of Language* trans. L. Matejka and I. Titunik, Harvard University Press, Cambridge, Mass.

3

COMMUNICATION AS SOCIAL PRACTICE

INTRODUCTION TO SOCIAL SEMIOTICS

In this chapter we will introduce you to a set of ideas which can be tied together under the heading 'social semiotics'. Social semiotics is perhaps best described as a set of related approaches rather than a single unified theory. These approaches are concerned with questions such as:

- How does the performance of any socially meaningful action make sense to the members of a community?
- How do people interpret it?
- What could have been done/said in its place, and how would these alternative choices have differed in meaning?
- When do people make this particular meaning or engage in this particular action?
- How does the meaning change in different circumstances or contexts?
- What larger social and cultural pattern/s does the action relate to?
- How might it tend to re-create or change these larger patterns?

LEMKE 1990:186

Social semiotics can be summed up simply as the study of how people make meaning. We make meaning as members of a particular culture, a particular society, a particular social grouping or community. Social semiotics looks at how and why we make meanings differently according to who and where we are socially and culturally. Are we Australian, Malaysian or Canadian? Child or adult? Nuclear physicist or hairdresser? Of indigenous, white or migrant background? In church, at the bank manager's cocktail party or in the pub? A city or a country dweller?

Social semiotics talks about the process of *making* meanings, rather than assuming that the meanings are already there, attached to words and texts. Of course, H-O-R-S-E spells 'horse', but does 'horse' have the same meaning for everyone who uses the word? Does it mean the same to a ten-year-old who lives in the city but whose dream is to own a pony as it does to a child whose father is a jockey who owns and trains his own horses? Does it mean the same for a medieval knight, an inner-city dweller who once went on a disastrous pony-trek holiday, and a drug user for whom it is a code word for heroin?

On one level, members of a culture can be said to speak the same language (such as English), but when two English speakers of different backgrounds have difficulty 'communicating' we also say 'they don't speak the same language'. And both statements are valid. While we must have a shared system of meaning in order to communicate at all (a common language such as English, or accepted conventions about the meanings of certain gestures), we always have to deal with the fact that those people we communicate with are also different from ourselves in many ways. So meanings can't simply be taken for granted as shared. Instead, we always have to work at making meanings 'available' to others.

That is why social semiotics talks about communication, or meaning making, as a social practice or social process. This reminds us that communication is something people do, rather than a thing.[1] This perspective sees communication as:

- a social practice
- carried out by social agents (members of a society)
- within a social context.

Social semiotics, like all semiotics, makes use of the concept of the *sign system* or *semiotic system*. Sign systems are resources for making meanings within a culture. They provide the range of potential meanings available to us as users of that sign system.

Cultures make meanings from an enormous variety of sign systems; elements as apparently basic to human survival as food, clothing and shelter are transformed into complex sets of resources for meaning making. What does it mean for a man to cook a meal for his partner at home instead of going to McDonald's or to an expensive restaurant? Why are there so many taboos and conventions about what people can wear? Why are there so many different styles of houses in areas with similar climates? Why does furnishing a house with fake tiger-skin rugs and purple chandeliers mean something different from having beige interiors, polished wood surfaces and oil paintings on the walls?

The answers to all of these questions have to do with the ways in which all these systems—systems of food and eating, of dress and adornment, of architecture, of verbal language, as well as many others—are used to make meanings within a culture. As sign systems, they offer a range of potential choices: for example, the choice between wearing diamonds or pearls, eating Kentucky Fried Chicken or home-cooked spaghetti or snails, speaking colloquial English or a more formal version.

This perspective, where we view the actual choice against the background of all the possible alternatives and see its meaning as deriving in part from its relationship to the rest of the system, goes back to Saussure. However, unlike Saussure, social semiotics does not maintain a fixed distinction between the code or *langue* (some sort of idealised grammar or set of rules) and performance or use (*parole*).

In order to avoid this dichotomy, the social semiotician M.A.K. Halliday talks about the code as a system or potential and sees behaviour as the 'actualisation of that potential in real life situations' (Halliday 1984:5); that is, 'code' equals 'potential for behaviour' or **meaning potential**. The things people actually say or do, then, are seen as the output of a system of relations. Instead of seeing 'what people actually say or do' as somehow deviating from or not able to be accounted for in an idealised theory of code, Halliday's systemic approach turns this around and sees the system as being determined by behaviour.

Sign systems, then, are sets of meaning potential, and the output of these systems is actual choices, what people say or do. We need to qualify and explain what is meant by 'choice'. Choices within semiotic systems are not made freely by individuals. They are 'choices' in the sense of one option among many potential options available within the system (meaning potential). In the actual performance or practice of meaning making, people don't make free choices as to how or what they will mean. There are always constraints on meaning making. Meaning potentials are just that—potential meanings. The actual meanings made are limited by two important conditions, the conditions of *access* and of *context*.

First, not everyone within a culture or community has access to all the possible ways of speaking, writing or meaning which that culture potentially allows. Not all of us will find ourselves in a position to agonise over whether to wear diamonds or pearls (or even want to do so). Not everyone has the same access to educational and other contexts so that they can command a range of ways of speaking, from technical, to formal, to colloquial discourse. Not everyone has grown up able to speak more than one language or dialect, or had access since childhood to the national language as a first language.

Second, acts of meaning making always take place within a context, and contexts constrain and limit the range of meanings that can be made. One cannot break into song in the middle of a formal written examination and sing the answers. Or at least, if you did do so, the consequences would be unfortunate, and you would be unlikely to pass the exam. There are ways of meaning making that are expected and appropriate to contexts, ranging from table manners at formal dinners, to the way people address and converse with their mothers-in-law, to what kinds of verbal and non-verbal interaction you are likely to find in a classroom. The contexts in which we communicate constrain what it is possible to say or do. (They do not, however, prevent the unexpected or 'inappropriate', such as the possibility that someone might actually start singing out loud during an exam.)

At this point, we need to introduce another element of the theory—the concept of text. While this is a familiar and widely used term in semiotics, literature and educational contexts generally, the way in which it is used (and thus what it can mean) within a social semiotic approach is distinctive and important.

Texts are produced through the choices made within system/s of meaning making (sign systems). A text is a unit of meaning which operates within a context. We can view texts from two perspectives:

- as product (synoptic perspective)
- as process (dynamic perspective).

Like communication in general, texts can be thought of as things/objects, or as actions. The synoptic perspective, or the view of text as product, is the one which most people are familiar with—when we talk about texts we think of a book, a poem, possibly a TV program. However, texts exist not so much as objects which can be picked up and carried around (a paperback, a video cassette) but as events which unfold in time and space. A conversation is a type of text which we can readily think of in these terms. It is a fluid, interactive process in which all participants take turns to contribute, shaping the direction and structure of the text jointly as they go along.

Other texts do not show their processes of production so clearly; for example, printed texts, such as books and newspapers, are presented to readers as completed objects. Nevertheless, they too go through stages of production, during which their 'final' form is cumulatively constructed, negotiated, and altered in different ways. And even this so-called final form is still subjected to ongoing cultural change and negotiation. One obvious example is the different versions of popular texts, such as films (there is the original black and white *Casablanca* and the 'colorised' text; the first release of *Blade Runner* and the more recently released 'director's cut') and music (the tape, record or CD version, the original recording or the remastered tapes) which makes it difficult to talk about any 'final' version of a text.

Perhaps less obvious, but even more important in some ways, is the way in which texts are changed through undergoing different kinds of commoditisation within a culture. A song might be written for a band and appear on their CD; but it also might then be picked up by advertisers and used in a television commercial. This change of context completely changes the text: it now (potentially) means a number of very different things. One interesting example of this kind of re-commoditisation is the character Patsy Stone in the television series *Absolutely Fabulous*. The chain-smoking, hard drinking and sexually aggressive and active character became a cult figure for the gay community; during the Sydney Gay and Lesbian Mardi Gras in 1995 there was a float full of Patsy Stones. Take a text to another place and use it in different ways, and you have a 'new' text.

Language as social practice

As we have noted above, all meaningful social practices constitute the object of study of social semiotics. However, most of the following discussion and examples will concentrate on verbal language as one of our primary semiotic systems. We will return to other, non-verbal systems of meaning in later chapters.

Who does social semiotics?

The term 'social semiotics' comes from the work of the linguist M.A.K. (Michael) Halliday, who published his book *Language as Social Semiotic* in 1978. Halliday was born in the United Kingdom and moved to Australia in 1976 to become Professor of Linguistics at the University of Sydney. Most people who call themselves social semioticians or who do social semiotics would acknowledge Halliday's work as foundational. Among his writings are a functional grammar of English (1985) and a very accessible short account of his theories, co-authored by Ruqaiya Hasan (1985). Hasan and Halliday have also written together on cohesion in texts (1976).

Work in this area began by focusing on language. J.L. (Jim) Martin has developed Halliday's theory, particularly in relation to register, genre, ideology and discourse (1985, 1986, 1992).

In 1988 Bob Hodge and Gunther Kress published their book *Social Semiotics*. This presented social semiotics as an analytical approach to a wide range of cultural texts and issues. It also linked with work which related social semiotics to other contemporary critical theories (Kress 1985, Kress and Threadgold 1988, Threadgold 1986).

Some social semiotic researchers have focused on specific discourses and genres, for example, scientific discourse in the classroom (Lemke 1990), mother–child talk (Hasan 1986), and drama (Birch 1991, Melrose 1994). Others have examined issues such as the cultural construction of race (Threadgold 1988b, McGregor 1991) and gender (Poynton 1985, Thibault 1988, Threadgold 1988a).

Social semioticians are also exploring a variety of systems of meaning, such as music (van Leeuwen 1991), visual images (Kress and van Leeuwen 1990), bodies (Wright 1991), sculpture (O'Toole 1992) and mass media (van Leeuwen 1986).

Language is so familiar and so much a part of our daily lives that we take it for granted much of the time, unless our attention is drawn to the way we are using it, for example, if an authority figure disapproves of our language (e.g. swearing), or if our production of written and spoken texts is under the spotlight within the context of a school, college, university or workplace.

However, there is more to the study of language than 'good grammar' and a sound grasp of vocabulary. Language practices, like all communication practices, need to be understood as patterns of meaning making which take place within a large and diverse range of social and cultural contexts. In order to understand how and why we use language, and to what ends, we need an understanding of the complex relationship between texts and contexts.

One of the reasons why we are able to communicate with others, despite the problem of 'difference' discussed above, is that there is a degree of probability or expectedness in the way meanings unfold within contexts (Halliday 1985:9–10). Thus, while texts and contexts can never fully determine one another, as members of a culture we are able to anticipate broadly the types of communication practices which will take place within a context. We are able to understand and respond to texts actively and appropriately to the extent that we are familiar with their contexts. That is, literacy about *texts* is inextricably tied up with the possession of literacy about *contexts*. Both constitute forms of cultural literacy.

Speakers and writers about language and communication often use the term 'competence' to refer to what we are calling 'literacy'. The term competence is associated with a tradition which studies the human ability to communicate and to use language in terms of the functioning of the human brain. A cognitive (mind-based) approach to these questions has been strongly influenced ever since the 1960s by the theories of the American linguist Noam Chomsky. Chomsky and others involved with cognitive linguistics and cognitive psychology have argued that all individuals have the innate ability to use language; that this is a set of skills our brains are 'wired for' from birth (Chomsky 1968).

There is no doubt that there are physical (or perhaps more accurately electrochemical) circuits and networks within the brain that must be in working order for us to use language.[2] But although much valuable research has been carried out, a cognitive perspective leaves many questions unanswered. First, cognitive accounts focus on the individual mind and tend to universalise this. (You will recall why this is a problem from the discussion of the 'process model' in Chapter 1.)

The social perspective on language is absent. Second, cognitive linguists separate competence from performance (just as Saussure distinguished between *langue* and *parole*). They focus on competence (taken at its simplest to refer to the mental ability to produce grammatical or well-formed sentences) at the expense of performance, which is seen as too 'messy' to deal with.[3] Thus questions of social and cultural diversity and the effects of these on language and meaning are not addressed. Context is entirely absent from a mind-based approach.

Since these are precisely the questions with which we are centrally concerned in this book, we will use the terms literacy and practice rather than competence.

TEXT AND CONTEXT

Contexts can be understood as the particular environments in which communication, texts and meaning making occur, and in which they function as meaningful. The context is the situation in which we make sense of a text or meaningful practice. For example:

- a group of protesters yelling 'Go, go, go!' at a politician they want to resign
- the same words shouted by a parent whose offspring are dawdling and about to miss the morning school bus.

The same words are uttered (or rather, screamed) in each context, but can we say that they mean 'the same' in both contexts? Certainly, what those words mean to the politician (hostility, disapproval) is likely to be very different from their meaning to the reluctant school children (parental nagging and over-anxiety).

In each case, the interaction between text and context produces more meanings than the dictionary definition of the word 'go' can possibly encompass:

> *v.i.* Start, depart, move, continue moving, with self-originated or imparted motion, from some place, position, time, etc., specified or obvious.
>
> *CONCISE OXFORD DICTIONARY*

There is a temptation to discuss contexts as if they are 'out there' in plain view, as part of 'reality'. But the view that contexts are non-semiotic, unlike texts, which are made of meanings, has a catch. Like texts, contexts are semiotic constructs. They are ways of making sense of the world. Context is a conceptual dimension, a way of reading what is going on 'out there'. There are as many potential contexts available to a person as there are meanings of a text, and these contexts may continue to inform or determine meanings, or may quickly give way to other contexts. Moreover, it is not as if we are aware of all the contexts that are influencing our actions or the meanings we make. One of the more interesting points about Freudian psychoanalysis, for example, is that it posits an unconscious aspect to our 'selves' which obviously can influence our actions, yet which we can never fully comprehend.

Why are contexts so unstable and difficult to explain? A protest rally against a politician or policy appears to be a stable and clearly defined context. How can this context be read in different ways? First, the way the politician reads this context will be different from the way the protesters read it. For a start, the context in which the politician hears the crowd's chant is probably one which includes her/his own psychological state, the number of protesters, the proximity of the media, and the support she/he is receiving from within the party. Other less immediate elements of this context could include her/his party's standing in the popularity polls and her/his recent performances in parliament, as well as that of her/his party and their opposition. Her/his supporters will read the context differently from the opposition's supporters, as will the political commentators who, a few days earlier, suggested that the politician might become party leader.

We select what constitutes context from aspects of the situation. These include:

- what is going on, and where
- those involved
- the role of the text in the situation
- the other texts (intertexts) which are related to this one
- the wider social and cultural context.

By acknowledging that contexts are semiotic and can be read differently, we acknowledge that contexts are subject to negotiation. Defining contexts is a political issue, since establishing the meaning of a context is a way of establishing the meaning of a text.

An example is the way the terms 'rape' and 'sexual harassment' can be applied to particular contexts within Australian culture. Recently, a judge stated that the penalty for a man found guilty of rape should be lessened because the woman he raped was a prostitute. The judge decided that in determining the degree of seriousness of this rape, the woman's profession was a relevant aspect of the context. Others in the community, particularly women's groups and prostitutes, strongly disagreed with the judge's definition of the relevant context in this matter.

As another example, consider sexual harassment. What one person sees as a playful joke may be seen by another as unwanted and threatening behaviour. This has a great deal to do with gendered power differences in contexts such as the workplace. A power inequity, as we saw in Chapter 1, means that the same context is effectively not 'the same' for the more powerful participant as it is for the less powerful.

The relationship between texts and contexts is thus an interdependent one. Each affects the other, although it cannot be said either that contexts determine texts, nor that texts determine contexts. As Halliday expresses it, 'the text creates the context as much as the context creates the text' (1985:37).

It might be useful to reiterate, however, that while everyone can bring different contexts to bear on texts, there is a considerable political dimension to the way in which some contexts are privileged over others. There are a number of contexts in which the various colonial activities in Africa, America, Australia and New Zealand might have been 'understood'; indeed, the context we bring to bear on this issue will determine, for instance, whether we use the word 'invasion' or 'settlement' when we refer, say, to Australian history in the eighteenth century. Australian Aboriginal peoples brought their contexts to bear on understanding and explaining British actions in 1788, but the British decided that those contexts didn't count.

Similarly, the various forms of discrimination and exploitation that have been practised against women in western cultures over the centuries have been perpetuated, to no small extent, because it was argued that women could only understand things in terms of 'private' contexts, whereas men could bring wider, public contexts to bear on issues; or, to put it another way, women could only understand things emotionally, while men were supposedly capable of bringing reason to bear on their thoughts and actions.

CONTEXT OF SITUATION

A number of scholars have attempted to provide a theoretical account of context, including the anthropologist Malinowski, the linguist Firth and the ethnographer Hymes. Halliday examined their frameworks for describing context (Halliday and Hasan 1985:5–9) and came up with his own simple but comprehensive model. Although it is not without its problems, it provides a very useful tool for analysing contexts. Halliday suggests that we can separate context into three aspects or dimensions:

- Field—what is happening? what is the communication about?
- Tenor—who is taking part? what is their part in the interaction? what positions are they taking up?
- Mode—how is the text structured? what part is the code or language playing?

To exemplify these dimensions of context, let's look at the range of potential contexts in an office workplace. What texts might be produced, and how could we describe their contexts?

The field or social action could be a chat over morning tea, or a board meeting. In the first case, the subject matter could be someone's drinking habits, or what happened on *Melrose Place* the previous evening, and in the second case it might be concerned with the latest sales figures, or an impending takeover bid.

The tenor, or participants involved, and the social relations between them, could include a range of combinations, such as colleagues of equal status, or managing director and clerical assistant. Different patterns of meaning making would be observed according to who is interacting with whom. The field of gossip over morning tea is more likely to take place where the tenor relations are informal and fairly equal. Workplaces which observe hierarchies strictly also place firm limits on which participants have access to which fields of discourse. (The chairman presiding over a board meeting is likely to call in a junior clerk to request a printout of the latest sales figures rather than to gossip about the TV soaps.)

The mode, or the structure of the communication, could take a number of forms: written memo, e-mail message on a computer screen, telephone conversation, face-to-face talk. Again, certain choices of mode will hook up with field and tenor options. Thus, a memo will be used for 'official' business, but gossip is unlikely to be communicated on letterhead stationery.

Every context can be analysed in terms of its field, its tenor and its mode. When contexts are analysed in this way, it becomes clear that the range of field, tenor and mode options cannot freely combine with one another. That is, some combinations are more likely than others. For example, we would not expect a context in which an executive listens patiently while a cleaner plays a guitar and sings a ballad about how to balance the budget (although it is possible to imagine a context for this—a TV comedy). The field (giving advice about the budget) does not match the tenor (an executive whose job it is to know how to balance budgets being advised by a cleaner whose tasks do not include being expert at this). Nor does the mode (guitar ballad) match either the field or the tenor. Our sense of these kinds of incongruity constitutes a form of cultural literacy about communication and context.

Let's now examine each of these dimensions of context in more detail.

Field

Field refers to the social action of the text, what the language (or other semiotic resource) is being used to do. More specifically:

> The field of discourse refers to what is happening, to the nature of the social action that is taking place: what is it that the participants are engaged in . . . ?
>
> HALLIDAY 1985:12

In identifying the field, or social action, we recognise that it is an activity which is meaningful within a social system. 'What's going on' may be wholly 'language-in-action' or it may be an activity structured through other semiotic resources (visual, non-verbal).

Typically, the kind of social action going on also influences the subject matter, or what the interaction is about. While these two aspects of field, the social action and the subject matter, are linked, they do not necessarily determine one another. If the social action is 'doing the washing up', the participants may be discussing whether the washer has cleaned a plate adequately, or the quality of the detergent, but are just as likely to be discussing topics unrelated to what they are doing, such as the state of the economy or the neighbours' divorce.

Other fields do constrain subject matter, in particular those fields which are under the overt control of an institution. Obvious examples can be found in the fields of religion, law and education. For example, in a school science lesson, the subject matter is expected to be, and largely will be, science, although the participants will probably also be talking about various other (unofficial) topics.

Teacher:	Yesterday we were talking about, uh, *wave* motion. And we said that *sound* was a particular *kind* of wave motion. Can anybody remember what kind of wave motion sound *is*? [To student with hand raised.] D'you remember? [Student indicates she only wants the pass to the bathroom.] Why should I give you a pass? [4 seconds, laughter] When you can't answer a question like that? [2 seconds, then to class:] What kind of wave motion is sound?
Student:	It's—it's a *wave* motion.
Teacher:	Sound is a *wave* motion. What *kind* of wave motion?
Student:	Sound wave.
Teacher:	Sound is a wave, what *kind* of wave?
Another:	Vibration.
Teacher:	What *kind* of vibration?
Student:	Waves.
Teacher:	What *kind* of waves?
Eugene:	Are you asking which one of those four?
Teacher:	*Mhmm.*
Eugene:	Oh . . . um, uh long- long-i-tud-inal wave.
Teacher:	Eugene is correct. [Others comment, whistle] [31 seconds, writing at board]

LEMKE 1990:246–7

To analyse the field of this text, we can ask:

- what is going on? and
- what is the subject matter?

The social action is that of instruction, through a classroom lesson, and more precisely a teacher questioning students to test their recall. The associated subject matter is the discourse of science, evident in word choice ('wave', 'vibration', 'longitudinal', 'motion'). Here is a text whose field is under the official control of the teacher, in whom the authority of the institution is vested.

The social action, however, is not exclusively or purely the 'official' field. There are moments when the field escapes from the teacher's control, for example when a student raises her hand as if to respond to the teacher's question but instead performs the social action of 'seeking permission to go to the toilet'. Students often use such techniques to challenge the teacher's control of the field without appearing to do so—what we can call a **tactic**. A tactic is an attempt, by those who do not have 'official' power, to achieve their own ends (de Certeau 1988).

Field, then, is strongly linked to the institutional context in which it takes place. Institutions such as the law, the family, religion, education and sport have particular discourses associated with them, discourses which define and limit ways in which it is possible to mean within the context of the institution. These discourses are an important aspect of any analysis of field. Questions of the role of institutions and discourse in shaping contexts will be taken up again in Chapter 5.

Tenor

Meaning making is a form not just of social action but of *interaction*. When we make meanings we address them to some other—a listener, reader, or audience, actual or implied; sometimes we simply address meanings to ourselves. Communicative acts are not just simple exchanges of information, but are about the allocation, negotiation, acceptance or rejection of a variety of social relations. Tenor refers to this interactive dimension of communication. Here is Halliday's definition of tenor:

> The tenor of discourse refers to who is taking part, to the nature of the participants, their statuses and roles: what kinds of role relationship obtain among the participants, including permanent and temporary relationships of one kind or another, both the types of speech role that they are taking on in the dialogue and the whole cluster of socially significant relationships in which they are involved?
>
> HALLIDAY 1985:12

When we 'read' a text, whether it is a written text, a spoken interaction, a set of gestures, a photograph or a television program, we enter into a relation with that text and with the agent which produced it. To communicate is not merely to give and receive neutral information, but to enter into a relation with some other. This social relation is mediated in and through texts or meaning-making practices. For example, a street sign: HARBOUR BRIDGE LEFT LANE sets up a relation between the motorists who read it and the sign itself. The sign addresses motorists on behalf of the social agent who installed the sign, presumably the road traffic authority. It directs the motorist; that is, it gives the motorist directions ('traffic in the left lane goes to the Harbour Bridge') and at the same time it gives the motorist an instruction ('take the left lane if you want the Harbour Bridge').

If we refer to Halliday's definition of tenor, we can make several observations about the tenor relation between the motorist and the sign. First, we can note that this is a temporary, if not momentary, relation which is set up between motorist and road sign. The driver notes the sign, makes a decision about which lane to take, and drives on. Second, the tenor involves one participant 'telling the other what to do' and thereby taking on the status of authority over the other (with respect to the social action or field in which both are involved).

As you can see from this example, tenor relations need not outlive or transcend the interaction which produces them. The concept of a relation does not imply a 'relationship' in the everyday sense of the word—that is, a socially identifiable, personalised connection between individuals. Instead, the concept of tenor arises from the function that language (or some other semiotic resource system) has in specific contexts, as interaction. Many of these kinds of interaction do carry with them relationships which we readily recognise and name (mother–daughter, boyfriend–girlfriend, prosecution lawyer–witness). Other, more transitory and less socially stable relations such as the relation between the motorist and the road sign do not have labels. That is why we need a critical vocabulary in order to specify this dimension of context.

We can analyse tenor relations in more detail using the categories suggested by Poynton (1985). She identifies three aspects which constitute tenor:

* power
* social distance (contact)
* emotion or attitude (affect).

Power
- force, physical strength or skills, e.g. in contexts such as the boxing ring, the school playground, sport
- authority (socially vested or institutionalised), e.g. parent–child in a family context, teacher–student in a classroom context
- social status, e.g. class or socioeconomic or hereditary social status, e.g. Porsche driver, professional (doctor, lawyer), member of British aristocracy or royalty, street kid
- expertise (possession of a relevant knowledge or skill), e.g. person who has memorised the Melbourne tram timetable, local spider expert, professor of cardiology

(Note that attributes such as gender, race and age can carry multiple markers of power (or powerlessness). For example, to be female, in many contexts, is to be attributed with a lack of force, of authority and of expertise.)

Power refers to the extent to which the participants are positioned as equal or unequal. Contact, or social distance, refers to how intimate or distant the participants are, in a social sense. Affect refers to the kind of attitudes and emotions that are being displayed as part of the interaction.

Each of these aspects can be brought into play in a context through a variety of specific markers, or socially constructed attributes. Some examples are given in the boxes below.

These tenor factors are not necessarily set or predetermined elements of context which then shape texts and meaning making in predictable ways. Tenor relations may evolve and shift during the interaction.

For example, consider a situation in which a student comes to see a lecturer to ask for an extension. The context is already pre-structured to an extent in terms of the relative power and status of the two people concerned. Lecturers have a higher status than students because of their role within the educational institution, their qualifications and their level of relevant expertise. The lecturer has

Contact
- extent and frequency and means of contact, e.g. lifelong friend and neighbour, mail or milk deliverer (seen daily very briefly), parent who lives interstate, TV newsreader (seen every night but never met), members of an industrial union
- personal contact versus professional or task-oriented contact, e.g. friends and family members versus a doctor–patient relationship

power over the student, being in a position to evaluate the student's work, allocate grades, decide course content and so on.

These tenor factors mean that the student would probably not come in and yell at the lecturer, demanding an extension, and the lecturer would be very unlikely to apologise profusely to the student for not granting one. The student would probably address the lecturer by title and surname (indicating the lecturer's higher status and also a degree of formality and distance). The lecturer might use the student's first name, or not address the student by name at all (how does this position the student?). The lecturer would remain seated and the student would stand unless invited to sit. These would all be markers of the unequal status and power relations of the two participants.

However, this relation may be negotiated and changed as part of the communication process. For example, the student may burst into tears, explaining that the recent death of a family member has made it extremely difficult to concentrate on study. The social distance (contact) may shift from relatively formal and distant to a slightly more personal relation. The lecturer may offer the student a box of tissues. With increased intimacy, the dimension of affect is likely to become more overt, with the discussion of feelings and the use of non-verbal markers of sympathy (possibly touch and facial expression).

As this example suggests, the relation between context and meaning making is a dynamic one, in which elements of context may shift as part of the process. Further, each element of tenor—power, contact and affect—may be taken for granted as part of the 'accepted' background or may be brought into focus as under negotiation. Here

> Affect
> - may range from positive expressions (joy, pride, pleasure, desire, approval, etc.), to indifference, to negative expressions (distaste, contempt, hatred, anger, disapproval, etc.)
> - may or may not be explicitly expressed, but the absence of overt markers of emotion is as meaningful as their presence, e.g.:
>   academic scientific writing strives to be emotionally neutral and 'objective'
>   popular science reporting may show 'excitement'
>   pro-conservationist speech will be strongly marked for affect, ranging from praise for the wonders of nature to indignation and contempt for organisations responsible for polluting the environment

is an example where different aspects of tenor are brought to the fore as the interaction proceeds.

Mother: Don't do that. Move it away, if you want to rock it. [The child is rocking on a chair.]
Child: No.
Mother: You'll go straight to your room if you bang my chair . . .
Child: I hit you with a teddy.
Mother: Poor teddy! Teddy's crying. You hurt his head. He's got a headache now. He wants to be my teddy.
Child: No [taking teddy]. He hasn't got a tummyache. He's got a fat tummy. I want to see the water in there . . .

POYNTON 1990:68

The mother begins by directly asserting her power over the child by issuing a command ('Don't do that') and then a threat ('You'll go straight to your room if you bang my chair'). However, she then changes to a different strategy, downplaying her own power in order to shift the interaction away from a conflict over the child's behaviour. She turns the child's act of aggression ('I hit you with a teddy') into the topic (field), and talks about the teddy's feelings ('Poor teddy . . .') and how the teddy will want to be hers now. In this way the mother shifts the tenor so that it is focused on affect and contact rather than on power/control. (The clear moral lesson for the child in this brief but suggestive interaction is that if s/he is angry or violent then others will not want to be close to him/her.)

You can see from this example that there is more to the analysis of tenor than simply identifying a relation in terms of the social roles involved, such as mother–child. There is no one-to-one, deterministic relation between an identifiable social relation, such as parent–child, and the ascription of power, authority and control. Social relations are always negotiated through individual interactions and meaning-making practices.

Mode

Finally, we will briefly discuss the third element of context, mode. Mode concerns the formation of the communication as a text, including the code/s and the medium/s involved. Halliday offers the following definition of mode:

> The mode of discourse refers to what part the language is playing, what it is that the participants are expecting language to do for them in that situation: the symbolic organisation of the text, the status that it has, and its function in the context, including the channel (is it spoken or written or some combination of the two?)
>
> HALLIDAY 1985:12

While Halliday is primarily concerned here with language, mode is concerned precisely with the choice of a semiotic system or code. Within any system, more delicate (precise) mode options are available. Within language, a text may be formed through the medium of speech or of writing, just as in painting an image may be done in oils or in watercolours. Verbal texts may be dialogue or monologue, printed or handwritten, scrawled on the back of an envelope or typed on official letterhead stationery.

It may be useful to define the terms code, channel and medium briefly. A code is a system of signs governed by rules. It is also often used to refer to these rules. A distinction is sometimes made in the study of communication between channel and medium. A channel is defined as the physical means of carrying a signal, for example sound waves or light waves, while medium is a more general term referring to the means of communication. Channel is a term which is used mainly in the study of the physical problems in communication, and is therefore less relevant for our purposes in this book.

Together, the concepts of code and medium remind us that texts are material forms as well as meaning-making practices. The code and the medium make possible, and also limit, the range of meanings. They provide a diversity of materials (mediums) and ways of shaping these materials (codes). Technology is continually expanding the ways in which these mediums and codes can combine, as well as opening up new mediums. Prehistoric humans had a fairly limited range of mediums with which to make meanings. They had visual media, such as carvings and cave paintings, and possibly other systems such as dress, adornment and dance, and no doubt used their bodies as a medium of nonverbal communication, through gesture, touch and so on. By contrast, in the twentieth century, and heading into the 21st, we have not only what we can call 'simple' mediums such as speech, writing and graphic representation, but also complex mediums which combine several mediums using technology. Television and film are the prime examples of such mediums, since they can combine speech, music, and a range of visual media.

The analysis of mode is critical to understanding the ways in which texts come to mean as they do, since the other two elements of context, field and tenor, need always to be read against the possibilities offered by the mode. Let's examine how this works in an advertising text (see Figure 6).

The Sony ad appears in a print medium, a magazine, and employs both verbal and visual codes. The photographic image of the compact hi-fi system is the central and dominant image in the text. Its central placement relates to the field; the social action is that of 'advertising a product to potential consumers'. The product takes centre stage against a plain background. Another code, music, is also alluded to by the images of musical notes.

The verbal text supplements the visual text by amplifying (no pun intended) the information the image presents and extending the field of discourse. The verbal text also sets up specific tenor relations of persuasion which the image alone probably could not accomplish.

Putting field, tenor and mode together

Let's now fill out our analysis of the Sony text in relation to the dimensions of field and tenor. We have noted that the field is promoting a product for sale, and that this is pursued in part through the visual image. The verbal text constructs a field of music

FIGURE 6

COURTESY OF SONY AUSTRALIA

equipment technology (there are references to 'digital audio technology', 'ultra high output', '5-band spectrum analyser'). The text also invokes the field of music genres and appreciation ('heavy metal album', 'concert hall'). The term 'heavy metal' is used in the large print at the top of the text as well as in the body text underneath, and can be read as belonging to two different discourses. In the heading, SONY NOW MAKE A MACHINE THAT CAN TURN HEAVY METAL INTO CRYSTAL, the association between 'heavy metal' and 'crystal' comes from the discourse of medieval alchemy, the science of turning base metals such as lead into precious metals such as gold. The pun on 'heavy metal' comes from its double meaning, as a term from both musical and chemical discourse, at least for those readers who have the cultural knowledge of both discourses. The double meaning is also carried through, for those who have a different set of cultural literacies, in the images of crystal notes floating away from the CD player. Contrasts, or binaries, such as heavy/light, classical/popular music can be picked up on by readers of the advertisement. These all help to produce the field, or social action, by suggesting the transformations that this marvellous piece of equipment can perform for the buyer. That is, they are all motivated by the function of 'promoting a product to a potential consumer'.

What kind of tenor relations does this text produce? The advertisement is worded as if the *power relations* between the producer of the text and its audience were equal. The 'speaker' of the ad seems to assume that the readers have similar expertise in hi-fi, since many technical terms are used without explanation. While we, the audience, may not know this much about hi-fi, we may find it flattering to be treated as if we do.

In terms of the *contact*, we might consider that it is not very close, since there is no direct contact with the speaker. The text is produced by an anonymous agent and disseminated to thousands of people through the mass media. Nevertheless, in the last two paragraphs the ad addresses us in a personalised and familiar way, and talks about 'your favourite' music, 'we' and 'your neighbours'. We can call this kind of contact **synthetic personalisation** (after Fairclough 1989:62, 195), the process of framing a text or interaction as personalised and individualised although it actually involves large numbers of people who are treated identically. Another example of this is the convention in many shops, supermarkets and fast food outlets of saying to each customer, 'Have a nice day.'

Returning to the Sony ad, the *affect* is very positive, with terms of praise used for the product ('studio quality', 'high quality') and suggestions about the pleasure the buyer will derive from the product ('the perfect way to enjoy your favourite . . . album or CD').

As we are used to advertisements using this kind of tenor, with its characteristics of apparent equality, pseudo-personal appeal and 'feel-good' affect, we don't usually give it a second thought, but you can see that these features of tenor relate directly to the ad's selling function. The tenor contributes to the social purpose of this text, its field. All of the features of context—field, tenor and mode—work together to create a text which is functional. We recognise it as a particular type of text because it has these characteristics and it relates to its context in a relatively predictable way. Such recognisable text types are genres. (The concept of genre will be the discussed further in Chapter 5.)

SUMMARY

This chapter introduced readers to a social semiotic approach to communication. This perspective sees communication as:

- a social practice
- carried out by social agents (members of a society)
- within a social context.

We examined the concept of the *sign system* or *semiotic system* as a resource for making meanings within a culture.

The relationship between text and context was identified as a dynamic one, in which texts and contexts interact with one another. A social semiotic model of context was introduced as a way of analysing this dynamic relationship. This model analyses contexts in terms of field, tenor and mode:

- Field—what is happening? what is the communication about?
- Tenor—who is taking part? what is their part in the interaction? what positions are they taking up?
- Mode—how is the text structured? what part are the code and the medium playing?

We suggested that our awareness of the relation between text and context, as users of language and other semiotic resources systems, constitutes a form of cultural literacy.

FURTHER READING

Halliday, M.A.K. & R. Hasan 1985 *Language, Context and Text: Aspects of Language in a Social-semiotic Perspective* Deakin University Press, Victoria, Part A

Hodge, R. and G. Kress 1988 *Social Semiotics* Polity, Cambridge

Lemke, Jay L. 1990 *Talking Science: Language, Learning and Values* Ablex, Norwood, Ch.8

Poynton, C. 1985 *Language and Gender: Making the Difference* Deakin University Press, Victoria, Ch.6

4
SPEECH GENRES

This chapter will consider speech from a number of angles: as a member of the binary speech/writing, as a medium of communication, as a mode of interaction (dialogue), and as a site where power relations are negotiated, challenged or enforced. We will address questions such as:

* How does speech differ from writing?
* Is speech less complex than writing?
* What influences determine how people speak?
* How does dialogue work?
* What is the relation between speech and power?
* Whose speech matters, and in what contexts?

SPEECH VERSUS WRITING

Speech and writing are two of the primary means or mediums which people use to communicate. They are two alternative ways in which people can communicate using language. Thus they share a common code (a particular language, for example English, Chinese, German). However, they also differ in a number of important ways, ways which can affect the purposes to which we put them.

1   Speech is transmitted as sounds (aural channel) while writing is transmitted as marks (visual channel).

Sounds are transient, not permanent, unless one of the various audio technologies (such as audiotape, compact disc) is used to make a more permanent record of them. So speech demands the hearer's immediate understanding and relies on memory.

In contrast, writing is usually produced in a more permanent form (on paper, walls, plaster casts), although there are exceptions

(for example, sky writing, messages written on the sand as the tide is coming in, and so on.)

Writing allows readers to re-read a text, to check their comprehension, find a piece of information that they missed the first time, and so on. On the other hand, listeners don't have the same kind of control over an oral message without the aid of technology such as recording devices. Instead, they may interrupt the speaker to ask for something to be repeated, clarified or explained.

2   Unlike written communication, oral communication is accompanied by paralanguage and bodily communication.

There are many resources available to speakers for making meanings. Speech involves not just sounds which combine to form words, but the tone, pitch, rhythm, pace and volume of the voice (this is known as **paralanguage**). In fact, when speech takes place face to face, the whole body becomes a resource for making meaning (this will be discussed in more detail in Chapter 9).

In written communication, the reader is using a different set of resources to read meanings. Paralanguage is absent, although writers can use punctuation and lettering styles to 'reproduce' paralanguage. For example:

- a question mark can show rising intonation: Will you be back later?
- capitals may indicate loudness: HEY, YOU!
- italics may be used for emphasis: No, *I* don't want to go, *you* go instead.

But writing as a form of communication does not employ the resources of the body to make meaning in the same way that spoken communication does.

Nevertheless, with the advent of new technologies, what seem to be fairly clear cut differences between the medium of speech and the medium of writing are becoming less distinct. For example, the Internet, a vast web of interactive computer networks which spans the globe, links individual users to other users, so that by typing a message into a home or office computer linked to this network, one user can 'talk' to another. Once a message is completed and sent, it travels almost instantaneously, and if the other user is using the network at the same time, s/he can reply almost immediately. Communication via the Internet can thus take on the interactivity of a telephone conversation while allowing the option of keeping a permanent record of the message, like a letter.

Users of the Internet have even developed a common code to supply the paralanguage and bodily communication (the facial expressions, tones of voice and gestures) which supplement the verbal meanings in face-to-face interaction—see Figure 7. These are typographic symbols combined to form miniature icons for various emotions (to make sense of these read them sideways).

3 Speech is the usual medium of communication when the participants are face to face, while writing is more commonly used when those communicating are separated physically. Written communication enables a message to be produced in the absence of the receiver and to be read in the absence of the sender.

Although we often take writing very much for granted, its ability to cross barriers of space and time makes it a powerful technology; and for many centuries it was the only technology which could do this (before the invention of other technologies such as telephone, radio, television, audio recording, fax and computer).

Of course, there are contexts in which written communication does take place in the presence of both sender and receiver, for various reasons. For example, writing allows for private communication within the context of a group (passing a note to a friend in class), or for a degree of formality (handing an employer a letter of resignation), or to enable ideas or information to be put 'on display' for consideration or discussion (the use of blackboards, overhead transparencies or handouts by teachers and seminar presenters).

4 The medium of writing allows a message or text to seem like a product, while speech is like a process.

Although we are using the term 'speech', in everyday life we more usually talk about speaking to refer to the same activity. This signals a common way of thinking about talk as something people do (a *process*) rather than a thing (a *product*).

On the other hand, writing is commonly used to produce a finished text (product), a message which can be thought about as a discrete whole, rather than something which is experienced

FIGURE 7 Emotions on the Internet: 'Smileys' are faces turned sideways

Characters	Meaning
:-(	frown
;-)	wink (denotes a pun or sly joke)
:-O	yelling or screaming, completely shocked
:-P	sticking your tongue out
:-D	big
%-(	confused and unhappy
:'	crying
:'-)	crying happy tears
*	kiss
{{{***}}}	hugs and kisses
<g> or <G>	grin

COURTESY OF ALBION BOOKS. SHEA 1995

as a more or less continuous flow (process). Of course, to construct a piece of writing, writers have to go through a process, for example, writing multiple drafts of an essay or several versions of a personal letter.

Most written communication hides the processes that produced it (it's considered unacceptable to hand in an essay with paragraphs scratched out and rewritten, and sections cut and pasted on). Again, this relates to the function of the communication—its formality and its degree of permanence. For example, you might post a personal letter leaving in numerous crossed-out sections rather than copy it out neatly, but a published book (a much more permanent and public piece of writing) is checked and re-checked for errors before being printed.

Depending on the task which you are using speech or writing to perform, there will be differences in the ways you use the medium to achieve a similar purpose. For example, as part of your university assessment, you may be required to present your ideas on a particular topic to a class orally, and in writing to your tutor/lecturer. Let's compare the features of the oral task and the written task—we could expect them to differ in the ways shown in Figure 8.

The features of speech work well because we make sense of it through anticipation. The features of writing work well because we make sense of it retrospectively—we are able to look back over what we have already read. Speech is no less structured and

FIGURE 8   Speech and writing

Speech	Writing
• uses repetition of words and ideas	• uses variation in word choice
• ideas are introduced one at a time	• denser—packs ideas in more tightly
• ideas linked or strung together	• ideas joined together in complex ways (longer sentences)

organised than writing; it is just that it is structured and organised *differently*. It is important to remember that what works in writing won't always work orally, and vice versa.

The differences discussed above are partly to do with the limitations of each medium (the **materiality** of speech and writing), and partly to do with the purposes to which we put speech and writing within a culture (their social functions, their structuring as **social sign systems**). These purposes come to take on a particular value within a culture. Within western culture (European and English-speaking cultures), it is conventional to presume that writing as a means of communication has been more highly valued than speech: those areas of a culture (such as law, science and literature) which primarily employ the medium of writing have often been highly regarded. Interestingly enough, the French philosopher Jacques Derrida suggests that, to a certain extent, speech is still valued over writing because it is understood as being more spontaneous, and more 'honest' in that it is closer to the 'truth' of our intentions (Derrida 1976).

THE SOCIAL LIFE OF SPEECH

Speech is regarded as the most basic and primary means of communication. It is the one we acquire, as individuals, before many other semiotic systems. It is also regarded, in accounts of the evolution and development of human beings, as having developed earlier than writing—some millions of years earlier, by some accounts (Halliday, 1985:vii). Speaking and listening are activities we usually perform without reflecting very much about what we are doing, and which seem to 'come naturally'. In contrast, writing is something we are very conscious of having had to learn how to do (although this is true of speech also).

As children, we learn how to mean primarily by learning how to speak. Of course, babies also rely heavily on facial and gestural signs as a means of communication and interaction. Beyond behavioural symptoms such as crying when they are wet or hungry, babies develop ways of interacting symbolically with those around them. Even before they are able to demonstrate control of 'adult' language, very young children use vocal sounds to respond to and interact with those around them, apparently gaining pleasure merely from the process of 'having a conversation'.

Speech, then, is a fundamental human activity. However, we should not be fooled by the deceptively 'natural' character of speech as a phenomenon and speaking as a practice. Neither speech as a social practice, nor our capacity for speaking, develop in a social or historical vacuum. Languages and specific modes of speech develop in particular social and historical contexts.

It is impossible to talk about 'speech' without considering *what* we speak, that is, which language, and the history of that language. For many, but by no means all of the readers of this textbook, English will be your first language; that is, the language you learned to speak first. But English is not a pure phenomenon—Australian English is not the same as American English, or New Zealand English, or so-called Standard British English. To trace the history of any language, and its various inflections and dialects, is to trace the history of the colonising of some groups by other, dominant groups.

For example, Standard British English was once a **dialect** (variant language type) spoken predominantly by the merchant class in London. With their increasing social power in the late Middle Ages, the variety of language members of this class spoke gradually became associated with—indeed, colonised—not only trade and finance but other influential institutions, such as government, administration, law, religion, literature and education. It became accepted as standard, or 'correct' English, at the expense of other varieties of English, and these other dialects came to be regarded not only as incorrect but as reflecting the morality and lifestyle of their speakers, who were largely working class as opposed to merchants, who were the emerging capitalist class (see Fairclough 1989:56–8). Other types of speech, and those who spoke them, were regarded as 'vulgar', 'ignorant' and 'slovenly', and yet, but for a turn of history, one of these 'non-standard' dialects might have become established as Standard English and revered in the place of the East Midland dialect.

Thus the values attributed to a language are largely determined by the social and political status of the group which speaks that language—the language of a dominant group becomes the 'prestige' language, and the languages of the dominated are devalued.

A similar story can be seen in relation to the pidgins and creoles of colonised countries such as America and Australia. **Pidgins** and **creoles** are composite languages, a mixture of two or more languages, usually as a result of colonisation. The colonised people adapt elements of the language of their colonisers and combine it with their own language. The result is a pidgin which is used as a 'common language' for communication between the colonisers and the colonised. When a pidgin becomes the first language of a generation it becomes a creole. For example, most non-European Torres Strait Islanders speak a language called Torres Strait creole or *Broken*. It is increasingly accepted as the official language of the islands. For the indigenous inhabitants of the islands, for many years, it was regarded as 'standard English', until increasing contact with mainland European English speakers led to the realisation that it was not the English of the mainland Anglo-Celtic community. Instead, it was (and in many cases, still is) regarded 'as a "bastardised", "fractured", "ungrammatical" form of English' (Shnukal, 1983:30). This produces a form of linguistic racism, which has very real effects for Torres Strait creole speakers in terms of access to employment and access to education, in mainland society if not in island society.

Speech, whether it takes the form of standard or non-standard varieties, regional dialects, accented varieties, pidgins or creoles, is produced out of a particular set of past historical and political conditions, which continue to affect the way that variety of speech is regarded in the present.

How we speak—our specific speech practices—is influenced by a number of social and cultural dimensions. Pierre Bourdieu, in *Language and Symbolic Power* (1991a), suggests that speakers acquire a 'practical sense' which is the capacity to make our utterances relevant or appropriate in particular contexts. Acquiring this 'practical sense', or linguistic **habitus** (a term which will be explained in more detail in Chapter 7), means acquiring a sense (so ingrained it is not conscious) of the conditions which attach to contexts, of what speech behaviour is appropriate and of the consequences of behaving appropriately or otherwise. This 'practical sense' guides us through what can sometimes be a minefield of social interactions, so that we know, for example, what kinds of things it is appropriate to say at a funeral, and in what tone of voice, and how to close off a telephone conversation. Whether the interaction is a selfconsciously ritualised one, or a routine daily one, speakers' linguistic habitus enables them to negotiate these situations.

The ability to speak, then, is much more than the ability to use our physiological resources (vocal cords, lips, tongue, mouth) to produce a series of vocal sounds recognisable as a well-formed and meaningful utterance in a particular language known to our hearers (although this is no mean feat in itself!). Thus what Bourdieu refers to as a practical sense or habitus is part of the notion of literacy which we have been developing throughout this book.

This literacy about how to speak in different contexts is not possessed equally by everyone, nor is what constitutes this 'practical sense' the same for all speakers of a language. Not everyone is equally proficient at speaking in public, and most people know someone who can never end a telephone conversation easily and without awkwardness (someone who never seems to notice hints such as 'OK, well, I'd better get going then . . .'). Linguistic literacy, or the ability to perform successfully in a wide range of speech contexts, is a resource which is differentially available. It constitutes a kind of 'cultural capital' (Bourdieu's term), a valuable resource which can give the speaker a high degree of control over her/his social interactions.

When we learn to speak, we do so in particular contexts, including the family, the peer group and the school. There are many factors which exercise what Bourdieu calls a 'determining influence' (1991a:95) on speakers' linguistic habitus. These include:

- gender
- level of education
- social position
- social origin (rural or urban)
- ethnic origin.

None of these factors can completely define how a speaker will handle a particular speech event, but their influence is too strong to be ignored in any explanation of 'what is going on' here. Our gender, schooling, what our parents do/did for a living, whether we are city born or country born, where we live now, and our ethnicity are all influences which produce our orientations to meaning making, or **coding orientations** (Bernstein 1971).

The utterances which speakers produce, according to Bourdieu, are the result of the relation between the linguistic habitus and a linguistic **market**. By the term market, he means a field of action or social context in which resources (different kinds of **capital**) are distributed and exchanged. Just as the stock exchange is a market for distributing and exchanging economic capital, other fields can be seen as linguistic markets.

Bourdieu gives the example of a pub landlord, whose 'possession of a talent for being "the life and soul of the party" . . . is a very precious form of capital' (1991a:99).

> Thus a good pub landlord finds, in the mastery of the expressive conventions suitable for this market (jokes, funny stories and puns . . .), and also in his special knowledge both of the rules of the game and the peculiarities of each of the players (names, nicknames, habits, oddities, specialities and talents from which he can profit), the necessary resources for exciting, sustaining, and also containing . . . the exchanges capable of producing the effervescent social atmosphere which his clients come for and to which they must themselves contribute
>
> BOURDIEU 1991:99–100

A speaker's sense or expectation of the value that linguistic practices will have in different markets is thus also part of the linguistic habitus. Speakers attempt to position themselves to profit from the linguistic capital they possess (or at least, to minimise their losses). For some speakers, faced with a market for which they don't have the required linguistic capital, silence is the only possible response. To return to the example of Torres Strait creole, children who grow up with this as their first language and who enter the mainstream white education system may find themselves lacking the linguistic literacy to participate alongside middle-class white children speaking 'standard English', unless the school system is flexible enough to include their own culture and language in the learning process. What is more, in a market dominated by the values of the mainstream, any speech they might produce might be less valued and regarded as 'impoverished'. Similarly, a blue-collar worker wanting to defend his/her own case in a court of law would be strongly disadvantaged, not only because of a lack of detailed knowledge of and expertise in law, but because he/she would lack the linguistic capital of the expressions, demeanour and mode of argument appropriate to this 'market'.

We move now from a consideration of speech as a resource acquired by speakers, and from the broad social and cultural context in which the acquisition of speech takes place, to a consideration of the text types of spoken interaction.

SPEECH ACTS AND SPEECH GENRES

For many decades it was assumed, mainly as a result of the influence of formal linguistics,[4] that studying writing was the best way of going about understanding language as a system of communication. Studying speech as a means of communication provides a very different perspective than can be gained from assuming that writing is the paradigmatic example of language as communication. This position is strongly developed by Mikhail Bakhtin.

For Bakhtin, the basic unit of speech communication is the **utterance**, a term which connects explicitly with spoken language, although for Bakhtin it applies equally to written communication. The utterance is not to be confused with the sentence. Unlike the sentence, which is a formal unit of written language, the utterance is a unit of 'living language'. The notion of 'living' language or speech is very significant here. Bakhtin often talks about 'speech life' or the 'life of signs', indicating first that language and communication cannot be understood only from an abstract perspective, but must be considered as part of what people do in their lives. Second, he is indicating that speech, words and signs take on 'a life of their own', not subject to the control of individual speakers and their wills. Speakers may attempt to bend speech to their will, but speech is an intersubjective phenomenon, that is, the meanings that speech takes on are the result of not just speakers but also listeners, and a variety of social forces.

This last point is an extremely important one for Bakhtin. Speech always involves both a speaker and a listener, and the listener is no less active in this process than the speaker. That is, the listener responds actively to the speaker's utterance, and is her/himself potentially a speaker in turn. Dialogue or conversation provides the clearest example of this, but whole texts can also be seen to be participating in a dialogue with other texts either directly, such as letters in a newspaper, or less directly, as when a film such as *Big Trouble in Little China* is produced partly as a (comic) response to earlier films in the same genre, such as the *Rambo* films (see the discussion of **intertextuality** in Chapter 5).

Unlike Saussure, who believed that what people actually did with language (what he referred to as *parole*, or actual speech practice) was too chaotic and unpredictable to be studied, Bakhtin argues that the choices speakers make are not completely free but are governed by broad regularities. Despite the enormous variety of uses to which we put language, Bakhtin points out that 'each sphere in which language is used develops its own *relatively stable types* of utterances' (1986:60). These he refers to as **speech genres**.

The term speech genres refers not only to oral genres but also to written genres. Bakhtin stresses that there are very many different and varied speech genres, and in fact they cannot really be numbered and catalogued, because there will always be new genres developing, as the spheres or areas of human activity with which they are associated grow and develop and change. Bakhtin's own list of speech genres which need to be included already begins to look rather limited and out of date:

> . . . short rejoinders of daily dialogue, . . . everyday narration, writing (in all its various forms), the brief standard military command, the elaborate and detailed order, the fairly variegated repertoire of business documents . . . , and the diverse world of commentary (in the broad sense of the word: social, political). And we must also include here the diverse forms of scientific statements and all literary genres (from the proverb to the multi-volume novel).
>
> BAKHTIN 1986:60–1

Bakhtin's work is very useful, then, not only for thinking about speech, but for the ways in which it allows us to think about all language, whether spoken or written, as **dialogic**. To summarise our discussion of his work:

- the utterance is the basic unit of speech communication
- speech genres are types of utterances developed for use in particular contexts

M.M. (Mikhail Mikhailovich) Bakhtin

Mikhail Bakhtin (pronounced buk-teen) was a Russian scholar, literary theorist and philosopher of language. He was born in 1895 and died in 1975. His work did not become well known in the west until the 1980s, largely because translations of his work from the Russian did not become available until this time. Bakhtin lived and worked in some very difficult times: the Bolshevik Revolution, the Stalinist purges and the Second World War (during which he made cigarette wrappers out of the pages of one of his manuscripts, owing to a paper shortage!). He worked with several other scholars, including V.N. Volosinov, in what has become known as the Bakhtin Circle. It is not quite clear whether some of the work produced by this circle belonged to Bakhtin or Volosinov, as members of the circle sometimes attributed their work to one another in order to protect themselves from persecution. He has been hailed as 'the most important Soviet thinker in the human sciences and the greatest theoretician of literature in the twentieth century' (Todorov 1984:ix).

- speech, and indeed all language, is potentially dialogic (that is, involves and anticipates a response).

The utterance as a unit of interaction

We now move to a consideration of the ways and extents to which this responsiveness can take place, and how it is tied up with the issue of different contexts. According to Bakhtin, any utterance is shaped with a listener in mind, and with the expectation that that listener will be in some way responsive. This may mean that the listener becomes a speaker in her/his turn, in speech genres which are overtly dialogic, such as conversation, dramatic dialogue (plays, films, TV), school debates, question time in parliament, and so on. Other, more apparently monologic texts, that is, texts shaped by a single speaker/writer, nevertheless always implicitly address some audience. Newspaper articles, poems and political speeches all address an audience. Some speech genres may shift between these two modes of interaction; for example, conversations are usually dialogues, but may also involve chunks of monologue, where a single speaker tells an anecdote or story. The distinction between dialogue and monologue, then, is not absolute—monologue is, in a sense, simply an extreme pole in a range of modes of linguistic interaction.

Bakhtin's notion of the utterance has some similarities with the concept of the speech act. Speech act theory (first developed by the English philosopher J.L. Austin, in his 1962 book *How to Do Things With Words*) argued that language did not merely represent or describe something in the world of experience but could also be used to perform actions. Austin identified a special class of utterances which he called performatives because of their function in performing the action they name. For example:

'I christen this child Mary Joe' (uttered by a priest in a christening ceremony).
'I name this ship the *Lazy Slob*' (uttered while smashing a champagne bottle against the hull of a vessel).
'I pronounce you husband and wife' (uttered by a minister of religion or marriage celebrant in a marriage ceremony).

Other speech acts include threatening, promising, cursing, blessing, warning and congratulating.

The utterance, then, is an act performed in saying something, an act performed through language. What speech act theory left out of the picture was the social or interactive dimension inherent in all speech acts or utterances. Bakhtin's dialogic view of speech adds this important dimension. At the risk of the reader suffering 'metaphor overload', let's take the notion of the utterance as a dialogic, interactive speech act a step further. To do so, we will focus on a particular speech genre, that of conversation.

Conversation as speech genre

Participants in spoken interaction take turns to speak, thereby jointly producing a text. What is it that propels such interactions along? Some speech genres, such as casual conversation, appear to be 'about' very little—just talk for talk's sake, like this dialogue from a play:

Man:	You was a bit busy earlier.
Barman:	Ah.
Man:	Round about ten.

Barman:	Ten, was it?
Man:	About then.
	(*Pause*)
	I passed by here about then.
Barman:	Oh yes?
Man:	I noticed you were doing a bit of trade.
	(*Pause*)
Barman:	Yes, trade was very brisk here about ten.
Man:	Yes, I noticed.
	(*Pause*)
	I sold my last one about then. Yes. About nine forty-five.
Barman:	Sold your last then, did you?
Man:	Yes, my last *Evening News* it was. Went about twenty to ten.
	(*Pause*)
Barman:	*Evening News*, was it?
Man:	Yes.
	(*Pause*)
	Sometimes it's the *Star* is the last to go.
Barman:	Ah.
Man:	Or the . . . whatsisname.
Barman:	*Standard*.
Man:	Yes.
	(*Pause*)
	All I had left tonight was the *Evening News*.
	(*Pause*)
Barman:	Then that went, did it?
Man:	Yes.
	(*Pause*)
	Like a shot.
	(*Pause*)

HAROLD PINTER, *LAST TO GO*, 1961

And so it goes on, for another page and a half! The playwright, Pinter, is pushing to a comic extreme the capacity of conversation to be sustained when there seems to be very little information being exchanged. If you look at the conversation, the sum total of the information that emerges is that the Barman was busy around ten o'clock, and that the Man sold his last newspaper, the *Evening News*, at around twenty (or a quarter) to ten! Note also that both these items of information are provided first by the Man, and that the Barman cooperates in the conversation by replying to the Man's questions and confirming or acknowledging his statements, although in a very minimal way (reluctant? embarrassed, perhaps? bored?).

This kind of communication is known as **phatic communion**, where the function of communicating seems to be solely to keep the channel of communication open and to keep the conversation going. Much of our brief daily spoken interactions are like this: 'hello'—'isn't it hot/cold/humid'—'have a nice day'—'see you later'.

So what is at stake in this interaction? What keeps it going? It seems to involve utterances which are concerned not so much with exchanging information, as with using the exchange of information to negotiate the continuation of the interaction. It seems fairly clear that the Man is keener to negotiate this than the Barman.

At this point, it is useful to introduce some technical terms so we can be precise in our analysis of language as interaction. Halliday (1985) has suggested that when analysing utterances as interaction, we need to identify what he calls their **speech function**. Utterances, or **moves** (another term for the same concept) may function in a variety of ways for different participants, depending on their specific agendas. These agendas might include negotiating to obtain or to provide information, or seeking or offering a form of action. Figure 9 shows some possibilities, in table form, along with the names used for each speech function.

This gives a broad picture which encompasses most (but not all) of the basic ways in which speakers can use moves to interact. For each of these speech functions, there is also a range of possible responses, some more likely and more cooperative than others (see Figures 10 and 11).

Here we can see how Bakhtin's insight that all utterances anticipate a response operates in practice. While the speech function of a move does not completely determine the response, it sets up a range of possible or probable responses. The listener, who becomes speaker in turn, can be compliant, or s/he can be less cooperative with the speaker, by not negotiating along the lines set up by the speaker. She or he may not answer the question, or not do so directly, or may even challenge the speaker's right to ask the question. She or he may even avoid the question altogether, and ask another question instead.

But a participant in a conversation has to balance her/his own purposes against those of the other participant/s. In order to get what you want, you have to give the other person enough of what they

FIGURE 9 Basic speech functions

giving information:	statement
demanding information:	question
giving action:	offer
demanding action:	command

FIGURE 10 Speech functions and responses

Speech function	Compliant response	Non-compliant response
statement	acknowledgment	contradiction
question	answer	disclaimer
offer	acceptance	rejection
command	undertaking	refusal

FIGURE 11 Examples of speech functions

Statement	Acknowledgment	Contradiction
School sucks.	Sure does.	You've got to be kidding!
Question	Answer	Disclaimer
Where was Sally yesterday?	She had to go to a funeral.	None of your business! or I don't know.
Offer	Acceptance	Rejection
Want a beer?	Thanks or Why not?	No thanks or I'd better not (or shakes head).
Command	Undertaking	Refusal
Help me lift this rhinoceros.	OK (or performs action).	No way or I can't, I've got a bad back.

want to keep the conversation going. If the conversation breaks down, negotiation stops.

Furthermore, speakers often use less than direct ways of framing their moves. Consider how often we frame negotiations for action in terms of information. For example:

- if we want someone to turn the television down, we might use the statement 'The TV is too loud'
- if you are trying to get a wealthy companion to buy you an

expensive gift in a jewellery shop, you might say 'Isn't that diamond necklace fabulous?'

Such indirect ways of negotiating speech purposes relate to cultural conventions concerning power differences and politeness. By expressing a request as a statement, a speaker allows the addressee the option of refusing the request less bluntly by simply treating it as a statement or question. For example, the addressee could respond to the examples above by saying, 'Yes it is, isn't it?', thereby refusing to enter into the negotiation on the speaker's terms. 'Escape clauses' like this allow the appearance of politeness and communicative harmony to be maintained—particularly important where there is a power differential between the participants.

Note here that we are not assuming that conversation is all about consensus and agreement. By talking about negotiation and moves that participants make, we are recognising that what is at stake for people in any interaction may differ among the participants, and that they are therefore involved in a process of negotiation in order to achieve either shared ends or different ends. The basic speech functions need to be interpreted quite differently when the interests of the two participants are in conflict, for example:

Question → *interrogation*
A: Where were you on the night of the robbery?
B: Having dinner with Elvis.

Statement → *insult*
A: You're an absolute loser!
B: Up yours!

Offer → *threat*
A: Want a gunshot wound to the head?
B: (*terrified look, flees*)

It is important not to assume that all participants in a conversation have equal power and thus equal control over what's going on. In casual conversation the power relations between the participants may not seem to be very marked or unequal. Nevertheless, this does not mean that the issue of power is not 'at stake' or 'under negotiation' in this speech genre. Having provided you with some tools for the analysis of dialogue, let's now address the question of speech and power.

SPEECH AND POWER

Magistrate:	I'm putting it to you again—are you going to *make* another offer—uh—to discharge this debt [1]
Defendant:	Would you in my position [2]
Magistrate:	I—I'm not here to answer your questions [3]—you answer *my* question [4]
Defendant:	One rule for one and one for another—I presume [5]
Magistrate:	Can I have an answer to my question—please [6] The question is—are you prepared to make an offer to the court—to discharge—this debt [7]
Defendant:	What sort of minimal offer would be required [8]
Magistrate:	It's not a bargaining situation [9]—it's a *straight* question, Mr H [10]—can I have the answer [11]
Defendant:	Well, I'll just pay the court a pound annually [12]
Magistrate:	That's not acceptable to us [13]

HARRIS 1984:5

This dialogue takes place in the formal context of the courtroom, under the constraints of an institution—the legal system—which sets up power relations that are clearly defined and institutionally enshrined. In such a context, we expect to find that magistrates have greater power than defendants, and that this difference in power will be manifested in the magistrate's control over who speaks and when, and over the kinds of issues that will be discussed. We also expect that it will be the magistrate and the prosecution and defence lawyers who ask the questions and decide if the answers are adequate ones. After all, for the defendant, a great deal is at stake; her or his liberty (or good name, or bank balance) may depend on these answers.

In terms of these kinds of expectations, what is odd about the interaction above between the magistrate and the defendant? Using the categories of speech functions provided above, we can analyse what is going on in this interaction (italics indicate speech functions of moves). The magistrate asks a *question* of the defendant [1], but instead of complying by providing a direct *answer*, the defendant asks a *question* of the magistrate [2]. The magistrate points out that this is inappropriate behaviour [3]. Instead of accepting this *statement*, the defendant challenges it [4], forcing the magistrate to *command* him to answer, 'please' [6]. After repeating similar tactics, the defendant eventually makes an *offer* [12], which is *rejected* by the magistrate [13].

Clearly, the defendant's speech behaviour is at odds with the compliant and submissive position which a defendant in court might be expected to take (watch any TV courtroom drama series for dramatised examples of how defence lawyers 'coach' defendants in this respect). The defendant in the example above uses the resources of the system of speech function in language to challenge and resist the court's legal right to make him pay his debts. This interaction demonstrates that while institutions constrain contexts and the types of speech interactions which can take place within those contexts, they do not completely determine them. Participants can and do attempt to challenge and negotiate the power relations which are assigned to them in specific contexts. The extent to which they are able to do so depends chiefly on the institutional power which underlies the speech situation. In the law court, the defendant may challenge the power of the magistrate, but these tactics will probably merely delay the eventual result—the enforcement of the magistrate's judgment—rather than be ultimately successful.

Our analysis of the courtroom example demonstrates a number of features that Poynton (1985) identifies in language where there is a power difference. Power is manifested in general by asymmetry in the meaning choices available to the powerful and the less powerful. Those who exercise power in a speech interaction:

- control turn-taking in dialogue
- interrupt
- control what is under negotiation (through speech function)
- control the topic being discussed
- control the degree of directness or indirectness (indirectness, euphemism and 'watching your words' are associated with the less powerful)
- control the use of address terms (use of titles rather than first names shows status).

This is neatly summed up by Fairclough's statement that 'power in discourse is to do with powerful participants controlling and constraining the contributions of non-powerful participants' (1989:46).

It is revealing of the relative status of women and men in western society that studies of women's and men's speech have shown that men interrupt women more frequently than vice versa, that indirectness is more characteristic of women's speech, and that in conversations between women and men, it is largely men who determine the topic (Poynton, 1985:26–7).

It is useful at this point to return to the notion of the linguistic habitus and the linguistic market introduced by Bourdieu. Bourdieu (1991a) makes the point that an important element of the habitus is the speaker's practical sense of the conditions which attach to markets, that is, of who can speak under what circumstances. Linguistic markets determine who can speak, whether or not they will be listened to and to what extent their speech will be valued or seen as legitimate. Here is a final example which illustrates the operation of a linguistic market. It concerns a study of the TV football viewing practices of a family and their friends.

> Competence to read the game well enough to participate in 'viewing' rituals may, apparently, be quickly taught (especially if the novice is familiar with any form of football). But the right to be 'heard' when you speak about the game depends on other initiatory rites. The level of competence appropriate to televised football spectatorship is reasonably openly shared with women by men. However, the competence of women to speak about the game is recognised by neither Richard nor Peter. In my interviews with Peter considerable time was spent establishing just whether or not women had been present during the observation and what the nature of their participation had been. Peter had 'defined' his viewing group as 'men only', even though all were accompanied by their wives and girlfriends. The wives and girlfriends offered beer, and watched them viewing from the sidelines. This positioning offers an interesting parallel with the positioning of the cheerleader squad during the televised game. On one occasion the women went to the movies while the men watched football. On another occasion they visited a friend. When the women did come into the room it was not registered in Peter's account. When women did speak about the game it was considered not significant for the study, even though all participating students had been asked to note down everything they observed, without exception. However, when the women spoke about the advertisements broadcast and the relationship of the advertisements

to the program, their voice was noticed. And when the women commented on the viewing behaviour of the men their comments were also recognised. The women were granted the right to speak and be heard about consumer related matters and about their men, but not about the game.

When I asked Peter how the women could comment on the advertisements and how they could notice the behaviour of the men if they were not present, he disclosed that the women had traversed the domestic space of viewing, the lounge room, and had often stopped long enough to notice and comment.

VN:	When the women would come into the room, did they ever make comments about the game or ask questions about what was happening?
Peter:	Maybe not so much about the game but particular players.
VN:	What would they say?
Peter:	I don't know.
VN:	So they knew the main footballers.
Peter:	Oh yes, well not all of them—but high profile players that are in the news all the time, on television and doing ads.
VN:	What sort of things would they say?
Peter:	Pretty critical things . . .
VN:	Come on, I want to know . . .
Peter:	Oh you know 'you log' or . . .
VN:	So they were critical of the way a particular player was playing the game . . .
Peter:	No, just critical of the player . . . and football . . .
VN:	So they'd say 'oh, not so-and-so again' . . .
Peter:	Yeah and that they considered . . . I suppose they looked at the players . . . like they looked at players a long time ago in the sense that there's nothing—all brawn and no brains.

The discursive space constructed around televised football is then gender-coded 'male', though male dominance of the space is certainly contested by some women. The women's authority to speak about football was considered to be based in the mediated authority of newspaper reports and spoof sporting programs on radio, though it remains unclear why women would want to read newspaper reports about football if they had no more than a passing interest in the game and never became involved in it. Peter was convinced that women are interested in footballers as individuals, but not in football itself.

NIGHTINGALE 1992:162–3

The author of this study, Virginia Nightingale, discovered that not only did women's equal competence about the game of football (at least as spectators) not count according to the men, but their presence as part of the spoken interaction around football watching was actually ignored, or edited out in the men's report of the interaction. In this case the women's speech, no matter what their contribution, is discounted almost as if they had not spoken. They are rendered silent, metaphorically if not literally.

We began this chapter by looking at the opposition between speech and writing, and it seems appropriate to close it by invoking another fundamental opposition—that between speech and silence. Silence is often the only response possible for the powerless.

SUMMARY

This chapter has examined the differences between speech and writing, in terms of:

- their materiality
- the values assigned to them.

We noted that writing is valued through its association with 'prestige' areas of western culture, while speech is linked to a different set of values, such as sincerity and spontaneity.

Oral literacy is thus both valued and devalued. The values attributed to speech cannot be separated from the social and historical conditions which produce both dialects and speakers.

By analysing communication from the perspective of speech, we can apply the metaphor of negotiation to linguistic interaction, in which the utterance or move is the fundamental unit. All speech genres, and all genres, deploy moves in order to negotiate meanings. An analysis of the speech genre of conversation shows that this genre is as much constrained by rules as it is spontaneous.

Finally, the chapter dealt with the question of power in discourse, and in particular with the ways in which power is tied into control of, and also access to, the linguistic market of speech itself.

FURTHER READING

Bourdieu, P. 1991 *Language and Symbolic Power* ed. and introduced by J.B. Thompson, trans. G. Raymond and M. Adamson, Polity, Cambridge: Introduction by John B. Thompson (pp. 1–10) and Appendix: 'Did You Say Popular?' (pp. 90–102)

Halliday, M.A.K. 1985 *Spoken and Written Language* Deakin University Press, Geelong

Fairclough, N. 1985 *Language and Power* Longman, London & New York, Ch. 3

5
FRAMING CONTEXTS

This chapter examines the ways in which we read and make sense of texts not only in terms of an immediate context but also in terms of a wider context of culture. Contexts function as cultural frames within which to make sense of texts, frames which operate through our knowledge of and literacy in a variety of other contexts. This chapter considers the patterns that shape our cultural literacy.

CONTEXT/S OF CULTURE

In Chapter 3 we looked at the ways in which texts relate to their contexts, and introduced a social semiotic model of this relation which suggested that three dimensions, field, tenor and mode, can be used to analyse how texts shape contexts, and how contexts shape texts. Texts, we argued, are socially situated practices which carry out social functions; that is, they function as representation, as interaction and as message. Our focus was on what is sometimes referred to as the **immediate context** or **context of situation** (what's going on and where, those involved, the part the text plays). Is this all we need to know in order to think about contexts and how we make meanings? Consider the following text:

Q: What were two dingoes arguing about outside a tent?
A: Eat in or take away?

Texts such as this riddle are recounted by all kinds of people, and circulate widely within a variety of contexts and situation types. Like a yo-yo craze or a political catchphrase, they last for a time and then disappear from circulation, perhaps to reappear later in a different form. Riddles, jokes, limericks, songs, advertising slogans and jingles, memorable lines from movies, characteristic sayings of public figures, whole texts and fragments of texts of all kinds are used and re-used within cultures in ways which take them away from any definitive original context.

For any text to be recognisable and readable it must draw upon already established and shared sets of meanings. It must therefore be repeatable beyond its context of production, or what the French theorist Jacques Derrida calls **iterable**. That is, it must be capable of functioning repeatedly in the absence of an 'original' sender, an 'original' receiver and an 'original' context. Jokes and riddles are particularly good examples of texts which are iterable; for them to be meaningful, it is not necessary that we know who first told the joke, to whom, in what immediate situation. We know, from the Q and A format of the riddle above, that it is a riddle, and we prepare to laugh upon hearing the punchline (so strong is this expectation that many people will laugh even if they don't 'get the joke', simply because it is the expected social behaviour in the context of 'being told a joke').

All texts, including jokes and riddles, carry elements, or traces, of context with them. Mikhail Bakhtin, the Russian critic and theorist, coined the term **dialogism** to refer to the way in which texts, through their relationships with other texts and other contexts, become charged with these traces. Any text resonates with the meanings of other texts and other contexts or places in which that text has been. Thus a text does not mean in isolation, but exists in a dialogue with other texts.

How can we make sense of the dingo riddle without reading it in the context of a number of other texts and contexts? Hardly anyone in Australia could have remained unaware of the mysterious disappearance in 1980 of baby Azaria Chamberlain from her parents' camp site near Ayers Rock/Uluru and of her mother's controversial claim that 'a dingo has taken my baby'. The extensive media coverage and high level of informal debate about the event and the subsequent trials provide a huge body of **intertexts** (related texts), among them riddles and jokes such as this one. The riddle makes sense as part of an ongoing dialogue with other texts such as news reports, headlines, media interviews, legal trials, and conversations. Did Lindy Chamberlain kill Azaria, or was she taken by a dingo? The riddle is a chunk of dialogue that functions as part of a much wider ranging intertextual dialogue which debates this and other questions, and in which many different voices take part.

As literate members of a culture, we employ our knowledge of other texts to make sense of what we see, read and hear, and when speaking, writing or communicating through visual or other media, we expect others to draw on **intertextuality** to make sense of our semiotic behaviour. But how does this intertextuality work? We won't necessarily have a shared set of specific texts with those we are communicating with, as happened to a large extent with the almost blanket media coverage of the Chamberlain case, where a body of texts was made very public on a mass scale. The next section will examine how intertextuality works.

INTERTEXTUALITY

In Chapter 3, we made the point that, in a given context, members of a culture can predict to an extent what kinds of meanings will be made. That is, we can 'unpack' texts by analysing their functional relation with a context.

Intertextuality provides another dimension to this process of making sense of what is going on; we do this by reference both to the immediate context of situation and to the wider context of culture, through intertextuality.

How can we define intertextuality? Interttextuality refers to the process of making sense of texts in reference to their relations with other texts. It involves the circulation and exchange of meanings, not as atomised bits (words/signs) but as packages of meaning.

Let's look at intertextuality from the perspective of the individual language user. As individuals, we each have different life histories, which are histories of the texts and meaning-making practices we've experienced—produced, viewed, read or witnessed. For each event or process of meaning making in which we are involved (and we are involved in a web of these virtually from birth to death), we draw upon our knowledge/embodiment of other texts—their similarities and differences—in relation to the event or process in which we are taking part. What we know/embody about other texts allows us to produce intertextual frames which can be used to read still other texts. These intertextual frames constitute knowledge about ways of speaking and types of texts; thus the intertextual 'baggage' that we carry with us is condensed into more general understandings of cultural patterns of meaning making.

In order to understand how this works, let's look at some of the ways in which cultural meanings are patterned or 'packaged'. These include:

* codes
* narratives/myths
* genres and
* discourses.

A **code** is a set of rules or principles governing a sign system. For example, English grammar is a code governing the English language. Codes are oriented towards particular mediums, that is, they define how a medium is to be read, for example, traffic lights. The medium is visual (coloured lights), but it is the code which maps meanings onto the medium (red = stop, green = go, amber = prepare to stop). As the concept of code was discussed in Chapter 3, we won't deal with it in any detail here. It remains a useful general concept, however.

Narratives

Narrative refers to a way of structuring meanings in the form of a story. Narratives involve the telling of a tale, with a sense of a sequence of events in some kind of temporal order, as in the nursery rhyme:

Jack and Jill went up the hill to fetch a pail of water.
Jack fell down and broke his crown
And Jill came tumbling after.

While we could read these sentences as unrelated events, there is a strong convention which says that they should be read as linked events that follow one another in time, although the story lacks explicit markers of time (such as 'one day', 'then', 'next' etc.). Instead, we read the order in which they are presented as the order in which they happened.

What is more, we frequently also read in a **causal** connection between the narrated events; that is, a prior event is read as the cause and a subsequent event as the effect. Why is this convention about narratives significant? Consider the following narrative:

A storekeeper had just turned off the lights in the shop when a man appeared and demanded money. The owner opened a cash register. The contents of the till were placed in a bag, and the man left hurriedly. The police were notified of the incident immediately.

Note how we make a number of assumptions or **inferences** based on a reading of this text as a narrative. We assume, for example, a 'cause-and-effect' relation between sentence 1 (a man appearing and demanding money), sentence 2 (the owner opening a cash register) and sentence 3 (the contents of the till being placed in a bag). We also assume that within sentence 3, there is a causal connection between the contents of the till going into a bag and the man leaving (although we are not explicitly told this). In order to maintain these inferences, we also need to assume certain things about the identity of the participants; for example, that the storekeeper is also the owner, and that the man who demands money is the same person who leaves hurriedly. In other words, we read this text as meaningful in part because of a number of textual clues (the mention of a store owner, a till being emptied, an incident being reported to the police), and in part because we make sense of it as a narrative composed of events in a causal relation with one another. Nowhere is it actually stated that a robbery has taken place, yet most readers of this text will argue that that is what the text is about. The text fits a recognisable story type—a narrative of a robbery.

This brings us to a related use of the term narrative: to refer to the way in which particular generalised stories circulate widely within a culture and are seen as valid and predictable. Another term for such culturally ratified stories is **myth** (from the French semiotician Roland Barthes). An example of such a myth or narrative is 'heterosexual romance':

Boy meets girl. Boy falls in love with girl. They get married and live happily ever after.

or 'capitalist success story':

Working-class boy studies diligently. Leaves school. Gets a job. Works hard. Is promoted/starts own business. Becomes rich and successful.

Such 'story types' are to be found not just in novels, films and TV soap operas, but also in news and documentaries, not to mention gossip, folklore and oral history. The heterosexual romance narrative has provided the format for countless movies and novels. Many variations of such narratives are possible, but cultures tend to validate some stories over others. To test this claim, try rewriting the heterosexual romance as a homosexual romance. How does replacing the term 'girl' with 'boy', or 'boy' with 'girl' affect the cultural values attached to this narrative? Which cultural groups would such a narrative be acceptable to, and which would not accept it?

Another variation is exploited to comic effect in the TV science fiction comedy *Red Dwarf*, when the android character, Kryten, sums up the plot of one episode as follows:

> Ah, it's the old, old story. Droid meets droid. Droid turns into chameleon. Droid loses chameleon. Chameleon turns into blob. Droid gets blob back again.
>
> *RED DWARF IV*, BYTE ONE, 'CAMILLE'

Narratives are used as ways of interpreting and structuring everyday life, and can take on a very powerful function in validating the events in people's lives. An example of the validating power of narratives is the way in which the heterosexual romance myth is used within some cultural groups as a measure of a woman's 'success' in life; those women whose lives don't match this narrative may be judged, or even judge themselves (in some sense) 'failures'.

Genres

Genres are ways in which we make sense of types of texts, as culturally defined and expected combinations of field, tenor and mode. In Chapter 3, we gave examples of genres such as:

> road sign
> office memo
> classroom lesson
> guitar ballad
> parent–child talk
> committee
> meeting
> advertisement.

Other genres are:

> sermon
> rental lease

conversation
poem
flirtation
newspaper article
jar label
bus ticket
argument
soap opera
science fiction
riddle

and the list could go on.

Within a given culture, not every possible combination of field, tenor and mode is equally likely. Certain field, tenor and mode choices constitute text types which are meaningful within a culture, as we saw in Chapter 3.

Genres are ways of meaning associated with a social purpose and a social occasion. Becoming literate within a culture thus involves (in part) learning which genres are appropriate to which social occasions. This may range from quite clear-cut rules for highly structured and ritualised occasions (such as religious ceremonies) to less formalised occasions in which the range of generic choices may be wide.

For example, a genre such as a committee meeting follows a conventional format with a set structure and a number of obligatory elements:

- recording of the names of those present
- apologies
- confirmation of previous meeting's minutes
- business arising from minutes
- other items of business.

Such an occasion is also structured in terms of rules about who may speak and when.

In contrast, a spontaneous meeting of friends may provide the occasion for a range of genres, such as gossip, casual conversation, jokes, appointment making, narratives of various kinds, and perhaps also argument or insult. Who speaks and when is not structured formally, and everyone involved is likely to compete for turns at talking. At the same time, however, these less formalised events are structured by certain more or less unconscious rules or conventions, and not everyone is likely to succeed in gaining equal 'air time'. Some speakers are likely to dominate informal conversations because they possess what Bourdieu refers to as **cultural capital** (a set of resources or literacies which are culturally valued).

How are supposedly informal social events and conversations structured by unconscious rules? A group of people at a cafe can be expected to behave, and talk, in certain ways about certain subjects which correspond to that social genre (the genre of a 'cafe gathering'). Now, as Bourdieu points out, their behaviour and conversation (no matter how apparently eccentric or spontaneous) are already predetermined to some extent by their literacy in the genre (Bourdieu 1991). Different 'positions' can be taken up (one person might intentionally 'bait' another, that person might retaliate, the rest of the company might urge them on, but all in 'fun'), and different subjects can be used to drive this interaction (sporting team allegiances, romantic entanglements, a person's sense of fashion). What is important here is that this conversational behaviour, despite appearances to the contrary, always takes place within the framework of a shared cultural literacy and set of generic rules. However, these rules can never really be acknowledged, because if they were acknowledged, the spontaneity would disappear.

What would happen if a member of the group refused to abide by these unconscious rules? The genre would fall to pieces, and so would the social occasion, in all probability. If, for instance, one of the members insisted on bringing their highly detailed company financial figures into the conversation, or someone actually started to mock another person's fashion sense in a way that was obviously not 'in jest', these 'intrusions' would have to be quickly rejected. The 'rules of the game' of a cafe gathering could be almost as difficult to defy or challenge as the (formal) rules of chess.

How are speaking rights determined within such informal social genres? Some people may be (unofficially) 'assigned' the role of dominance or centrality, precisely because they possess a literacy which helps keep the conversations, and the interactions that make up the genre, going. A person who is seemingly able to pluck interesting or funny observations 'out of the air', or to successfully redirect a fading conversation, might be expected to occupy a central place in the genre regardless of that person's cultural capital; or rather, they might occupy a central position because of the capital associated with helping to keep the genre running smoothly.

While genres provide frames for social interaction, and constrain the ways in which this proceeds, genres can never entirely control or predict how meanings will be made in a context. This is because genres are never entirely single or pure. As long as we retain the perspective of communication as a dynamic process, we must recognise that the performance of genre can involve one genre giving way to or interrupting or blending with another. This is a defining characteristic of the medium of television; Raymond Williams has referred to it as 'televisual flow' (Williams 1990). Not only are programs continually interrupted by advertising, but a parade of different genres passes across the TV screen (game shows, cartoons, soap operas, news, current affairs, crime dramas, movies). Elements of one television genre may occur in another, for example, footage of a police car chase is a generic element from crime dramas which may occur in television news.

This mixing or embedding of one genre within another was identified in a number of genres by Bakhtin (1986:72–3), who argued that what he called 'secondary speech genres' (rhetorical, artistic and scholarly genres) characteristically make use of embedded 'primary speech genres' (such as conversation). Certainly we are familiar with the use of quoted dialogue in novels and children's stories, in fact in narrative texts of all kinds. However, the use of embedded or mixed genres is much more widespread than Bakhtin is suggesting, and is probably endemic in contemporary cultures. Consider the humble jar of Vegemite (Figure 12).

The genre of jar label is one which is so familiar and taken for granted that most people will hardly stop to examine one closely. But if we do, we see that there are a number of generically predictable elements:

- the product name, prominently displayed—VEGEMITE
- the brand name—KRAFT
- the weight/size of the product (required by law)
- the ingredients (required by law)
- country of manufacture (required by law)
- a use-by date (again, required by law)
- a slogan, or epithet of praise ('*All Natural*').

FIGURE 12 The Vegemite jar

COURTESY OF KRAFT FOODS

These features all relate to the social purpose of the genre: that is, to announce and identify the product (and to do so in a way which complies with consumer legislation), to inform the consumer of its qualities, and in doing so to signal its value in relation to the needs/desires of the consumer (a function less easily legislated). We can identify three functions served by the jar label: it functions to represent the jar's contents (field), to position the consumer in relation to the product (tenor) and to draw attention to itself as message ('this is a jar label'—mode).

Embedded in this rather minimalist and functional genre, we find another genre, a recipe (for 'MUM'S PRIZE MEATLOAF Serves 4'), in which Vegemite is (of course) a key ingredient. While the genre of recipe brings its own characteristic field, tenor and mode, it is also contextualised by the genre in which it is embedded. That is, the inclusion of the recipe here functions not only on its own terms but as part of the social purpose of the jar label, by demonstrating the value of the product and also positioning the consumer more explicitly as a 'Mum' and a prize-winning cook, someone who is handy and versatile in the kitchen with even the most prosaic of ingredients.

Genres are thus important ways of ascribing social value and social position. The Vegemite jar label, with its embedded genre of recipe, functions to construct 'the ideal Mum', contributing in its own small way to sociocultural values and ideologies of gender. In fact, the very ordinariness of this 'text' makes it powerful. Texts such as this, since they are both familiar and apparently insignificant, are likely to be accepted into the everyday fabric of people's lives without being questioned.

Such embedded genres are a common device in a range of marketing genres, including advertising. While the ostensible purpose of such genres is to sell/promote a product to a potential consumer, this is seldom achieved by a direct appeal or exhortation to buy. When watching or reading advertisements, note how often other genres are reproduced within the 'main' genre, to achieve the social purpose through more indirect means (such as a testimonial letter, a conversation, a cartoon, and so on).

The advertisement shown in Figure 13 appeared in an in-flight magazine. The Vegemite jar is placed alongside two other images or 'texts', which at first glance have little relation to one another. It is useful here to recall Saussure's point that signs take on meanings in

FIGURE 13 Travelodge advertisement

For more than three decades, Travelodge has built a reputation for being at the forefront of the hotel industry in Australia, and we continue to offer business travellers, holiday makers and families reliability and honest value-for-money in many great locations. We're still out there in front, with today's Travelodge continuing to lead the way in Australia, New Zealand, the South Pacific Islands and, increasingly, in Asia.

For information and reservations, telephone Australia Nationwide Free Call 1 800 222 446, or Sydney area (02) 267 2144. In New Zealand on Nationwide Freefone 0800 801 111 or Auckland (09) 377 7717.

Travelodge hotels and resorts. **Australia:** Sydney • Parramatta • Newcastle • Coffs Harbour • Canberra • Melbourne • Adelaide • Brisbane • Townsville Surfers Paradise • Daydream Island • Darwin • Kakadu • Ayers Rock • Perth. **New Zealand:** Auckland • Masterton • Christchurch • Mt. Cook Te Anau. **Papua New Guinea:** Port Moresby • Rabaul. **Fiji:** Suva. **New Caledonia:** Noumea. **Indonesia:** Jakarta (1994). **Malaysia:** Kuala Lumpur (1995) Kanga. **Thailand:** Bangkok • Phuket. **India:** Bangalore (1995) • Madras (1996).

*Trademark Kraft Foods Limited.   SOUTHERN PACIFIC HOTELS   Concept 6789406.4

COURTESY OF SOUTHERN PACIFIC HOTELS

relation to other signs, that is, signs function both in terms of what they are not, and in relation to other signs with which they occur.

What do you think is the function of the Vegemite jar in this advertisement? What is the relationship between Vegemite, an old Holden car and Travelodge? Does the written text of the ad help you decide this? (Written text which helps pin down or constrain the possible meanings of a visual text or image is said to **anchor** it.) Would the meaning of this ad have changed a great deal if you substituted a meat pie for the Vegemite? What if you changed the car to a luxury yacht and the Vegemite jar to a bottle of French champagne?

This advertisement demonstrates intertextuality in action, since it brings together texts (a Vegemite jar, a car, a Travelodge sign) which are already in circulation within our culture. The meanings you attribute to the advertisement as a whole would be constrained by your intertextual experience of the texts embedded within it— whether or not you hate Vegemite, for example, or whether you are too young to remember seeing that model of Holden car being driven around.

If genres are types of texts, how are they different from discourses?

Discourses

Discourse is a term which is frequently used in the general sense of text as a social process. More specifically, the concept of discourse can be used to distinguish discourse types, or different ways of speaking or meaning associated with particular institutions. For example, associated with institutions such as the law, religion, the education system and the family are discourses or ways of speaking which are characteristic of those institutions and their practices.

The French poststructuralist Michel Foucault was responsible for developing the concept of discourse as we are using it here. Foucault's concern with discourse is with its power to structure, classify and normalise the social world (Foucault 1972). Discourses, he argued, owe their control over their material and subjects—their portion of the social world—to their ability to seem natural and self-effacing. By identifying the ways in which discourses operate, we are able to make them 'visible' and to reduce their degree of control.

An important function of discourse is to express the meanings and values of the institution. Kress says of discourses that they are:

> systematically organised sets of statements which give expression to the meanings and values of an institution. Beyond that, they define, describe and delimit what it is possible to say (and—by extension—what it is possible to do or not to do) with respect to the area of concern of that institution . . .
>
> KRESS 1985:7

For example, the discourse of education (or more specifically, western compulsory public education) is likely to encode a set of common values, to be found across a number of institutional sites and occasions, such as teachers' discourse in the classroom, the policy documents of education bureaucrats, or principals' addresses at school assemblies and 'speech nights'. Lemke outlines some of these values:

> We believe that education and all its rules are constructed for the good of students and in their interests. We justify and rationalize every restriction on students' rights and freedoms as being 'necessary' in their

own interests. We believe that the use of power and even force to compel students to do as we wish is justified by their natural irresponsibility and the good we are doing them.

LEMKE 1990:84

Values such as these (and others) are likely to be implicit rather than explicit, but govern in a powerful way which practices and meanings are likely to be acceptable within the institution. Discourses thus encode power relations; they specify what relations are possible and valued in specific institutional contexts. They classify and assign value not only to objects and practices but to social relations. In the case of educational discourse, what it means to be a student is defined and classified, as well as what rights and what social relations are possible or desirable for students.

Discourses never exist in isolation. So while a discourse may attempt to impose its values within its sphere of influence, and even beyond—as Kress puts it, 'a discourse colonises the social world imperialistically, from the point of view of one institution' (1985:7)— other discourses may challenge it, check it, coexist with it either peaceably or otherwise. Students, for instance, don't have access to, nor are they usually literate in, the official discourse of education; however, they have their own set of discourses (less easily labelled, because less obviously institutionalised) which again usually go unrecognised by those occupying official positions of power within the institution (teachers, bureaucrats). Student discourses (which might be specifically derogatory about teachers, for example) are normally denied any official value within the institution (for the obvious reason that teachers and bureaucrats make those decisions). When students do come forward to speak 'officially' (at school functions, for instance), they are normally expected to make use of discourses closely associated with the institution (they might talk about the community of the school, the much-loved and hard-working teachers).

Some discourses are more strongly institutionalised than others; for example, legal and religious discourse are strongly regulated through their respective institutions. Other discourses, such as feminist discourse, environmentalist discourse, the discourse of indigenous rights, may fight to be heard against more established discourses, and are produced by those groups whose (repressed or oppressed) status within a culture is subject to struggle or contestation.

Although some discourses may be regarded as less institutionalised than others, this does not mean that they are somehow more open, or less complex or structured, than overtly institutionalised discourses. For example, student discourses within the education system have their own rules and characteristics, which, although susceptible to change, are likely to be relatively homogeneous and enjoy widespread (unconscious) acceptance.

In this context it is worth recalling Frank Zappa's rebuke to members of the crowd at a concert who were abusing the 'boys in uniform' (police who were attending the concert): 'Everyone's in uniform here.' Of course, there is no official body or figure at rock concert crowds or in school yards to oversee or scrutinise discursive practices (as there is in a law court, for instance, where a judge might disallow certain discourses as illegitimate), but the amount of capital involved in using student discourses appropriately and effectively, and the loss of capital involved in not 'performing' adequately, ensures that rock-concert-crowd or student discourses are likely to be 'reproduced' through the weight of that social pressure.

It is also important to note that even (and perhaps, particularly) discourses which appear to be strongly institutional in character are not necessarily attached to one group or institution, or to one function within a culture. Graeme Turner makes this point when he defines discourse as:

> socially produced groups of ideas or ways of thinking that can be tracked to individual texts or groups of texts, but that also demand to be located within wider historical and social structures or relations.
>
> TURNER 1990:32–3

Discourses travel through and across cultures, and there is really no limit as to the uses that can be made of them. As an example of this, look at the way technological discourses are deployed in advertising genres, regardless of the audience's potential literacy in such discourses. Advertisements for cars and stereo equipment (such as the Sony ad we discussed in Chapter 3) routinely make use of quite technical discourse in order to carry across the values associated with the institution of science and technology (values such as progress, excellence, 'proven reliability') and to reinscribe these upon the product being promoted.

As another example, look at the way in which medical discourses have been picked up by New Age culture. On the surface, official medical culture and New Age culture are involved in a kind of antagonistic relationship: medicine tends to equate New Age alternative remedies with 'quackery', and New Age culture tends to characterise official medicine as arrogant, inflexible and inhuman. At the same time, advertisements for alternative-medicine products often make use of medical or scientific discourses precisely because such discourses ('scientific tests demonstrate') still carry a significant amount of cultural capital—even with New Age audiences.

Discourses thus range from those which are widely regarded within a culture as prestigious and authoritative, to those whose power and authority is limited to certain social groups. Some discourses have the institutional power to enact the realities and values which they represent (such as a judge, pronouncing someone 'guilty', or a priest, pronouncing two people to be married). The authority of others may be limited to certain contexts; as we have suggested, the discourses of New Age or alternative medicine, which may have credibility and acceptance within certain communities and groups, are largely excluded from the discursive realms of institutionalised medicine. Articles on iridology and healing by touch are likely to be excluded from traditional medical journals, and research by practitioners in these areas is unlikely to be funded by wealthy medical foundations.

Let's summarise our discussion so far.

- Narratives are ways of structuring experience into a sequence of events, or story. These are often culturally predictable to some degree.
- Genres are types of texts deployed for specific social purposes in specific social contexts.
- Discourses are ways of speaking associated with particular institutions and the conventions and values of those institutions.
- Genres and discourses can combine so that the values of a discourse are used to achieve a particular social purpose.

All of these concepts—narrative, genre and discourse—function as framing devices which link the texts in which they operate to the wider context of culture. Cultural patternings of texts—the frames by which we recognise, classify and make sense of texts—are not fixed but are all the time being produced by us as members of a culture. Terry Threadgold expresses this as follows:

> These intertextual frames are never part of an abstract 'system' (in the Saussurean sense). They are always and only constructed and reproduced in texts as social processes, that is, as events, performances. They 'pre-exist' any particular 'use' only as 'chunks'—familiar, taken-for-granted 'ways of speaking'—in other texts.
>
> THREADGOLD 1989:117

To see in more detail how these concepts can be applied to texts, we will use a case study, involving a comparison between two genres and the discourses and narratives involved.

CASE STUDY: THE REPRESENTATION OF TWO ABORIGINAL WOMEN

In this case study we will look at two texts, one in a women's magazine and one in a newspaper magazine, in order to examine in detail how narrative, genre and discourse can function to frame meanings. These texts are about two Aboriginal women, both 'successful' in the public eye: the first (see Figure 17, page 113) is an article on former tennis player Evonne Cawley in the *Australian Women's Weekly* (July 1992:12–13), and the second (see Figure 18, page 115) is an article on magistrate Pat O'Shane which appeared in the *Australian Magazine,* the magazine supplement to the *Weekend Australian* newspaper (July 31–August 1, 1993:8–12). The values which are given to these two women and their lives are rather different. We will examine the ways in which narrative, discourse and genre shape the ways in which these two women are represented.

Let's start by looking at the genres of the two texts. Both share the genre of magazine article, but there are also generic differences between them. The *Women's Weekly* article, 'Evonne goes back to the beginning', fits within the women's magazine mass market formula identified by Windschuttle (1988:247); as a celebrity and sportsperson, Cawley has had recurring coverage in the *Weekly* throughout her career. She is also constructed (visually and verbally) within a traditional paradigm of femininity as the gentle wife and mother. At the top of the double-page article is a photograph of Evonne with her smiling family clustered around her. She has her arms around her young son, and her daughter is resting her arms on Evonne's shoulder. She is framed within discourses of conventional femininity and the family, discourses which are closely associated with the traditional women's magazine. The discourse of Aboriginality also provides an intertextual frame for reading this text, and one which can potentially emphasise her difference from the dominant white culture of the magazine and its readership. But the article frames this discourse in terms of a search for personal identity, through phrases such as 'I can remember, I can remember' and 'One of our tennis greats is staging a personal comeback.' In this way, Cawley's story fits within the consensual values of the *Weekly*.

By contrast, the article 'In the case of Pat O'Shane', which appears in a magazine that is part of a newspaper, is produced in terms of the generically constrained news values of conflict and controversy. The article is concerned with O'Shane's somewhat controversial career as a magistrate who believes in speaking out on social issues. As in the Cawley article, O'Shane's Aboriginality is brought forward as an issue, but unlike Cawley's, O'Shane's identity is not produced through discourses of femininity which render her less problematic. She is presented not as a wife and mother (although she is both of these) but as a 'career woman', a vocal feminist and an Aboriginal activist. Where Cawley's narrative is framed through discourses of femininity and personal self-fulfilment, O'Shane's story is framed by the discourses of Aboriginal rights and feminism, discourses which are overtly political.

It could be argued that these two articles are different because the women they purport to be about are different, and have very different personal styles or politics. But can this be the only reason for the different meanings and values constructed around their stories? We need also to ask why each magazine has chosen to do an article on Cawley or on O'Shane. Is it only random choice that has Evonne Cawley's story in the *Women's Weekly* and Pat O'Shane's in the *Australian?* Our answer to this question is that the selection of these particular women is motivated. That is, the choice of subject/inter-viewee is generically and ideologically constrained—Evonne Cawley is selected because her narrative can be framed within the consensual values of the *Women's Weekly*, while Pat O'Shane can be framed in terms of political debates about feminism and Aboriginal rights in the *Australian* and other newspapers. These two texts, then, construct meanings around gender and ethnicity in ways which are constrained quite broadly by the ideological values of the particular mass medium (news magazine versus women's magazine).

We'll move now to a consideration of the narratives each text deploys. Each article is structured around discourses of Aboriginality which involve narratives of the subjects' lives. Although these are both stories of Aboriginal women who grew up in humble circumstances in the country, and went on to achieve success in their chosen fields, the two narratives differ significantly.

Evonne Cawley's narrative is highly personalised, and recounts a search for increased knowledge and awareness of her Aboriginality as a narrative of personal growth (see Figure 14). No causal connections are established between the events of her childhood and her current 'awareness'. In her narrative, Aboriginal oppression and racism are not named (but Cawley refers to these issues vaguely as 'what happened', 'all these things'). According to Cawley, 'It was something I've always wanted to do, to make people realise that all these things happened in the past purely through ignorance.' By making racism a historical 'hiccup' which can be cured through education, Cawley's narrative edits out the political elements of an understanding of racism.

In contrast, Pat O'Shane's life narrative is an overtly political one, in which issues of race and gender are foregrounded and direct causal connections are made between her political beliefs and her personal experiences of poverty and racism. However, unlike that of the Cawley article, this narrative is not constructed as uncontested (see Figure 15). (At least) two fairly polarised readings of O'Shane's life are put forward—in which not only evaluations of O'Shane but categories and events pertaining to her life are contested as part of an ideological battleground. O'Shane's words and opinions are cited, and form one version of her story, but alongside this narrative is one produced by the journalist (Legge), who reframes O'Shane's story to construct a different narrative.

So a single 'happy-ever-after' type of narrative is produced in the *Women's Weekly* story, while two narratives at political odds with one another are produced in the *Australian Magazine* article. The differences between the narrative treatment in each article can not only be related to the broad generic features of the magazine type and audience noted above, but are also produced through the specific

FIGURE 14 Narrative of Cawley's life (awareness of her Aboriginality)

- idyllic rural childhood—a period of innocence
- schooling—when she learned of shooting of Aborigines—felt 'strange, bewildered', not knowing more of her own culture was 'frightening'
- during her tennis career, Cawley 'resisted pressure from Aboriginal groups to take a stand'
- after returning to Australia from the US, she goes through a process of self-discovery through learning about Aboriginal culture ('angry I didn't learn at an earlier age')
- involvement in Aboriginal issues—presented as passive? ('her return to Australia dovetailed neatly with the establishment ... of the ... Council for Aboriginal Reconciliation ... with which Evonne has become involved')

genres employed by each article. The Cawley text functions as a 'personal problem' or confessional—a type of article generic to women's magazines (Muller 1991:82). In keeping with this, the tenor of discourse is personalised and emotional, and the narrative is one of personal development. Cawley is quoted talking about her feelings, family moments and personal experience in an intimate way.

The *Australian Magazine* article enacts the genre indicated by its apparently playful title, 'In the case of Pat O'Shane'. There is a generic slippage between the genre of feature article and the judicial genre of court case. Terms such as 'case' and 'doubt' seem to slide between non-technical discourse and technical legal discourse, and the structure of the article incorporates the testimony of various 'witnesses', with prosecution alternating with defence. The writer of the article seems to set herself up not only as a reporter writing about an interview but also as a judge interpreting the witnesses' testimony for the readers (jury).

Another significant feature in these two texts is the use of **citation**, the quoting or reporting of the speech of another. Citation is a technique for introducing other voices into a text. These two texts both make use of citation. The ways in which the journalist/narrator frames the voices of others in each article relates directly to the specific genre. The combative, legal genre of the O'Shane article is characterised by its writer's use of a controlling narrative voice. The narrator does not allow the voices she cites to stand in an open dialogue with one another. Despite the pseudo-dialogic mode, with the semblance of journalistic 'balance' through quoting voices both

FIGURE 15 Narratives of O'Shane's life

O'Shane's narrative of her life	Legge's narrative of O'Shane's life
• rural childhood: conflict, racism, sexism, poverty, unemployment	• ? 'difficult' childhood
• political awareness and commitment	• a 'fighter', 'rabble rouser', 'stirrer', 'boat rocker'. 'Always the victim'
• achievement despite the system	• succeeded among many others less 'noisy about [their] success'
• holds a position which enables her to speak out, to critique social/judicial systems	• has achieved a privileged position, and is exploiting it and her status as female/Aboriginal ('she's something of a protected species—Our Lady of the Politically Correct')

in support and in criticism of O'Shane, the writer continually inter-rupts this apparent dialogue to frame, interpret and redefine. Her narrative voice-over frequently functions to undercut O'Shane's voice and O'Shane's narrative in order to impose her own (see Figure 16).

The confessional genre of the Cawley article calls for rather different narrational politics. The narrative voice here is unobtrusive, supportive, non-judgmental, implicitly endorsing Cawley's values and actions. The mode is one of monologue rather than dialogue, with Cawley's the only cited voice. The narrator's identification with the subject is constructed through her indirect reporting of Cawley's speech/thought. This sets up a patronising tenor relation which involves speaking for the other, as a mother might answer for a child in the child's presence ('Evonne is hoping . . .'; 'Evonne said it was interesting . . .', 'Evonne is now looking forward to going bush'). The use of first name in the Cawley article constructs an intimacy in the tenor relations between the writer/narrator and Cawley, and draws the reader into this intimacy also. Compare this to the use of O'Shane's surname to refer to her in the *Australian Magazine* article. This functions to construct the more distant tenor relation appropriate to its 'combative' genre.

In both stories, narratives of Aboriginal women's lives are con-structed; narratives which could be contextualised in terms of a wider debate about social justice and the workings of oppression. In both stories, there is an attempt to depoliticise these narratives by reducing them to the level of the personal, the individual. In the *Women's Weekly*

FIGURE 16 Citation (underlining identifies the reporter's voice)

Reporting O'Shane's speech:
O'Shane vehemently denies that she is the beneficiary of largess. <u>Always</u>
<u>the victim.</u> (p.11)
Plus, she points out, you battle your way through preselection, then you
have to cop the party line. <u>Not O'Shane. No fear.</u> (p.12)

Quoting O'Shane's speech:
'...I haven't been allowed any latitude at all and I'm not going to be stopped
by any adherence to unstated or unwritten rule.' <u>That is for sure.</u> (p.11)

*Reporting and quoting O'Shane's father (to challenge her account of her
childhood):*
He <u>does not think his children suffered racial abuse at school</u>: 'Nothing
very serious.' <u>He denies the poverty.</u> 'There was plenty like us and some
worse off.'

Quoting a newspaper:
'If she takes up the appointment,' reported a newspaper before Pat
O'Shane's acceptance of a job as a magistrate in NSW, 'it would not be
the first time she has broken new ground. She was the first Aborigine to
graduate at law at an Australian university, the first Aboriginal barrister
and the first Aborigine to head a government department—not that she
enjoys this categorisation.' <u>Not much.</u>

---

text this is achieved apparently as a joint construction by writer and
interviewee, while in the *Australian Magazine* there is contestation
over the narrative.

This case study has demonstrated the ways in which genres,
narratives and discourses interact in quite complex ways in texts. It
has also tried to show that narratives, discourses and genres are not
'given', that is, they are not already there in some sort of objective
reality but are selected and coded into texts as ways of seeing, ways
of framing meanings, and particularly, ways of assigning ideological
value.

SUMMARY

This chapter has built on the understanding of context developed in
Chapter 3 to argue that the concept of context involves:

- the immediate context of situation, semiotically conceived in terms of three dimensions, field, tenor and mode
- intertextual resources or frames, in particular:
    narrative/myth
    genre, and
    discourse.

Narrative, genre and discourse always carry the traces of other contexts, and any text can be read in terms of such traces, which constrain its meanings along with the constraints of its immediate context. As readers of texts and makers of texts, we bring these frames to bear on our understanding of 'what is going on' in any process of making meanings.

FURTHER READING

Fairclough, N. 1989 *Language and Power* Longman, London, Chapter 2
Kress, G. 1985 *Linguistic Processes in Sociocultural Practice* Deakin University Press, Geelong, Chapter 1

FIGURE 17 'Evonne goes back to the beginning'

'I CAN REMEMBER, I CAN REMEMBER'

ONE OF OUR TENNIS GREATS IS STAGING A PERSONAL COMEBACK

Right: Evonne Cawley with her husband Roger and children Morgan and Kelly. The family is looking forward to 'going bush'.

To Evonne Cawley, the sweet smell of home is that of dust on earth floors when water is laid on it in the heat of the day.

This and fishing in the inland rivers and creeks of NSW with her grandmother and aunts are cherished memories of a childhood which ended when she was 11 and left home eventually to become one of the world's greatest tennis players.

Now she is about to take a new direction, to seek out her Aboriginal heritage, of which she says she knows very little.

'All I remember of growing up is living part of the time in the Aboriginal mission in Griffith,' she told The Weekly. 'We left there when I was about two, when my father found work at Barellan. But we spent a lot of time at the mission and they were probably the happiest times of growing up.

'Everybody was having fun. There were plenty of kids to play with, and I learned to swim in the irrigation canals. I remember playing rounders and dancing around fires at night. I even remember the smell of the dirt floor when it was brushed over in the heat of the day, and then water put on it, and there was this beautiful fresh smell.'

Evonne is one of four Australian athletes chosen to represent Australia as Olympic torch-bearers at Barcelona, an honour which thrills her.

She and her husband, Roger, moved back to Australia from the US last December to live in Noosa with their children, Morgan, 10, and Kelly, 14. They made the decision to return for good after taking a long holiday here.

'I was quite happy in America—I just didn't realise how much I missed Australia until I got back to it,' Evonne said. 'I've done pretty well everything I set out to do, I'm satisfied with my life. But there has always been something missing, a gap.'

Evonne is hoping that gap can be filled by writing a book and making a television documentary about her attempts to understand and know her Aboriginality.

'I realised after Mum died last year that making the documentary

114 COMMUNICATION AND CULTURAL LITERACY

would be a great opportunity to learn about my heritage, not only for my sake, but for my kids', too.'

Last year for the first time, the family saw a performance by Aboriginal and Island dancers in Cairns. 'After that, we had to get Morgan a didgeridoo,' she said. 'He's putting out little calls and sounds, but he can't keep it going.'

Evonne began her education about her people by reading a book about the killing of Aborigines by white settlers. Among the tribes to suffer were her own Wiradjuri people.

'It made me sad, but more than that, it made me angry that I didn't know this before,' she said.

In school, Evonne's only lesson about the Aboriginal role in white settlement of the country involved writing an essay.

'We were asked to pretend to be an early settler and give an account of everything that happened during our day. One of the things we had to include was shooting the Aborigines,' she said.

'I felt quite strange at the time, a little bewildered. But that was what we learned about.

'Many different emotions are coming out as I read now about what happened. Mainly, I think I am angry I didn't learn at an earlier age. That's why I think it's so important that they teach this in the schools, so they can appreciate their heritage and feel proud, so that they can do a lot of other things with confidence. I know just from my experience that not to know was frightening.'

Evonne said it was interesting to see Aboriginal beliefs being adopted by the modern world. 'Now, everybody is looking after the environment—Aborigines lived in harmony with themselves and the land for so many years.

'And now you hear psychics say you were somebody else in another life. Aborigines weren't really afraid to die, because they believed their spirit would come back through another child, or an animal.'

After months of reading about her people, Evonne is now looking forward to going bush with the family to find out first-hand about their traditions. 'I am really keen to see the Aboriginal lands. I've always had dreams about living off the land,' she said. 'I love nature, I love roughing it.'

The documentary, also featuring Morgan and Kelly, will be produced for an international audience, according to Roger.

In the past, Evonne has resisted pressure from Aboriginal groups to take a political stand. But her return to Australia has dovetailed neatly with the establishment, last year, of the Federal Government's Council for Aboriginal Reconciliation. The council, with which Evonne has become involved, aims to foster better understanding between Kooris and non-Aborigines.

'It was right up my alley,' Evonne said. 'It was something I've always wanted to do, to make people realise that education is the most important thing, that all these things happened in the past purely through ignorance.'

ELIZABETH JOHNSTON IS A BRISBANE BASED
FREELANCE JOURNALIST. JOHNSTON 1992:12–13

FIGURE 18 'In the case of Pat O'Shane'

MANY ADMIRE HER, MANY FEAR HER. EVEN SOME FELLOW BLACKS WISH SHE WOULD SHUT UP. BUT UNPREDICTABLE PAT O'SHANE, AUSTRALIA'S MOST OUTSPOKEN MAGISTRATE, ISN'T ABOUT TO ZIP HER LIP WHILE MISOGYNY AND RACISM PLAGUE THE JUDICIAL SYSTEM.

'If she takes up the appointment,' reported a newspaper before Pat O'Shane's acceptance of a job as a magistrate in NSW, 'it would not be the first time she has broken new ground. She was the first Aborigine to graduate in law at an Australian university, the first Aboriginal barrister and first Aborigine to head a government department—not that she enjoys this categorisation.' Not much.

. . .

She's a fighter. A rabblerouser. A stirrer. Always has been. As a schoolgirl she used her fists, as a teacher she used her tongue. It has stood her in good stead. As a young lawyer in the Alice Springs Aboriginal Legal Aid office she told the white advisers to make their own coffee. As a political activist in Sydney she got angry when her black male comrades tried to steal the limelight after the hard yakka had been done. As a senior bureaucrat during the Wran Labor government she spoke out often and vehemently, attacking the Liberals, the federal Labor leadership and her Aboriginal crit-

ics. As a magistrate she has stated publicly that male judges are misogynists and women are more intelligent than men.

In January, she dismissed charges against four women who defaced a Berlei Bra billboard, insisting the real crime was committed by the advertisers for promoting pictures of a woman scantily dressed being sawn in half. She has rubbished the self-governing Aboriginal body, the Aboriginal and Torres Strait Islander Commission (ATSIC), and denounced the reconciliation process initiated by the Keating Government. Recently a federal Labor MP nominated O'Shane as his choice for Australia's next and possibly last governor-general. No way, mutter those a little closer to the action. Not because she's black or a woman. Indeed Lois O'Donoghue, the Aboriginal woman heading ATSIC, is the favourite.

Boat rockers make people nervous. That is the risk they run. At the height of the Berlei Bra fracas O'Shane said she was the victim of a sexist and racist campaign. 'I receive the kind of inordinate public attention I get because I am an Aboriginal woman, for no other reason.' It is a very effective shield. Racism still rules in the suburban heartlands and far reaches of rural Australia but rich veins of white guilt run deep through the educated elite. In a postscript to O'Shane's biographical contribution to *Tall Poppies* the book's editor, Susan Mitchell, described her subject as tough. 'Nobody or nothing would ever destroy her belief in herself. She was a tall poppy who had been cut down to the roots and, having bloomed again, God help anyone who ever tried to cut her down.' Staunch conservatives and Aboriginal leaders are least afraid to challenge her views. Others who disagree with her shy away from taking a shot because she's something of a protected species—Our Lady of the Politically Correct.

. . .

If the pluck is Irish, the anger is not. Talk to O'Shane about her childhood and she tells about poverty. About tents and dirt floors. About going without meals. She seethes over the racism. Over the sexism. She claims her father was ostracised by his workmates and found it difficult to get accommodation for his family. She remembers the taunts of 'black gin' at school.

Talk to Patrick O'Shane about the past and he puts a different spin on it. Maybe old age has mellowed him. Maybe it's because he's a white male. But he challenges the grim tenor of her account. He denies he had trouble from his workmates. He says the family's sporting prowess helped community relations. He does not think his children suffered racial abuse at school: 'Nothing very serious.' He denies the poverty. 'There was plenty like us and some worse off.' He denies he had any trouble renting places to live. As for the tent, well, he takes exception to that.

The tent was temporary, he says, lasting only until he had built a home on land at the northern end of Holloway's Beach. And the dirt floor? That riles him most. 'That's bloody nonsense,' he says of his daughter's description. They have had this argument before. 'I remonstrated with her about this,' he harrumphed. 'I carried kerosene tins of beach sand to put on the earth floor. I was right, and she realised there was a vast difference between clean yellow sand and earth. Even earth's not dirt.'

Pat O'Shane shakes with rage at having to account for the discrepancy. 'I mean he must have forgotten the stories that he told me,' she spits. 'We did have a f...ing dirt floor and we did carry water for a mile and a half . . . the fact of the matter is that we were bloody poor . . . I mean I kept that family from age fifteen to seventeen. I was the only one in that family who had a regular income. Why my father would say that I don't know, I can only say that he's a very old man and we've had this out before with other members of the family and their recollection certainly accords with mine.'

. . .

O'Donoghue suggests O'Shane is very capable, 'so long as she sticks to her field'. No chance of that. Reticence is not her speciality. But she must learn to take what she gives without screaming foul play. 'When you're in public life you've got to expect a bit of that,' says O'Donoghue. 'I don't think it's because you're a woman and you're black. I've never found it to be so. I think it's because of your actions.' O'Donoghue is a quiet achiever. A conformist who plays by the rules. 'You can't get away with speaking out so much on the bench or as a bureaucrat. If you want controversy . . . go into politics.'

This is not an option which appeals to O'Shane although it has been put to her time and time again. 'People write to me, they ring me up, they talk to me at parties, they stop me in the street, but I've never been interested in politics.' It's the system, she complains, 'So undemocratic.' Plus, she points out, you battle your way through pre-selection, then you have to cop the party line. Not O'Shane. No fear.

© AUSTRALIAN MAGAZINE. LEGGE 1993:8–12

6

WRITTEN GENRES

Written genres serve a diversity of purposes within our culture: they can function to inform, to entertain, to maintain social relations or to get all sorts of other things done. Effectively, each of these functions is a social practice, a way of acting within the social world. All genres set up or inscribe social relations; at the same time as they instruct, inform and/or entertain. In Chapter 4, we introduced you to the notion that texts, or utterances, are speech acts, that is, that texts *do* as well as *mean*. Written texts, as well as spoken texts, are performative, in that they are produced and read by social agents and have social and material effects.

In this chapter, we will examine the constraints and the possibilities of writing as a medium—what meanings does it enable and what are the cultural consequences of its material limitations? We go on to explore in detail one of the cultural constructs unique to writing— the notion of the author—and what the attribution of an author to a text tells us about its cultural value. In the next section, we look at the structure of writing as a code, and the ways in which written texts are typically organised as messages.

Finally, we look at the ways in which written genres function within both the public and the private sphere, and how they are active in the cultural construction of these domains.

WRITING AS A MEDIUM

We noted briefly in Chapter 4 some of the characteristics of the written medium. Let's begin this chapter by looking at these in more detail, under the following headings:

- writing as a resource
- written text as object and as commodity
- writing as a technology.

Writing as a resource

Writing is a relatively permanent, durable form of text, and therefore a re-usable resource. It is used by cultures for keeping records, storing knowledge and putting memories into permanent form, so that these can be consulted again and again if desired. This durability is important for genres such as tax records, financial book-keeping, history books, personal diaries, library catalogues, reference books and many others. Information retrieval is another important function which writing has had for centuries (since writing was invented, in fact). However, written and printed texts are increasingly conceding this function to computers, which are far more efficient at information retrieval.

Not all written genres place a high value on permanence. Some types of written text are ephemeral, and have relatively short 'lifespans' of use. They include bus tickets, shopping lists, phone messages and junk mail. The mass print media—newspapers, pulp fiction and magazines—fall somewhere in between.

Written text as object

Written texts are experienced as objects or products rather than as processes. Most written texts hide their processes of production; they are circulated in a final form that does not show obvious traces of the drafting and editing which is part and parcel of the writing process. This also enhances their status and value within a culture (or is it the other way around—their status within a culture requires this careful attention, because more is at stake in the meanings of such texts?). Written texts are subjected to 'gatekeeping' processes to various degrees; the more durable the written product is expected to be, the more it is subjected to checking and filtering. Book publishing exemplifies this.

The written text, in the form of the book, is one of the most important commodities in what is known as the cultural industry. As an object, it can be not only commoditised but aestheticised. Specialist bookbinders produce beautifully crafted editions of books, bound in hand-tooled calf leather with gold leaf on the pages and marbled end-papers. The contents of the book become insignificant in relation to its handsome appearance on a library shelf in a 'private residence'.

Within western culture, the book for centuries was a symbol of knowledge and thus power, a status object because it represented cultural capital. It progressively lost this status when the production of books shifted from the intensive labours of monks in monasteries, which were centres of learning accessed by a privileged few, to the mass production of books enabled by the invention of the printing press in the 15th century. This status has been further eroded in the twentieth century with the coming of the electronic age and the information superhighway.

Textual 'objects' as commodities

The status of written texts as objects enables them to be com-moditised—packaged as products which can be bought and sold. Once upon a time, this was not the case with spoken texts, but now the technology of sound recording means this process of com-moditisation is no longer a feature unique to written language.

Within contemporary western culture, it is important to note that many texts, whether written, spoken or visual, are produced as commodities to a certain extent. In addition to the idea of commodity as a thing that is produced by a commercial enterprise for sale to a target market (the commodity of the video game, for instance, is likely to be designed for a youngish, computer literate audience), 'non-commercial' texts may undergo commoditisation to some extent. As Arjun Appadurai expresses it:

> I propose that the commodity situation in the social life of any 'thing' be defined as the situation in which its exchangeability (past, present, or future) for some other thing is its socially relevant feature.
>
> APPADURAI 1988:13

If a company produces a video game, it does so in order to exchange that commodity—that text—for capital, both financial (sales figures, profits) and cultural (the prestige involved in having the biggest-selling, or an award-winning, video game). When a person dresses up before going to a disco, or cuts away the body section of a shirt to reveal incredibly tight stomach muscles, or goes to the gym to help produce those stomach muscles, we can say that the text's most 'socially relevant feature' (at least for the owner/author) is its 'exchangeability' (those stomach muscles can be exchanged for social popularity, sexual responses, admiring glances).

Moreover, there is nothing to stop what we might call the

're-commoditisation' of a text—almost to infinity. An example: a company manufactures 'Daffy Duck' caps, which constitutes a form of commoditisation. But once those caps have been purchased, they can be used for a variety of purposes, one of which might be 'exchange' (if tight stomach muscles don't impress the person you're lusting after, a 'Daffy Duck' cap just might).

Writing as a technology

Writing can be regarded as a technology which enables a text to be produced in the absence of the reader and to be read in the absence of the sender. This gives the potential for achieving both physical and social distance (in terms of tenor) between writer and reader. Thus writing is often used for contexts involving impersonal, distant or formal tenor relations. Examples are genres such as job applications, job advertisements, government policy documents and petitions. Petitions are worded in terms of exaggerated respect ('We, the undersigned, humble citizens of X, most respectfully submit to your honour our request for your gracious consideration'). If such a request were spoken, it would be labelled 'crawling' and not taken seriously, but in writing its formality and respectful tone are more appropriate, if archaic.

Body language and paralanguage, semiotic systems which realise interpersonal (tenor-related) meanings, are not available to readers of written genres. These systems are generally regarded as less easy for speakers to consciously control than their words. Hence writing is also used sometimes to 'control' or even to attempt to 'edit out' some kinds of interpersonal meanings which might be expressed, willy nilly, in a face-to-face interaction, such as affect, the dimension of tenor which relates to emotionality or attitude. Writing allows the writer to avoid the interactivity of speech, and its tendency to reproduce existing power relations because of participants' difficulty in speaking reflectively and in not reproducing habitual patterns of interaction. Writing enables a participant to attempt to negotiate a situation which she or he may think is loaded against her/him because of the greater power of the addressee.

Examples of genres and contexts in which writing might function in this way are writing a letter to break off a relationship, or a teenager writing a note to her/his parents to announce she/he won't be in for Sunday dinner with the grandparents. Writing can also be a way of avoiding respons(-)ibility (literally, being answerable) for the potential effects of one's message. Writing is thus a way to introduce distance into otherwise relatively intimate situations in which the expression of affect would usually be prominent.

Kress concludes that 'writing as a medium and writing as an activity both encourage and permit distancing—from the immediate context, from the audience and from the subject matter' (1988b:97).

WRITERS, AUTHORS AND TEXT PRODUCTION

Writing thus makes possible what Kress has called the 'effacement of the writer from the text' (1988b:95). Written texts may or may not explicitly identify their writers. Why are some written texts anchored to the name of an author, and not others? What is at stake for texts in their anchoring to authors? Why are academics so concerned about plagiarism? Does it matter 'whose words' they are in written texts? If we accept Bakhtin's argument that all texts are composed of **heteroglossia**, the 'many voices' of a language, and bear traces of 'where they've been'—the innumerable contexts which words carry with them (intertextuality)—then can anyone ever claim to be the author of a text, or its sole original source?

Michel Foucault has pointed out the apparently idiosyncratic use of the term author within western cultures:

> the name of an author is a variable that accompanies only certain texts to the exclusion of others: a private letter may have a signatory, but it does not have an author; a contract can have an underwriter, but not an author; and, similarly, an anonymous poster attached to a wall may have a writer, but he cannot be an author.
>
> FOUCAULT 1977:124

It is clear, then, that not all writers are regarded as authors. Kress argues that a writer's function is that of an 'assembler of text. That is, out of her or his experience of other texts, he or she creates a new text which meets the demands of a particular social occasion' (1985:47). Yet the role of author is clearly regarded as more than this. What is at stake in this distinction between authors and writers?

A key cultural value at stake here is the concept of originality. Written texts which are the works of an author are judged to have qualities of creativity and uniqueness. Such values are attributed in particular to literary genres, such as novels, plays and poems. (This is closely tied to notions of the individual subject who expresses him- or herself through unique utterances. This conception of the subject is an ideological one, which corresponds to (small 'l') liberal beliefs in free will and the importance of self-expression, an ideology which fails to recognise the ways in which social structure constrains behavioural and linguistic systems. Kress (1985) points out how disempowering this model of writing is for children learning to write, since they are expected to express themselves 'in their own words', yet their ability to do so depends on a wide experience of a variety of other texts.)

The term author is applied not only to poems, plays and novels, but to most published books of whatever genre, with the exception of reference works such as dictionaries and encyclopaedias. However, the same genres have not always required attribution to an author. In the past, literary texts did not need to be attributed to an author to gain their value.

Genres which require an author are those in which the identity of the writer contributes to the authority and value of the text (and this applies not just to written genres but also to films—critics study the films of Coppola, Eisenstein, or John Ford). The author is a function of our way of handling texts.

Other written genres gain their credibility from anonymity. Just as the naming of an author implies a particular writing position and an individualised style, genres which don't acknowledge their writer/s, such as dictionaries, encyclopaedias, 'hard' news stories (which often acknowledge a news agency but not a journalist), lay claim to values such as 'objectivity', 'fact', 'universality' or 'truth'.

Yet other texts, such as bus tickets, road signs and jar labels, are regarded as too 'generic' (read as the opposite of 'original') or too ephemeral to require attribution to a source.

Naming an author has another function: it identifies the person who has legal rights to a text and takes legal responsibility for its content. Authors are writers who own their texts, that is, who hold legal copyright for them. The term author thus belongs not only to cultural criticism (of literature, films) but to legal discourse. The author is the individual who can be sued for libel, and who can receive royalties from the sale of her/his commodity, the written text.

Plagiarism is thus the sin of failing to recognise the copyright holder—in effect, 'stealing' his or her work. Plagiarism sometimes surfaces publicly as a legal issue, in the form of court cases where one author sues over the claimed use of her/his work by another (the former Beatle George Harrison was successfully sued when a court decided that in his 1970s hit 'My Sweet Lord' he had made unacknowledged use of the tune of the 1960s Chiffons hit 'He's So Fine'). In academic discourse, however, what is at stake is, among other things, intellectual honesty and giving due acknowledgment to the work of other writers. Elaborate methods of acknowledgment, in the form of various systems of referencing, are used to identify who wrote what, and when.

The functions of acknowledging authorship here are slightly different, at least as they relate to the humanities disciplines. An author may be cited to give authority to an argument or to demonstrate that a range of positions or approaches are possible. Finally, by using a referencing system to identify the source of their material, students are being explicit about their function as writers—their role as 'assemblers of text'.

The agent of production could be an amorphous institution, a team of writers, a writer or an author. The agency of a text producer lies behind all written texts, regardless of how or if they are named or identified.

THE TEXTUAL RESOURCES OF WRITING

Speech and writing are not just different ways of making the same meanings, nor is writing a better way of communicating than speech. But each tends to be used for different purposes within a culture. As different technologies of communication, each constitutes a different set of resources for meaning. Written language has a number of characteristics which are directly related to the material possibilities and limits of the medium, as well as to its functions. These are:

- lexical density
- explicit meanings (few deictics compared to spoken language), and
- nominalisation.

The examples in Figure 20 demonstrate the ways in which we

FIGURE 19 Textual resources

> **Lexis** is a technical term for what is also called vocabulary. The words in a sentence can be either structural items or lexical items. **Structural** items have grammatical functions which don't mean much if you take them outside the sentence (words such as 'a', 'the', 'and', 'of' and 'but', to name just a few). Usually we have a limited choice of structural words to use in a particular place in a sentence. **Lexical** items are content words, and the choice of which lexical item to use is much more open (and therefore much more significant).
> **Lexical density** refers to the ratio of lexical items to the total number of words in a sentence or text.
> **Deixis** is Greek for 'pointing'. **Deictic** items are items used to point or refer to something else. They are meaningful to the extent that they set up a relation between the speaker/writer of a text and the time ('now'), place ('here'), people ('I', 'me', 'you') or things ('this', 'my', 'your') she/he is referring to. Deictics can refer to items within the text or outside it, but when they refer outside the text they require the presence of both speaker and listener to be unambiguous. (A classic example is that of a person walking on the beach who picks up a message in a bottle. The message reads 'Meet me here tomorrow.')
> **Nominalisation** is the coding of a process/action as a thing.

typically realise written language, and how this might be expressed in speech.

To calculate the lexical density, count the number of words underlined (these are the lexical items—some of these are not clear-cut cases, since the distinction is fuzzy, particularly with words like 'once' or 'same'). Then count the total number of words and write the two totals down as a ratio. Notice that the written versions have a very high proportion of lexical items to total words (7:9 in example 1a) and that the spoken versions have a much lower proportion of lexical items to total words (7:15 in example 1b).

There is a good example of nominalisation in example 2. In 2a, the meaning is realised (coded) as a thing—'improvements in technology'. In 2b, this becomes 'the technology has improved'. Note how the process ('improve') has become a thing ('improvements').

Although this is an artificial exercise, it provides a simple way of demonstrating the basic features we are discussing. (Of course, the analysis of actual texts is seldom so neat or straightforward.)

The first characteristic, **lexical density**, relates to the fact that written texts are usually in a more or less permanent form and so

FIGURE 20 Comparison of written and spoken forms

Written	Spoken
1a. Violence changed the face of once peaceful Swiss cities.	1b. The cities in Switzerland had once been peaceful, but they changed when people became violent.
2a. [Improvements in technology] have reduced the risks and high costs associated with simultaneous installation.	2b. Because the technology has improved, it's less risky than it used to be when you install them at the same time and it doesn't cost so much either.
3a. Opinion in the colony greeted the promised change with enthusiasm.	3b. The people in the colony rejoiced when it was promised that things would change in this way.

ADAPTED FROM HALLIDAY 1985b:81

can be read and re-read at the reader's own pace, giving the opportunity to reflect on the meanings of words.

The second characteristic, the **explicitness** of written texts, relates to their use in contexts in which writer and reader are not both present (unlike speech). The lack of deixis is one example of this need to be explicit. Written texts are not as likely to make use of the first and second person pronouns ('I' and 'you') and other deictic items as often as spoken discourse does, because their meaning is not so easy to retrieve when the context is not an immediate, shared one. Nevertheless, deictic items still occur in written language, particularly the first and second person pronouns, which function to make explicit the writer's position as 'speaker' and the text's function in directly addressing a reader.

Written texts therefore function by anticipating 'what the reader needs to know'. They construct what is shared context and what is not by making some meanings implicit and others explicit. Implicit meanings might be things like not needing to explain what some words mean, because the writer assumes the reader will know what a cat or a table is. On the other hand, in this textbook we explicitly define the technical terms which we don't expect readers to be familiar with. By making such assumptions, writers position readers in particular ways. It is important to make the point here that such positioning is one of the ways in which **ideology** works, because it sets up assumptions about what meanings can be taken for granted, or treated as naturalised, and what meanings have to be explicitly negotiated (see Chapter 8).

The third characteristic, **nominalisation**, like lexical density, is able to function effectively because written texts are able to be read and re-read at the reader's discretion. Therefore meanings can be packed into the typically denser nominal (noun-like) structures, which are linguistically economical ways of coding written language. Another important reason for the occurrence of nominalisation has to do with the structure of texts as messages (what we have called the **mode**, in Chapter 3).

Texts function as messages by signalling to readers/listeners what the message is going to be about, and they usually do so by placing this first. Halliday (1985a) uses the label **Theme** (with a capital T) for 'what-the-message-is-about'. Most sentences in English start with a thing/participant (a nominal or noun-like structure). In spoken face-to-face interaction the Theme or starting point is often 'I' or 'you'. In written English, as we noted above, direct reference to a shared context through deixis is less appropriate, so written language tends to place other items in the Theme position. Nominalisation opens up the possibility of making a process the starting point for your message, the meaning that you are going to talk about. This is what is happening in example 3. In 3b the Theme is 'the people', but in 3a, the sentence is organised differently. The structure of 3a signals that the writer is going to tell us about 'opinion in the colony'—a concept which is informationally denser than 'the people'.

These features show the ways in which writing comes to seem complex, more complex than speech. In fact, writing is simply organised differently from speech, which has its own complexity but is complex in different ways.

Two types of discourse which exemplify the features of written language are legal discourse and scientific discourse, both of which are often characterised by high lexical density, reliance on nouns, names and categories, and the avoidance of deictics and personal reference. Most written texts fall somewhere between the extremes of much legal and scientific discourse, and written texts which approximate features of casual speech. (An exception in legal discourse

FIGURE 21 Letter from Jason to Kylie

65 Blacksnake Drive
Riverstone 4999
8th November

Dear Kylie,

How's things? What's the weather been like at Barradale? It's been bloody hot here. Which particular freak weather pattern have you been experiencing lately? Has there been any rain? Any volcanic eruptions? Mum and Dad have had about an inch over the past couple of weeks, but no rain, which is discouraging.

Saw *Muriel's Wedding* last night. Despite the hype, or maybe because of the hype, I had some reservations, although I found it very entertaining when it wasn't dull, which was quite a lot, actually. I thought the lead role was extremely well done—in fact a bit overdone. Have you seen it? Don't bother.

Is Danni feeling any better? Does she really have glandular fever? Will she die, do you think? Has she left me anything in her will? I should be so lucky!

Great news—we've got a car! Found it on the median strip of the busy highway out near uni. Obviously dumped—people's cruelty never ceases to amaze me! It's a classic old FJ—black and slightly rusty. Our horses were cheesed off at first but are getting used to it being around. We haven't named it yet, except to refer to it as batty 'cause it looks a bit like a Batmobile.

Hope you are fine, and not too depressed about failing your exams. Let me know what you think about holidays—I like them myself—and we'll see if we can get together.

Love
Jason

is the recent trend toward using 'plain English' in legal documents such as insurance policies and contracts. These avoid the more confusing qualities of traditional legal discourse and are designed to be more clearly understood by their non-expert users.)

Let's now examine the two different written texts that appear in Figures 21 and 22, and analyse them in terms of some of the features we have been discussing. In addition to features of the medium (mode), we need also to consider the contextual constraints of field and tenor as sources of potential difference. We can ask questions such as:

- What are the concerns of the text as a message (what items function as Themes—underlined in the two texts)?
- How are the participants in the text referred to? What terms of address are used? Is there use of deixis?
- Are meanings largely explicit, or are some meanings treated as (and assumed to be) already given and shared?
- What is the subject matter of each text? What kinds of discourses is the lexis associated with?
- What tenor relations does each text presume or imply?
- Finally, how do these characteristics relate to the medium of the text? to the genre?

The two texts clearly differ in a number of ways. Since they are both written texts, we cannot attribute these differences to the medium. We can predict, however, that these differences arise from the different genre of each text. The text in Figure 21 is a personal letter, while that in Figure 22 is a front-page article in a regional newspaper.

Figure 23 suggests answers to the series of questions posed above.

Instead of attempting to account for these differences by arguing that the letter adopts some of the features of a spoken text while the newspaper article is a 'typical' written text, we might find a better explanation in the generic differences between the two texts, differences which relate as much to their field and tenor as to their mode (written or spoken). The letter field is that of maintaining social contact with a friend, therefore its subject matter is to do with the two friends' everyday lives and plans. Its tenor is personalised and familiar, in keeping with the close social distance (despite the physical distance between them). The newspaper article, on the other hand,

FIGURE 22 'Push for jobs'

CREAN SETS 1000 TARGET

Federal Employment Minister Mr Crean yesterday challenged Rockhampton businesses to throw their full support behind a campaign to create 1000 jobs in the area by October.

Mr Crean launched the '1000 jobs for Rockhampton' campaign at a luncheon for business, community and union representatives yesterday.

Staff from the Commonwealth Employment Service will knock on the door of 500 businesses in Rockhampton to make sure that both employers and unemployed people know of all the assistance schemes available to help create more jobs.

Mr Crean told the luncheon of the range of initiatives the Federal Government had introduced in its recent White Paper on Employment and Growth.

Mr Crean said that with the new training wage and with job subsidies, it was possible in some cases to put on a new worker for a cost of [as] little as $10 a week.

He said the purpose of his launch was to enthuse people with a commitment to the task of increasing job growth. He said a target of 1000 jobs was not beyond the capacity of this area to produce within the near future.

The last major job campaign in the region, 'A Million Dollars Worth of Work', had secured 120 jobs in eight weeks.

That was before the White Paper incentives, Mr Crean said.

The Minister told the luncheon that the Government had lain the framework for jobs growth.

But Mr Crean said the exercise would not work on the basis of Canberra determining a blueprint and saying go for it. Rather it had to be a partnership of those in the community who were aware of the inherent strengths and problems. There had to be a determination to cut through problems, he said.

COURTESY OF CAPRICORN NEWSPAPERS PTY LTD. FOX 1994:1

is not principally about the maintenance of social relations, but about presenting information to an anonymous public through the authoritative medium of the press. The news article's front-page billing signals that the information is considered important and of wide public interest.

GENRE, THE PUBLIC SPHERE AND THE PRIVATE SPHERE

These two genres appear to function in straightforward ways in two different social domains: the public and the private. What do we mean when we speak of the public sphere and the private sphere?

FIGURE 23 Comparison of personal letter (Figure 21) and newspaper article (Figure 22)

Letter	Article
• Themes: the people involved ('I', 'we', 'you'), other topics of concern (the weather, relatives, friends) and also processes ('saw', 'found', 'hope') • personal deixis ('you', 'me', 'we') • use of first names (Kylie, Danni, Jason) and personal terms of address (Mum and Dad). The latter are also deictic, since they make sense only in relation to the writer of the letter. • reference to a shared context, with information presupposed/assumed knowledge (such as that Danni has been ill with suspected glandular fever). Use of 'in-jokes' shared between writer and reader. • informal sentence structure, missing words ('[I] hope', '[I] saw', '[It was] Obviously dumped') • strong affect is expressed through use of exclamations ('I should be so lucky!'), terms of praise ('classic'), swearing ('bloody hot') • use of humour and word play (related to affect and to shared context) • subject matter (field) is writer's personal circumstances (weather, mutual friends, movies) • colloquial lexis ('hype', 'cheesed off') • speech functions: Questions (about addressee) as well as Statements (about self)—simulates the interactivity of dialogue/conversation, constructs solidarity and empathy	• Themes: most refer to the Minister (the newsworthy participant), also to CES staff and a job campaign • no personal deixis • terms of address are formal— title plus surname (Mr Crean) and position (Federal Employment Minister) • subject matter is explicit, and information is quantified (500 businesses, $10 a week, 1000 jobs) • sentences are complete (no missing elements) • attitudes and opinions (affect) not expressed explicitly • serious tone (absence of humour or word play) • topics (field) are 'public matters'—business, politics, employment • lexis associated with the discourses of business, politics, employment (campaign, assistance schemes, subsidies, targets, incentives, blueprints) • speech functions: all Statements (functioning to inform the reader)

The sociocultural world has been theorised as consisting of two interlocking domains; the public and the private. The public sphere is typically seen as the world of:

- work
- politics
- business
- citizenship
- legality, and
- rationality.

Traditionally, the public sphere has been the world of men, a world which was implicitly supported by the private sphere, the 'natural' domain of women according to a patriarchal model of social structure. The private sphere concerns itself with:

- the family
- child education
- morality
- sensuality and pleasure
- domesticity
- reproduction, and
- the personal.

The distinction between the public sphere and the private sphere is an influential one which has structured many western practices. Kress has argued that the values of the private sphere are closely aligned with speech, and those of the public sphere with writing: 'Participation in public life and the power which that distributes depend on access to and mastery of the forms of writing' (Kress, 1985:46).

While it is certainly the case that this kind of literacy is a vital skill in the public sphere, we will qualify that statement by arguing that access to the particular genres and discourses associated with the public sphere, in both their spoken and written forms, is a form of literacy which empowers individuals. The ability to speak in public contexts (such as meetings, political rallies, television interviews) is a literacy which carries a great deal of cultural capital. Conversely, being able to write really comprehensive shopping lists and highly enter-taining and intimate personal letters is a form of literacy which does not carry as much prestige and power within the culture. Speech and writing are not discrete activities in themselves, but activities whose forms and values are inflected (shaped) by their functions within the public or private sphere respectively.

While the division of the social world into public and private has been motivated by the sexual division of labour (women in the home, men in the 'workplace'), as a result of the social change which has been accelerating in the last 30 years under the influence of feminism, this division is no longer quite so clear cut. We have argued throughout this book that language and other semiotic systems actively symbolise the social, and that social change is negotiated through textual practices. We would therefore expect that these changes could be identified in specific texts. The print media are a linguistic market (in Bourdieu's terms—see Chapter 4) in which the distinction between public and private is frequently at stake. Let's examine some print media texts to see how particular written genres negotiate these changes.

Print media genres

The print media target various social groups differentiated largely on the basis of gender but also in terms of socioeconomic status. All the print media are 'public' in the sense that they are published and mass distributed, but some sectors of the print media are oriented to the public sphere (newspapers, news magazines, business magazines) and others (specialist magazines, women's magazines) are oriented toward the private sphere.

The picture becomes slightly more complex, however, when we examine these print media forms in terms of their component genres. Newspaper genres include:

- the public sphere genres: 'hard' news articles (with their discourses of business, law and order, and politics), opinion or comment articles, editorials, classified advertisements, real estate and employment sections
- the lifestyle, leisure and entertainment sections, the social pages, the comics.

The categories which newspapers use to define what is news largely reproduce the values of the public sphere: 'hard' news is the serious stuff and traditionally a field reported by men, while the social pages and the lifestyle sections were (and in some cases still are) seen as the province of female reporters, who were 'more suited' to deal with private-sphere issues.[5] A further complexity arises from the different markets of the 'quality' press and the tabloid (popular) press. The quality press is regarded (and regards itself!) as the archetypal voice of the public sphere. The tabloid press mediates public-sphere issues through a perspective and a mode of address which personalise issues and reduce the sense of distance between the public world and the private world (with stories about celebrities, tragedies involving children, the sex lives of politicians, and so on).

Magazines, more than newspapers, are oriented to the private sphere of leisure, sexuality and the home. Yet they too address both private and public sphere issues, through a variety of genres. For example, generalist women's magazines (which comprise the bulk of the magazine market) include genres such as:

- feature articles
- how-to articles
- recipes
- agony columns
- fiction (including romance).

Not surprisingly, these genres of writing are not those most highly valued by authoritative institutions (such as the education system) within western culture. In fact, they are frequently devalued and regarded as trivial, by both women and men. Yet contemporary women's magazines, aimed at working women, introduce discourses of business and employment alongside those of home, domestic skills, family, relationships, beauty and fashion. Figure 24 shows part of a text which addresses working mothers.

This text deals with an issue concerning a traditionally private-sphere activity—childcare—which also impinges on the public sphere through legislation enabling mothers (and, more recently, fathers) to take leave from work to look after their babies. How does this text negotiate the minefield that this intersection of public and private represents? It begins by invoking the public sphere, announcing that 'Australian women have officially had the right to maternity leave since 1979'. This is the discourse of the law and of industrial regulation, presented without qualification in a reporting mode which—so far—would not be out of place in a newspaper article. The

FIGURE 24 The (office) politics of pregnancy'

AUSTRALIAN WOMEN HAVE
OFFICIALLY HAD THE
RIGHT TO MATERNITY
LEAVE SINCE 1979. BUT IN
PRACTICE, TAKING TIME
OFF IS TRICKY BUSINESS.
CLAUDIA BOWE EXPLAINS
HOW TO PLAY OFFICE POLI-
TICS FROM THE MOMENT
YOU ANNOUNCE YOUR
PREGNANCY TO THE DAY
YOU RETURN TO WORK.

Liz never thought she would hate her job, but that's exactly how she felt upon returning to her real estate firm after having a baby. She had expected to enjoy working again; instead she became a guilt-wracked wreck.

After a year, she quit in disgust. 'I wasn't getting a feeling of success from any part of my life,' she recalls.

It *sounds* so simple: the career woman who wants to 'have it all' becomes pregnant, takes maternity leave and then returns to work—only now she has *both* a satisfying career and a delightful little bundle waiting for her at home. In reality, returning to work after a baby is a delicate dance of negotiation among newly competing demands and identities. There's the practical side of life to be worked out: you have to respond to the suddenly doubled demands on your time and energy. And there are the more thorny emotional dilemmas, such as how you weave in the tremendous importance of the new baby

with your dedication to work. You're being called upon to play two very different roles, and shifting identities several times a day can begin to wear on you.

Even for devoted careerists, going back to work after giving birth is often difficult; not every woman will be able to make good on her intentions to do it all. But for those who want to try, planning ahead and knowing how to play the office politics can make the road smoother.

Baby-love can come as a shock
Baby-love is unlike any love you've ever known and it can bowl you over; in its grip, many new mothers find themselves questioning goals that formerly were set in concrete. For career women who've been very driven for years, having a baby can be a shock. All of a sudden you realise you really love being with this baby and it may never have occurred to you that you would—you thought you'd just go back to work right away and get someone to take care of the baby for you. Instead, you become very attached. It's a real conflict.

When baby-love kicks in, it may prompt you to re-evaluate your life scheme. Quite a few women end up deciding that, at this point in their life, mothering is more worthwhile than working. These women probably will— and *should*—quit working for a time if it's financially feasible. The important thing to remember is that you most likely will want or need to return to work at some point, so take care not to burn any bridges.

There's no right or wrong about whether to return to work after having a baby—it's a decision that each new mother must make for herself. Remember, the women's movement was about freedom of *choice*, so don't let other women make you feel like you're letting down the sisterhood by choosing motherhood over work at this point in your life.

Be aware that in some people's eyes, you will be compromising your professional reputation by abandoning your career midstream. There will always ben those women who feel you've let down the female contingent with your about-face concerning your

career, and there will be male employees who will take your defection as further proof that time spent grooming women for upper management is time wasted.

THERE'S A SIGNIFICANT EXIT FROM THE LABOUR FORCE BY WOMEN AFTER THEIR FIRST CHILD IS BORN. THE WOMEN MOST LIEKLY TO RETURN? THOSE WITH HIGH-STATUS OCCUPATIONS, HIGH EARNING POTENTIAL, HUSBANDS WITH A LOW INCOME, WHO WORKED UNTIL JUST UP TO THE BIRTH AND HAVE BEEN WITH THE SAME EMPLOYER FOR A LONG PERIOD.

COURTESY OF MURDOCH MAGAZINES. BOWE 1992:3

qualification comes in the next breath: 'But in practice, taking time off is tricky business.' The phrase 'tricky business' and the reference to 'how to play office politics' are not part of part of the serious, 'straight' public sphere discourses of business and politics. Instead, these are metaphors for the 'business' of managing interpersonal relations, traditionally women's field of expertise and now applied to the workplace.

The body of the article begins with a (hypothetical?) anecdote about Liz, a mother who went back to work but left again after a year because she 'became a guilt-wracked wreck'. The anecdotal style immediately personalises the issues—a characteristic of private-sphere discourse, with its focus on the personal and private. The tone of the article is that of motherly or 'sisterly' advice: familiar in terms of social distance, with the frequent use of 'you' to directly address and involve the reader. 'Make use of my wisdom, I have been there and done that (or someone I know has),' the writer seems to imply.

Juxtaposed against the main text, and set in bold, are a set of 'industrial facts' whose tone is not easily assimilated into the body of the article. Their inclusion functions to give the seriousness and authority of the public sphere to the issue, but is not allowed to intrude upon the article's generic function of 'giving advice'. To incorporate public-sphere discourses into the advice genre would be to depersonalise the tenor and thus to destabilise the genre, which depends on personalised address to be successful.

Yet the article must still deal with the field and the subject matter of the workplace and its roles and activities. By looking at the lexical choices in it, we can see how it weaves together the two strands of office work and mothering (see Figure 25).

Each of these discourses is represented either in every sentence or in every alternate sentence, constructing the conflict between the competing demands of the two spheres. Apart from the repetition of 'baby-love', 'baby' and 'love', the text spends few words expounding the joys of motherhood, which are taken for granted (an ideological assumption? definitely!). On the other hand, the positive affect associated with the world of work needs to be explicitly constructed; much of the lexis associated with work is coupled with terms that associate work either with female identity or with a positive attribute:

> career *woman*
> *satisfying* career
> *maternity* leave
> *dedication* to work
> *devoted* careerists.

The text strives to be open in terms of emphasising that the choice between going back to work or quitting to stay at home with the baby is the reader's. However, subtle shifts suggest that it is oriented more towards those women who continue to work (predictable given the readership *New Woman* is targeting—young career women). Throughout the text, women are directly addressed as 'you', or referred to in the third person in their roles as mothers or 'career women'; but there is a shift to the more distant, less inclusive phrases 'quite a few women' and 'these women' (implying, 'but probably not you') in references to women who choose mothering over paid work. But the even more distant 'those women' is reserved for women who criticise mothers who give up their career (the 'sisterhood' musn't criticise 'motherhood'). (It is worth noting that the distinction between paid work and the unpaid work of mothering is never made

FIGURE 25 Discourses of work and mothering

Discourse of work	Discourse of mothering
career	delightful little bundle
leave	home
work	emotional dilemmas
careerists	giving birth
financially feasible	baby-love [repeated]
professional reputation	new mother
male employees	baby [repeated]
upper management	love [repeated]

in the text—throughout, there is an opposition between real work and the joys of motherhood, which is an ideological binary based upon a capitalist, patriarchal social and economic structure in which women's work in the home has no economic value.)

What we hope to have demonstrated in this analysis is that the modes of private discourse have a strong influence upon the way in which both public-sphere and private-sphere issues and discourses are organised textually (and that this has ideological effects). There is no way that readers familiar with and literate in print media texts could read this article in the same way as, say, a hard news story in a newspaper. The genre of advice, so typical and pervasive in women's magazines, constrains the ways in which this text means, individualising the issues and framing them as a matter of personal choice.

Is there anything wrong with this? Maybe not, but it does constitute an ideological move, since by personalising and individualising an issue, it also becomes depoliticised. The text plays down the roles of institutions like the workplace, the legal system and industrial regulations in determining what individuals can and can't do and how they can live their lives. A personal view of a problem is what advice columns provide, and the typical solution is to 'talk about it'. The problem and the solution are addressed locally. The social power structures which may underpin the personal problem are thus unlikely to be addressed or changed.

The different discourses and genres of the print media thus inflect the notions of public and private in complex ways. The print media function as multidiscursive and multigeneric institutions. That is, they employ a variety of genres, and these genres express a variety of discourses. These in turn constrain not only *what* we read but *how* we read.

SUMMARY

Writing as an activity, and written genres as types of texts, are shaped in part by the materiality of the medium.

Writing is a technology, neutral in itself, but assigned value by the uses and functions it has within a culture.

Most important, writing as a practice is determined and influenced by the discourses and genres which it realises, and the institutions which lie behind these discourses and genres.

Many of the differences we assume exist between speech and writing are not so much essential differences between the two mediums as differences that arise from the uses to which we put speech or writing within our culture. In particular, many written texts function in contexts which are formal and impersonal in their tenor relations, whereas speech is often the favoured mode in personal, informal interaction. To understand more fully the role of written language in our culture, we need to ask:

- which genres are written genres and which are spoken?
- which institutions, fields and markets make use of writing?
- what tenor relations attach to these genres and institutions?

FURTHER READING

Appadurai, A., ed. 1988 *The Social Life of Things* Cambridge University Press, New York

Foucault, M. 1977 *Language, Counter-Memory, Practice* ed. and trans. D. F. Bouchard and S. Simon, Cornell University Press, Ithica, NY

Kress, G. 1988a 'Language as social practice', in *Communication and Culture: An Introduction* University of New South Wales Press, Kensington, pp.91–104

Pateman, C. 1989 'Feminist critiques of the public/private dichotomy' in *The Disorder of Women*, Polity, Cambridge, pp.118–40

CULTURAL PRACTICE

In this chapter we are going to look at the notion of cultural practice and, more particularly, at the relationship between:

- cultural rules, conventions and structures, on the one hand, and
- individual communication and meaning-making activities of everyday life, on the other.

COMMUNICATION AS PRACTICE

In previous chapters we have emphasised the point that communication is concerned with making meanings, and that the kinds of meanings that are made depend very much on the specific cultural contexts and literacies involved; that is to say, we have argued that communication is first and foremost a cultural practice.

Let us recap this argument. We have been suggesting that communication cannot simply be confined to those situations where people talk, write, or overtly signal to one another. Most people, for example, would accept that two people talking to one another constitutes communication; and they would probably also accept such diverse activities as sports fans shouting abuse at an opposing team, members of an audience laughing at a scene in a film, or even a student yawning and then falling asleep during a university lecture, as examples of communication.

Communication practices are not, of course, exhausted by these more or less overt examples. Much of the work that has been produced in semiotics and cultural studies in the last twenty years has been concerned to demonstrate the communicative aspect of all cultural activities, including attending a concert, playing a video game, reading a magazine, wearing different styles or combinations of clothes, praying in a church or temple, or tattooing a picture of

Daffy Duck on your body. These can be understood as communication practices.
We might ask ourselves the following questions:

- How can we read these activities as forms of communication?
- What precisely do they communicate?
- To whom?
- How are specific meanings produced in communication practices?
- And how do these meanings influence or regulate the kinds of activities that people engage in or perform?

If the way these questions are set out in front of you seems to suggest a cat chasing its tail, then remember the point that communication is a cultural practice and culture is a communicative practice: neither concept can be thought of without regard to the other.

Activities are forms of communication because they are 'read' by members of the same or different cultures as signs, even when there has been no overt attempt to signal anything to anyone. Let us return to C.S. Peirce's definition of a sign that we introduced in Chapter 2: it is 'something which stands to somebody for something in some respect or capacity' (quoted in Hawkes 1977:126). The crucial thing about this definition is that it moves the emphasis away from the notion of communication as an exclusively intentional form of signalling, to the idea of communication as an exercise in the production and negotiation of signs.

Peirce's definition of a sign is important for at least four reasons:

- Meaning making (and therefore communication) is something that occurs all the time.
- The production of meaning often occurs outside overt forms of communication.
- Everything we do, every activity and move we perform, can be produced as a sign, as meaningful—that is to say, can communicate something to someone.
- Because of the preceding three points, communication must be understood as necessarily tied up with, and in a sense indistinguishable from, notions of **cultural literacy** and **cultural value**.

This last point is of particular importance with regard to the four questions about practice posed earlier, which could be summarised in terms of one question: how do we make sense of people's practices?

Let's look at a few examples of practice and use these examples as departure points for dealing with this question.

The first example we will look at is the film *The Flintstones*. At the beginning of the film there are two couples—Fred and Wilma, and Barney and Betty—who are very close friends and share attitudes, tastes and values. By the middle stages of the film, however, serious tensions have arisen between the two couples, who now tend to accentuate certain important differences that divide them. There is a crucial scene in which Fred, the newly rich executive, is having dinner at an expensive restaurant with Wilma. When Betty and Barney turn up, Fred patronises and eventually insults them to the extent that their friendship is apparently destroyed. When we try to make sense of what has happened here, the only major points of difference we can identify are that Fred now earns more money and has a better job. That might explain why Barney is resentful, except that Barney only becomes resentful after Fred changes his behaviour. How does the notion of communication as a cultural practice help us to account for Fred's behaviour, Barney's responses, and the breakdown of their friendship?

Second example: Imagine we are at the stately mansion of millionaire playboy Bruce Wayne, also known to viewers (but not identified by the residents of Gotham City) as Batman. Bruce is sitting in his plush lounge chair when the Penguin, the Joker, the Riddler and several of their lackeys intrude. They threaten, they intimidate, but Wayne remains calm, cool and decidedly detached. He eventually instructs Alfred, his butler, to see these 'gentlemen' (he uses the term facetiously) to the door. The next day the trio return, but this time they are met by the Caped Crusader, who is anything ('krunch'! 'blonk'! 'flam'!) but polite. Bruce Wayne and Batman might be 'different' people, but they share the same body. Why are they associated with such radically different practices?

Something happens to Fred Flintstone which changes his attitudes, values and practices and which therefore changes the way he 'reads' people (the Rubbles, for instance). Similarly, put Bruce Wayne into a dinner suit and have him sipping champagne at the ballet, and you have a particular kind of person whose behaviour owes something to his material context and background. Have the same Bruce Wayne change his dinner suit for a leotard, tight shorts, a cape, a mask and the Batmobile, throw in a gang of psychopathic criminals, and all that refined behaviour goes out the window. There are obviously strong connections between the kinds of social, political, economic and cultural details that characterise groups of people, and the kinds of practices (from eating habits to movie-watching preferences) that such groups engage in, but we are still in need of some specific theoretical concepts that will allow us to 'fill out' our generalisations. In other words, how do cultural **trajectories** (maps of people's cultural history, if you like) tie in with specific practices? It is at this point that we turn to the work of the French sociologist Pierre Bourdieu (see the box in Chapter 1).

Theories of practice have always found difficulty coping with the problem of the extent to which practices are the result of free choice or intentionality, on the one hand, or structured, predetermined and unconscious, on the other. Bourdieu's work, and in particular his theories of practice, is characterised by a determination to find a way between these competing explanations.

In what way is free choice or intentionality put forward as an explanation for practice? The process model of communication that we discussed in Chapter 1, for instance, proposes that people make decisions, engage in practices, and read other practices in terms of their individuality. According to this model, every decision we make can be more or less understood as an act of free will; which means that our decisions are not determined by what we previously referred to as our cultural contexts and trajectories.

This notion of individualism is the closest thing there is to a definitive American ideology, to the extent that it pervades or at least influences most cultural products that come out of the US. It is interesting to note that those cultural forms or genres we think of as being quintessentially American—the western film, say, or the private eye novel, film or television series—are all based on the notion of the hero as a strong, autonomous individual whose practices cannot be easily explicated in terms of general tendencies. On the other hand, 'types' (such as the gambler, the town drunk, the saloon girl) who are usually relegated to supporting or comic roles invariably behave in a predictable way. Classic American westerns such as *Shane, High Noon, The Man Who Shot Liberty Valance,* right up to more recent examples such as the Clint Eastwood films *Pale Rider* and *Unforgiven,* set up a distinction between the hero and ordinary members of the community. The hero is a law unto himself, an outsider, someone who acts almost in social isolation even when intervening to set society right.

Jimmy Stewart, who plays the the middle-class, East-Coast American lawyer and politician in *The Man Who Shot Liberty Valance*, is the closest thing, in those films, to a hero who is also a type rather than an individual. But the film makes clear, and he is aware, that his heroism—he is adulated as the man who shot Liberty Valance and in doing so rid the town of a murderer and troublemaker, allowing it to pass on to 'civilisation'—is 'stolen' from John Wayne's character. It is Wayne who actually shoots the very nasty villain, played by Lee Marvin, and it is therefore Wayne who is the real, if forgotten, hero. The central point to this John Ford film is that America may have been taken over and 'civilised' by lawyers and politicians—taken over by types—but it was built on a heroic individualism which goes largely unrecognised or unremembered.

How does Bourdieu theorise this split between individualism (as embodied, say, by the hero) and cultural determination (embodied in the notion of the type)? Bourdieu identifies certain notions as the keys to making sense of how practice is simultaneously free and regulated, conscious and unconscious. The most important of these notions are:

- objectivism, subjectivism and **structure**
- **habitus**
- **cultural** and symbolic **capital**
- **cultural field**, and
- **distinction**.

SUBJECTIVISM/OBJECTIVISM

In his introduction to *The Logic of Practice*, Bourdieu writes that 'Of all the oppositions that artificially divide social science, the most fundamental, and the most ruinous, is the one that is set up between subjectivism and objectivism' (1990:25).

What Bourdieu means by subjectivism is very close to what we might call decontextualised practice; as we suggested with regard to certain American cultural genres, often the only context for the actions and behaviour of heroes is their own individuality and heroism.

Bourdieu suggests, to the contrary, that there is always a close connection between:

- the structures of a culture, which include the values, ideas, desires and narratives produced by, and characteristic of, cultural institutions such as the family, religious groups, education systems and government bodies, on the one hand, and
- the specific tendencies, activities, values and dispositions of individuals, on the other.

This connection is usually denied in Hollywood films dominated by the notion of the hero. For an exemplification of this point, think of any Arnold Schwarzenegger film (for instance, *Predator, Total Recall, True Lies*). Try and imagine the possibility of Arnie's general behaviour, which we could characterise as heroic, individualistic, assertive, and violent but (for him) morally responsible, being understood in terms of cultural determination.

There are times when Arnie questions his own behaviour—particularly when his practices seem to be controlled by outside forces. Has he been set up by the CIA in *Predator*? Is he really in the middle of an interactive, total-reality video game in *Total Recall*? Why has he ignored his wife and perhaps driven her into having an affair in *True Lies*? The point is, however, that these moments are aberrations when Arnie has momentarily lost, or is in danger of losing, his individuality.

In *True Lies*, for instance, Arnie has become so much of a company (CIA) man that he has neglected his wife, Jamie Lee Curtis, and the intimacies of family life (shared birthdays, conversations, sex). Eventually he realises what is happening, throws off those influences ('company culture'), and regains his individuality (and his marriage).

For most of the 'ordinary' characters in the film, however, particularly the comic characters and the villains, the idea that they could act independently of their type (lecher, terrorist, coward, used-car salesperson) is virtually unthinkable. Terrorists, for instance, usually don't become terrorists by exercising their free will. Presumably they are born that way—though one wonders what a baby terrorist would look like.

In Hollywood films, types are often produced as being as free from sociocultural influence as is the hero. The list of types we referred to in the previous paragraph (lecher, terrorist, coward, used-car salesperson) doesn't refer to specific cultural contexts so much as to supposedly natural and ahistorical categories; after all, a coward is a coward whether that person ran away from the Normans at the Battle of Hastings or ran away from a feral hamster at the county fair.

You might want to argue that practices associated with a used-car salesperson have obvious connections with cultural contexts; it could be countered, however, that in western cultures used-car dealers are produced as an ahistorical category because of the idea that a certain type (dishonest, devious, tricky) is attracted to the job rather than the culture of the job producing the type.

The second category of human behaviour is referred to by Bourdieu as 'objectivism':

> Objectivism . . . sets out to establish objective regularities (structures, laws, systems of relationships, etc.) independent of individual conscious-ness and wills . . . It raises . . . the forgotten question of the particular conditions which make . . . experience of the social world possible.
>
> BOURDIEU 1990:26

Objectivism works, for Bourdieu, in precisely the opposite way to subjectivism, in that it can see practice only as the reproduction of structure and no more. Perhaps the most obvious examples of objectivist readings of practice—certainly the most obvious for Bourdieu—are to be found in the activities of anthropologists, who investigate, describe, analyse and explain mostly so-called 'primitive' or backward cultures.

Bourdieu himself did anthropological work in Algeria in the 1960s, and he was eventually struck by the incongruous, and even comical, aspect of anthropologists seeking out so-called primitive cultures, then observing, recording, describing, questioning and eval-uating what was going on in front of them, in order to bring it all back home as fresh anthropological 'knowledge'.

Bourdieu had problems with this kind of activity for two reasons:

• First, just as subjectivist accounts of practice edit out the rela-tionship between cultural structures and individual practices (that relationship is repressed), objectivist accounts of 'other' practices or cultures, such as those engaged in by anthropologists, have no place for 'the forgotten question of the particular conditions' which make, say, anthropology possible. In other words, in order for an anthropologist to objectify another culture as primitive, that anthropologist must naturalise the values that characterise one culture as civilised or advanced and another culture as its opposite.

Anthropologists observing other cultures have, to a certain extent, already written their books before they arrive. Designating a culture as primitive is a form of (usually negative) valuation which determines, to no small extent, what questions the anthropologists will ask, what things they will see and miss, and what aspects they will emphasise as important, as the 'keys' to the culture. In other words, anthropologists objectify others, but they always fail to objectify their own practices.

• The second major difficulty Bourdieu has with objectivist accounts of cultures and practices is that he sees them as failing to understand that descriptions of objective regularities (structures, laws, systems) do not tell us how people use—inhabit, negotiate, elude—those objective regularities.

An example of this point is to be found in the John Carpenter film *Starman*, and it is a particularly good example because it demonstrates that the difference between, say, laws and practices is forgotten even by practitioners. In *Starman* an alien, played by Jeff Bridges, is travelling across America by car with a woman played by Karen Allen. The woman does all the driving until Bridges points out that he has been closely observing her driving the car, has analysed and taken in all the rules and skills involved, and would like to drive himself. Allen reluctantly agrees, but almost immediately Bridges runs a red light and only narrowly avoids an accident. Allen abuses him, but Bridges replies that, after watching her drive, he had concluded that the rules about road lights were as follows: green means go fast, orange means go slightly faster, and red means go very fast.

Subjectivism and objectivism remain useful notions in attempting to account for practice, mainly because they point to the shortcomings of their 'other'.

• Subjectivism draws attention to the point that objectivist maps of a culture (laws, rules, systems) edit out intentionality and individuality (what we might call **agency**).
• Objectivism points out that individuality and intentionality are

regulated by cultural contexts (we can only intend what is available to us within a culture).

Bourdieu, reading across both approaches simultaneously, insists that practice is always informed by a sense of agency (the ability to understand and control our own actions), but that the possibilities of agency must be understood in terms of cultural trajectories, literacies and dispositions. The interplay between these two spheres—which makes practice possible—he refers to as 'habitus'.

HABITUS

Bourdieu once defined habitus as 'the durably installed generative principle of regulated improvisations . . . [which produce] practices' (Bourdieu 1991:78). In other words, habitus can be understood as the set of values and dispositions gained from our cultural history that stay with us across contexts (they are durable and transposable). These values and dispositions allow us to respond to cultural rules and contexts in a variety of ways (they allow for improvisions), but those responses are always largely determined—regulated—by where we have been in a culture.

The following list describes the main points Bourdieu associates with habitus (1990:52–3):

- Knowledge (the way we understand the world, our beliefs and values) is always constructed through habitus, and not passively recorded.
- Habitus can be understood as set of dispositions. We are disposed towards certain attitudes and values, disposed to act in specific ways, because of the influence exerted by our cultural trajectories. These dispositions are transposable.
- Habitus is always constituted in moments of practice. It is always 'of the moment', brought out when a set of dispositions meet a particular problem, choice or context. Habitus can be understood as a 'feel for the game' that is everyday life.
- Habitus operates at a level that is at least partly unconscious. Why? Because habitus is, in a sense, entirely arbitrary; that is to say, there is nothing natural or essential about the values we hold, the desires we pursue, or the practices we engage in.

Now this is not to say that these arbitrary practices are unmotivated, and that we act out of disinterestedness. On the contrary, all practices are informed by notions of power, politics and self-interest. But in order for a particular habitus to function smoothly and effectively, each person or agent must normally think that the possibilities from which she/he chooses are in fact necessities, common sense, natural or inevitable. Other possibilities are ruled out precisely because they are unthinkable.

The rules and structures of perception that pertain to a particular habitus are inscribed on and in individuals as if they were 'human nature' or civilised behaviour, and everything outside those rules and structures is usually understood, when it is forced upon us, as anything from horrific and barbaric to absurd and comic.

An excellent example of how arbitrary structures and rules are produced as a naturalised habitus can be seen in western meat-eating patterns; cows, pigs, chickens, ducks, turkeys and sheep are all slaughtered, packaged and consumed as staple components of a western diet, while domestic animals such as cats, dogs and hamsters are (unconsciously) excluded from this category. When stories circulate about 'foreigners' eating cats or dogs, the usual response is one of disgust and incomprehension.

What is implicit in this reaction is the notion that it is proper to eat some animals because they are 'depersonalised' (herds of cattle, flocks of sheep, but not hordes of hamsters); and we often reinforce this act of depersonalisation by naming the meat differently from the animal (we eat beef, not cow; mutton, not sheep). Animals which we personalise and regard as pets, on the other hand, are almost impossible to think of as food. Imagine, if you can, a camper starving in the Australian outback, faced with the possibility of having to eat a koala to survive! Cannibalism would probably be an easier alternative.

An example of such a dilemma occurs in *The Restaurant at the End of the Universe* (Adams 1980), the sequel to *The Hitchhiker's Guide to the Galaxy*:

A large dairy animal approached Zaphod Beeblebrox's table, a large, fat meaty quadruped of the bovine type with large watery eyes, small horns and what might almost have been an ingratiating smile on its lips.
'Good evening,' it lowed and sat back heavily on its haunches, 'I am the main dish of the day. May I interest you in parts of my body?'
It . . . gazed peacefully at them.

> Its gaze was met by looks of startled bewilderment from Arthur and Trillian, a resigned shrug from Ford Prefect and naked hunger from Zaphod Beeblebrox.
> 'Something off the shoulder perhaps?' suggested the animal, 'Braised in a white wine sauce.'
> 'Er, your shoulder?' said Arthur in a horrified whisper . . . 'You mean this animal wants us to eat it?' whispered Trillian to Ford . . .
> 'That's absolutely horrible', exclaimed Arthur, 'the most revolting thing I've ever heard . . . I think I'll just have a green salad,' he muttered.
> 'May I urge you to consider my liver?' asked the animal. 'It must be very rich and tender by now, I've been force-feeding myself for months.'
> 'A green salad,' said Arthur emphatically . . . 'Are you going to tell me . . . that I shouldn't have green salad?'
> 'Well', said the animal, 'I know many vegetables that are very clear on this point.'
>
> ADAMS 1980:92–3

Zaphod Beeblebrox is completely unconcerned at the prospect of eating the animal, but most of the party find it difficult to eat something that has been personalised to the extent that they have been conversing with it. Arthur switches his attention to something that is about as depersonalised as you could find, for him (a green salad), only for the animal to make the point that green salads can be personalised, too ('I know many vegetables . . .').

Systems, rules, laws, structures and categories of meaning and perception can only function effectively as habitus if we don't think about the sociocultural conditions of their production and existence; what Bourdieu calls 'the forgetting of history which history itself produces' (1990:56). Most western cultures accept, for instance, that life forms are divided into categories such as mammals, reptiles, amphibians, birds, insects and fish. These categories—which have their own specific characteristics—are used in producing stories about life on Earth, stories which start with primitive life forms (such as fish) that evolve, inevitably, into the highest form (mammals). There is usually a logic to these stories which explains, for instance, why dinosaurs died out and were replaced by mammals, and why human beings became the dominant mammals. Recently, however, evidence has come to light which suggests that dinosaurs sometimes behaved like reptiles and sometimes like mammals, and that their extinction, rather than being part of an inevitable replacement of reptiles by mammals, may have been accidentally caused by meteor falls or volcanic eruptions.

Those new details challenge the rigidity of the system used in the west to classify life forms, but still leave it more or less intact. Consider, however, the following excerpt from a short story by the Argentinian writer Jorge Luis Borges, quoted by Michel Foucault at the beginning of his book on western taxonomies of knowledge, *The Order of Things*. 'This book first arose,' Focault writes,

> out of a passage in Borges, out of the laughter that shattered, as I read the passage, all the familiar landmarks of my thoughts—our thoughts, the thoughts that bear the stamp of our age and our geography—breaking up all the ordered surfaces of existing things . . . This passage quotes a 'certain Chinese encyclopaedia' in which it is written that 'animals are divided into: (a) belonging to the Emperor, (b) embalmed, (c) tame, (d) sucking pigs, (e) sirens, (f) fabulous, (g) stray dogs, (h) included in the present classification, (i) frenzied, (j) innumerable, (k) drawn with a very fine camelhair brush, (l) et cetera, (m) having just broken the water pitcher, (n) that from a long way off look like flies.' In the wonderment of this taxonomy, the thing we apprehend in one great leap . . . is the . . . stark impossibility of thinking that.
>
> FOUCAULT 1973:xv

Foucault's reaction to this extract helps us understand how arbitrary rules and categories of thought are at the same time motivated, and tied up with questions of power and politics. Two of the main binaries used, in the last 200 years, to distinguish western cultures from Asian cultures were 'scientific/primitive' and 'civilised/barbaric'. Western explanations and narratives of the world corresponded to something called science, and possession of 'authentic' scientific systems for producing knowledge was a central marker, perhaps the most important marker, of whether a culture was civilised, like the west, or primitive and barbaric.

Moreover, it was only a short step from designating a culture as uncivilised to categorising its people as non-human or subhuman, and therefore without the rights accorded to civilised peoples. Most of the colonialism that occurred in the past 200 years—and still goes on today, in different forms—was rationalised in terms of particular categories or systems of western thought being privileged over those of so-called primitive cultures.

Perhaps the most crucial aspect of habitus, then, is that it naturalises itself and the cultural rules, agendas and values that make it possible. But there are also a number of other important points that can be identified in Bourdieu's definition.

First, conditioning associated with a particular type of existence, based on shared cultural trajectories, produces the habitus. Now this can seem a difficult notion, because we are not talking about something as straightforward as, say, the Marxist idea of class categories based on positions occupied within the economic sphere. Habitus is certainly informed by the idea of class, but members of a group share a particular habitus because of general cultural contexts and trajectories. A rather unusual example of this point is the John Carpenter film *Big Trouble in Little China*, which concerns the adventures of a swaggering, over-the-top American truck driver, played by Kurt Russell, in the demonised underworld of San Francisco's 'Little China'.

We refer to this as an unusual example because the film seems to be quite overtly concerned with denaturalising what we might call a macho American habitus (as exemplified by the practices of the Kurt Russell character) by demonstrating how that habitus does not take into account, nor cope with, 'oriental' experiences (involving magic and demons). All the while this is going on, however, it is evident that the American and Chinese communities share, to no small extent, a common habitus. How? One of the most important aspects of habitus is that it regulates the overall set of possibilities that a person can take up and negotiate; that is to say, it regulates what meanings, values and narratives—practices—are thinkable.

Kurt Russell and the Chinese characters in this film are separated by certain dispositions and trajectories (such as experiences of, and a belief in, magic and demons, on the Chinese side, and scepticism on Russell's side), but at the same time they have a great deal in common:

- the macho banter shared by nearly all the men,
- the acceptance by both American and Chinese characters of narratives and values associated with bravery, chivalry and romance, and
- the high degree of cultural literacy displayed by the Chinese characters in reading and making sense of Russell's overblown rhetoric and posturing.

These all provide evidence of a shared American/Chinese world view, a shared habitus, even as the film tries to suggest that America and 'Little China' are worlds apart.

What largely produces this shared habitus, of course, is the pervasiveness of American cultural institutions and products (coming out of film and television, for instance) and their ideologies. Chinese families interact like families in American sitcoms, elders come out with sage, homespun wisdom, and gender relations are dominated by the narrative of romance. Habitus is constituted, as Bourdieu suggests, out of 'durable, transposable dispositions'. *Big Trouble in Little China* suggests that even in the apparently diverse cultural mix of the US, those cultures (whether based on race, ethnicity, or economic capital) can still be understood, to some extent, as sharing a habitus.

Moreover, because a habitus is transposable, persons from different cultures can still adjust their practices so as to fit in with different contexts. Kurt Russell's character, on finding himself taking part in an underworld expedition against Chinese demons, faces a challenge to the validity and practicality of his habitus. However, he is able to transpose that habitus, and the dispositions and values that characterise it (machismo, individuality, anti-sentimentality, cynicism, aggression, self-confidence, an obsession with individual honour, a sexist attitude towards women), for two main reasons:

* because the rules of the two different games are not all that different (for instance, the villain is both an American capitalist and a Chinese demon, which suggests some kind of analogy between capitalist America and demonised China), and
* because Russell is able to pick up, in a selfconsciously clumsy and comic way, the knowledges and skills (involving ritualised combat, for instance) which allow his habitus to remain useful.

Habitus, as we mentioned earlier, is always 'oriented towards the practical'. In other words:

* dispositions, knowledges and values are constructed, not passively consumed or reinscribed, by persons, who use their understanding and feel for the rules of the game as a means of furthering and improving their own standing and capital within a cultural field.

It must be stressed that at the same time an agent is pursuing her/his own practical ends through a manipulation of the rules of the

game, what s/he constructs as her/his 'interests' are themselves produced by and through habitus.

Let's return to Kurt Russell and *Big Trouble in Little China*. Russell
is concerned to aggressively promote his macho reputation in order
to attract the sexual interest of the heroine (played by Kim Cattrall),
earn as much money as he can as quickly as possible (by gambling,
for instance), and repay any slight or damage done to his honour.
When Russell simply reproduces the postures, discourses and
actions—the practices—of this 'tough-guy adventurer', he is comically
ineffective (his rhetoric or pose, for instance, is often not attuned 'to
the moment', not appropriate to the overwhelming odds he finds
himself up against).

He is far more effective when he isn't constrained to act as a
fearless adventurer; when he acts, and makes use of his skills, 'of the
moment' (for instance, by instinctively catching a knife and throwing
it straight back at the villain).

Russell is most practical in his practices, and most furthers his
interests, when he 'feels' his way through the game rather than
deciding what to do before it is required. However, as we pointed
out, those interests (maintaining his masculine reputation and honour,
for instance) do not come out of a vacuum: Russell pursues them
precisely because they have been constituted as interests for him. At
various times in the film it makes more sense (in terms of personal
safety, for instance) for Russell to drop out of the adventure; but that
would mean, of course, rethinking what constituted his interests and
thus the most crucial, personalised, and therefore unconscious part of
his habitus.

Habitus always makes a 'virtue out of necessity'. This means that
just because there is a close relationship between 'objective prob-
abilities (for example, the chances of access to a particular good)'
(Bourdieu 1990b:54) and 'agent's subjective aspirations ('motivations'
and 'needs')' (54), people don't necessarily make those kinds of
calculations and decisions freely, uninfluenced by habitus. On the
contrary, Bourdieu makes the point that those decisions are always
already made:

> The most improbable practices are therefore excluded, as unthinkable,
> by a kind of immediate submission to order that inclines agents to make

a virtue of necessity, that is, to refuse what is anyway denied and to will the inevitable.

BOURDIEU 1990b:54

The Kurt Russell character's ultimate decision to reject the possibility of a relationship with the heroine, which would probably involve some form of domesticity, and take to the open road alone is an excellent example of making a virtue of necessity.

The romance narrative that runs through the film insists that the chance of a relationship between the two be played out right to the end, but Russell's final, and seemingly disinterested, rejection of a relationship is an example of the way in which what will inevitably be denied is denied in a disinterested way, as if a choice were possible. The heroine is middle class, professional, and a feminist. Marrying Russell (a loud-mouthed, sexist truck driver) would be unthinkable, if only because the benefits of having Russell as a partner (his sexual attractiveness) would be outweighed by the negatives (What would her friends and colleagues say? How long before she became bored with his macho rhetoric and posturing?). Russell knows this, which is why he rides off into the night.

We have spent considerable space and time describing and providing examples of Bourdieu's notion of habitus, but habitus is most effective as a means of analysing practice when it is tied in to two other concepts developed by Bourdieu: cultural field, and cultural and symbolic capital.

CULTURAL FIELD AND CULTURAL CAPITAL

A cultural field might best be defined as:

* a series of specific institutions, rules, categories, designations, appointments and titles which constitute an objective hierarchy, and which produce and authorise certain discourses and activities, on the one hand, and
* the conflict which is involved when groups or individuals attempt to determine what constitutes capital within that field, and how that capital is to be distributed, on the other.

Bourdieu understands the concept of cultural field to refer to fluid and dynamic, rather than static, entities. Cultural fields are made up not simply of institutions and rules, but of the interactions between institutions, rules and practices.

What do we mean by **capital**? Cheleen Mahar, Richard Harker and Chris Wilkes, in their book *An Introduction to the Work of Pierre Bourdieu*, describe Bourdieu's use of capital in these terms:

> the logic which orders . . . struggles (within a field) is the logic of capital. However, the definition of capital is very wide for Bourdieu and includes material things (which can have symbolic value), as well as 'untouchable' but culturally significant attributes such as prestige, status and authority (referred to as symbolic capital), along with cultural capital (defined as culturally-valued taste and consumption patterns) . . . For Bourdieu, capital acts as a social relation within a system of exchange, and the term is extended 'to all the goods, material and symbolic, without distinction, that present themselves as rare and worthy of being sought after in a particular social formation'.
>
> MAHAR, HARKER AND WILKES 1990:13

The amount of power a person has within a field depends on that person's position within the field, which in turn is based, to a large extent, on the amount of capital the person possesses. At the same time, one of the advantages of being in a position of power is that it enables groups or agents to designate what is 'authentic' capital. Further, cultural capital is sometimes difficult to identify because it is bound up, among other things, with a person's ability to effectively read what can and cannot be done, and what is and isn't valued, within a cultural field.

Perhaps the most important thing to understand about the relationship between cultural fields and cultural capital is that capital value is largely determined within, and often confined to, a particular field—although overlapping does occur. In contemporary western youth culture—say in a nightclub—a familiarity with current dance music, an ability to gyrate for hours without collapsing, a certain dress sense, an ability to hold your alcohol, an ability to carry on a conversation when you can't hear what the other person is saying—as well as a firm butt—would probably all qualify as capital. These abilities might not, however, constitute capital in, say, the diplomatic service; then again, they just might.

Another point worth mentioning is that in emphasising the importance of symbolic and cultural capital as means of understanding habitus, Bourdieu does not ignore the contribution of economic capital (that is, money). In fact he makes it quite clear that economic capital plays a considerable part in determining a person's access to other forms of capital. This is perhaps an appropriate time to return to *The Flintstones.*

In that film, Fred and Barney are working-class men with a more or less common habitus; that is to say, they share dispositions, values and practices. However, once Fred has become an executive and acquired a far greater income, the close relationship between the two families breaks down. The main reason for this is that Fred (and to a lesser extent Wilma) now has access to a whole range of possible goods and services (high-tech gadgets, expensive restaurants) which, at the same time, produce and demand new dispositions and literacies (Fred would eventually have had to learn to appreciate, and talk about, fine wines, for instance, rather than beer).

Within the field of 'quarry workers', Fred's habitus more or less matched the economic realities of his life. (Fred wouldn't have enjoyed high society, and wouldn't have been allowed in, anyway.) Once Fred moved into a different field, he was forced to transpose and develop his habitus to take into account the possibilities and new demands opened up by his increase in economic capital.

When the economic gulf separating the Flintstones from the Rubbles becomes too great, the two families cease sharing a habitus. Why? Because Fred's new position in life as a powerful and wealthy man more or less demands that he look down upon people like Barney and Betty whose economic situation is so inferior to his. In other words, once Fred becomes powerful and wealthy, he has to start acting as if he has always been powerful and wealthy, and part of that habitus involves naturalising both his own prosperity (intelligent people, the best people, 'winners', end up wealthy) and the poverty of others (poor people are stupid, are losers).

Cultural fields themselves are not autonomous, or uninfluenced by other fields. We made the point that fields are fluid and dynamic, mainly because they are always being changed by internal practices. Other executives at Slate's Quarry Company, for instance, might read Fred's promotion in terms of certain Flintstone 'qualities' being admired by senior management, and seek to copy them (being brash and loud would become significant cultural capital). At the same time, fields are influenced and changed by what happens in adjoining fields

(Flintstone's success in accidentally inventing cement might prompt other companies in other fields to start looking for Flintstone types). One of the ways in which Fred would be changed by his admission into this new field is that his habitus would be influenced by high cultural taste and notions of **distinction**. Bourdieu explains distinction as a kind of cultural habitus that is associated with the upper classes, but which has spread throughout various class groups and positions to the extent that it has been naturalised as good and valuable.

We really don't have the space to explain distinction in detail here; it is sufficient to say, by way of example, that certain texts get 'canonised'. Fred might end up reading *Hamlet*, staring at and appreciating the *Mona Lisa*, and drinking and collecting vintage French wines. Why? Because these (and many other) cultural texts get taught in educational systems, reviewed in newspapers, performed in theatres and exhibited in galleries and museums. The more cultural institutions tell us how valuable these products are, the more people come to accept the 'truth' of their value.

During the second half of the twentieth century the advent of so-called mass culture challenged this culture of distinction; for example, cultural institutions such as universities started including popular and mass culture texts in their subjects. Eventually, the automatic assumption that high culture (ballet, opera, poetry) was good and valuable, and popular culture (film, television, rock music) was rubbish, largely gave way to a consideration (at least in some cultural fields and institutions) of how people used all kinds of cultural products.

From this perspective, a Pearl Jam song or a 'Far Side' cartoon is just as interesting as opera or ballet; more interesting to many, because they are being used by greater numbers of people. And academics writing textbooks are likely to explain the theories of Pierre Bourdieu through reference to films like *The Flintstones*.

The Flintstones film narrative provides plenty of examples of the way the relationship between field and capital influences habitus. Perhaps an even more interesting example can be found in recent films based on the Batman character. Batman, also known as Bruce Wayne, occupies separate places within two apparently very different cultural fields—high society and crime (fighting). As Wayne, he possesses both symbolic and cultural capital within high society: an old family name, access to the most powerful people in the city, and a mansion constitute his symbolic capital, and speaking with the right accent, wearing the right clothes, and being seen at the opera constitute his cultural capital. None of this capital has any great value, however, in the underworld of Gotham City, or with the police fighting the evil machinations of the Joker, or with the crime reporters on the local newspaper.

As Batman, however, Bruce Wayne possesses just the kind of symbolic and cultural capital that counts in the crime-fighting field: a big, fast car with all kinds of tricky and useful gadgets, a black belt in karate (symbolic capital), and the ability to out-think and out-guess every criminal and police officer in town (cultural capital).

How does the relationship between field and capital determine the kinds of habitus that characterise Wayne and Batman? The most obvious example is the way the two personas interact within the two different fields. Bruce Wayne is in his element at cocktail parties and society balls precisely because he knows the rules of the field of high society, and is able to reproduce them 'naturally'.

If a male guest walked into a black-tie function wearing ragged shorts and an 'I Love Bambi' t-shirt, Bruce Wayne would not punch him (zock!), kick him (clunk!) or throw him over the balcony (kerplunk!). Wayne would know that the fellow was obviously a little eccentric, but probably harmless. Anyway, it would be virtually unthinkable—that is to say, not within Wayne's habitus—to zock! clunk! or kerplunk! anyone. He would walk up to the fellow, make a few patronising enquiries about his general well-being, and then instruct Alfred the butler to take him to the kitchen, feed him, give him a few dollars and see him (discreetly) out the servants' entrance.

Wayne would probably try and do the same thing if the Penguin turned up to gatecrash the private concert given by Madame LeFarge at stately Wayne Manor. Sadly, things would not work out quite so well, because the Penguin would probably shoot Alfred, set fire to the kitchen, and steal Wayne's van Gogh painting.

If Bruce Wayne were Batman, however, things would be different, because Batman's habitus would enable him to read the Penguin's intentions. And whereas as Bruce Wayne he abhorred violence, and lived to patronise people, as Batman he'd know how to respond effectively to a criminal (zock! clunk! kerplunk!).

Bruce Wayne and Batman employ practices which are effective

within the specific fields they inhabit, precisely because they both demonstrate an ability to understand, successfully negotiate, and demonstrate a 'feel for', the rules of the different games they are playing in. Wayne does not exactly reproduce the habitus characteristic of high society; after all, he really could have thrown the person in the t-shirt out the front door. The dispositions and values associated with his particular habitus, however, place a great deal of stress on paternalism, shouldering the rich person's burden, and displaying the kind of tolerance and social sophistication associated with 'good breeding'. It is in Wayne's interest that he carefully negotiate the rules of high society so as to produce practices that are not necessarily written down or objectified, but the interests which produce those variations of habitus are themselves products of a habitus.

SUMMARY

In this chapter we have attempted to move from understanding communication as a cultural practice to a description and analysis of the more specific ways in which communication practices are produced within cultures.

Theorising communication practices is a difficult task precisely because:

* Any practice is always something decided and negotiated 'of the moment', and therefore cannot be reduced to the level of a simple reproduction of the objective structures (say, the laws, rules and systems) of a culture.
* At the same time, practices are not produced 'in a vacuum': there are strong connections between a person's cultural trajectories, the kinds of attitudes, values, and agendas they have, and their activities and behaviour.

Pierre Bourdieu's work is extremely important to any theorising of practice because it offers the kinds of theoretical notions, for instance:

* habitus
* symbolic and cultural capital, and
* cultural field

which enable us to identify and analyse perhaps the two most important aspects of virtually every practice. These are:

- that the attitudes, values, ideologies and dispositions which shape and determine practice need to be naturalised before they can become effective. In other words, we have to forget or edit out a whole range of other views and possibilities in order to produce our practices comfortably and 'naturally'.
- that there seems to be a perfect match between the attitudes, values, agendas and desires we have, and what is more or less objectively available to us. This is brought about not because each group in a culture has a 'natural' habitus, but rather because, as Bourdieu makes clear, the habitus functions by making a virtue of necessity and by ruling out what would be difficult to achieve as 'already impossible' because it is unthinkable.

FURTHER READING

Bourdieu, P. 1990a *In Other Words* trans. M. Adamson, Polity Press, Cambridge
Bourdieu, P. 1990b *The Logic of Practice* trans. R. Nice, Polity Press, Cambridge
Certeau, M. de 1986 *Heterologies* trans. B. Massumi, University of Minnesota Press, Minneapolis
Certeau, M. de 1988 *The Practice of Everyday Life* trans. S. Rendell, University of California Press, Berkeley

8

IDEOLOGY

This chapter looks at the notion of ideology, which we understand as a process which naturalises the connection between certain signs and meanings within texts.

In our chapter on communication and practice (Chapter 7), we made considerable use of Bourdieu's notions of **field, habitus** and **cultural capital** to suggest how and why practices come about. Every cultural field 'writes itself' into existence, in a sense, because each field produces and deploys stories and narratives that determine what can and can't be thought, without appearing to be doing anything of the sort. These stories and narratives, which operate as if they were as natural to us as breathing, we can call ideologies.

Ideology functions to convince its audiences that the ideas it offers up are timeless and ahistorical; that is to say, they have always been, and always will be. Different aspects of our everyday culture—our eating habits, religious beliefs and material goods, for instance—are usually experienced in this way. We see ourselves as 'civilised', for instance, because we celebrate Christmas, have the scientific and technological capacity to mass-produce sophisticated goods, and eat with a knife and fork. These aspects are all produced, within western cultures, as natural and valuable. A culture which didn't celebrate Christmas, didn't have access to science and technology, and favoured eating with the fingers would not only be produced as different and exotic; generally speaking, it would also be understood as inferior and less valuable, perhaps even less human.

Why is this the case? How does the material context of a culture come to be naturalised and valued to the extent that it can be used to differentiate the human and the non-human? After all, our material and cultural contexts are anything but natural. Take Christmas, for instance. The celebration of Christmas is generally presumed to date back to early Christian times, but in its present form dates to nineteenth-century Britain. And eating with forks was considered bad manners by Louis XIV, king of France in the seventeenth century; well-mannered people used a knife and their fingers.

As for the western claim to scientific and technological mastery, this again is only a recent phenomenon, dating from about the Renaissance (in the fifteenth century). For the three and a half thousand years before the Renaissance, Asian areas (such as China and India) led the world in the development of technology, a situation which appears to be repeating itself late in the twentieth century.

We have described ideologies as stories and narratives that circulate in a culture and determine, to a large extent, what can and can't be thought, and what can and can't be done. In order for ideologies to be effective—in order, for instance, that Christmas, or eating implements, or access to science and technology be understood as having a natural value that extends across cultures and across history—ideologies have to decontextualise their own culture, their own material conditions, their politics, laws, pleasures and values. Ideologies try to hide the **contingent** nature of thoughts and activities within a culture; that is to say, they try to convince their audiences that certain values, ideas and activities are more or less natural, and that things have always been this way, or should remain this way. To sum up: ideologies function in an attempt to make the specific or the particular seem generally applicable.

All ideologies have some kind of group basis within a culture; in other words, ideologies construct and promote meanings which privilege one culture, or one section of a culture (which can be based on class, occupation, race, skin colour, gender, age, sexual preference, religious affiliation, nationality or general physicality) over another.

We can come up with some specific examples to demonstrate this point, using Australian history as our text:

- in Australia during the nineteenth century the families of free settlers were considered better sorts of people than those who were descended from, or had been, convicts,
- until the last 30 years, woman were excluded from many occupations and nearly all the professions because they were not considered (mainly by men) to be capable of carrying out the required work, and
- until the 1976 referendum, Aboriginal people were not allowed to vote because they were not considered the equal of whites.

All these conditions were produced, perpetuated and naturalised through the circulation of ideologies.

HOW DO IDEOLOGIES WORK?

How do ideologies try to promote and naturalise differences between groups? Ideologies usually work through the construction of binaries, or pairs of terms (such as us/them, male/female, white/black). These binaries are always hierarchical; that is to say, one part of the binary is privileged (it is good, natural, valuable, strong) over the other (which is bad, artificial, insignificant, weak). A particular ideology may be deployed by one or more groups within a culture, but it is usually addressed to all or most groups, regardless of whether those groups share any of the ideas or goals of the ideology.

Why do ideologies attempt to target most groups within a culture? We made the point that ideologies functioned predominantly to naturalise and perpetuate differences within a culture; paradoxically, however, this is usually done through the attempted erasure of differences. Ideologies are often deployed, for instance, to convince other groups that their interests are the same as those of the group producing the ideology.

One obvious example is those television commercials for kitchen or cooking products which usually feature a male voice telling women what wonderful cooks they are (because they use the right brand of margarine or butter or pasta), how important they are to their family (who presumably would all starve without the mother's cooking), and what a wonderfully harmonious group the family is, with the father having an outside (therefore 'real') job, the children going to school, and the mother at home devoting her life to the others.

THE FIRST FUNCTION OF IDEOLOGY

Perhaps the first function of ideology, then, is to create a notion of community where everything is harmonious, just and workable as long as different groups stick to their 'natural' place. Even though it is obviously in the interest of men that women don't compete with them in the workplace (that is to say, it is in the interests of certain groups of men that women stay in the home), the ideology of many kitchen and cooking advertisements pushes the idea that this arrangement is in the interest of everyone; it is best for women that things stay this way, and women would suffer if other arrangements held sway (if the woman wasn't at home, the family would be unhappy, and consequently the woman would be unhappy).

This kind of ideological narrative isn't just played out in commercials. A considerable number of contemporary Hollywood films—*Fatal Attraction* and *Cape Fear* are two obvious examples—are pre-eminently concerned with two closely interrelated themes:

- the movement of women into the workforce, and
- the decline, within the family, of the authority of the father.

A third factor that is tied up with these themes is the threat posed to the family by sexually active and assertive women who aren't 'maintained' within the confines of the family unit. In both *Fatal Attraction* and *Cape Fear*, the father's infidelities threaten to destroy the family, and in the end it is only the loyalty and courage of women—the mother and/or the daughter—that saves the father and the family, and restores the father to his position of 'rightful' authority as head of the household. *Fatal Attraction* and *Cape Fear* are examples of ideological narratives demonstrating what things would be, or are, like in a 'post-margarine-commercial' community where some men and women have refused to fulfil their (natural) duties.

THE SECOND FUNCTION OF IDEOLOGY

We have suggested that ideological narratives perpetuate inequalities and differences through pretending to erase those differences. The example we used referred to the way in which gender inequality was erased through reference to the good of the community. But there is a second function to ideology, and that is, to convince and demonstrate to groups in a culture that the value that is assigned to certain signs or markers of difference (skin colour, for instance) is just and natural. This allows the members of privileged groups to behave as if they were naturally superior to other groups.

We previously referred to the important role played by science and technology as a marker of civilised, and therefore human, behaviour. Michael Adas, in his book *Machines as the Measure of Men* (1992) points out that from the eighteenth to the middle of the twentieth century western colonialist activities—in Asia, Africa, America and Australia—were largely justified and rationalised in terms of the west's scientific and technological superiority. Markers of science and technology came to mean that one group was human and superior, and other groups which didn't possess those markers were inhuman and inferior.

There are two main points to this function of ideology:

- it encourages one group to exploit and sometimes even exterminate other groups, supposedly because this is sanctioned by a natural 'order of things' (an order created, say, by God or evolution).

    Since the eighteenth century western cultures have had to pay at least lip service to notions of liberty, equality and fraternity; which means that, theoretically at least, every individual is a free and equal member of the community. If unequal power relations were to be maintained, and one group's pre-eminence was to continue, then reasons had to be found to effectively disenfranchise other groups. The two most obvious examples of this disenfranchisement involved women and colonised peoples:

  - women were not considered full members of western communities because they lacked an education, or were considered naturally stupid and immoral, and

  - colonised peoples (Australian Aborigines, American Indians, Africans and Asians) were not considered part of the community of the human race because they were considered inferior, incapable of scientific thought, and lazy, immoral and untrustworthy.

- a second important aspect of this function of ideology is to convince supposedly inferior groups of the truth and justice of their inferiority.

    In western cultures, women were forever being told that they were unsuited to, and unworthy of, any kind of role in public life. Similarly, colonised peoples were told repeatedly that being ruled by the west was good for them because eventually it would raise them to a level of civilisation (as long as they accepted the values of the west, and did what they were told). Not all women and colonised people accepted this kind of ideology, but it did doubtless have the effect of helping to maintain inequalities and oppression.

Michel de Certeau, in his book *Heterologies* (1986), makes the point that when military groups interrogated peasants, trade unionists and other dissidents in South American countries, the idea was not to get information from them—the interrogators knew they didn't have anything of value to tell them—but to convince the dissidents that they were worthless, because if they believed this, they wouldn't have any reason to resist their oppressors.

An indication of how effective ideologies can be in undermining the resistance of groups can be seen in the importance attached to the dissemination of negative propaganda (your cause is lost, things are desperate for you, you are fighting for people who have betrayed you) in wars during the twentieth century.

In the 1991 Gulf War, it seemed that far more effort went, on the allied side, into convincing home audiences that they were involved in a just fight, and Iraqi audiences that the war would be disastrous for Iraq, than went into the fighting. The US military obviously won the publicity/propaganda war in that conflict; and the seriousness attached to that publicity war was doubtlessly born of an awareness of how significant the supposed loss of the publicity war was to the US military during the Vietnamese war (see Chapter 1 for a discussion of this point).

IDEOLOGY AND REPETITION

We have suggested that ideologies are stories and narratives produced by groups within a culture in order to privilege their own position of power or authority. But how are obviously contingent ideas and values naturalised and decontextualised?

Ideology works mainly through repetition. Ideas are repeated, with variations, in as many mediums, genres and fields as possible, so that the ideology comes to pervade the culture. In the end the ideological position or value becomes so familiar that most members of the culture no longer question the assumptions on which it is based. Every part of the culture repeats the ideology, everybody accepts it, so it must be true. In other words, the repetition of ideology across the culture, as Bourdieu suggests, helps to ensure that we forget that ideology . . . is ideology.

Ideology doesn't usually criticise alternative ideas—they are normally treated as if such alternatives were unthinkable. And if, for some reason, they are thought or suggested, they are usually disqualified from consideration by being branded as . . . ideology.

We might refer back to that visit to Gallipoli by an Australian delegation headed by the then prime minister, Bob Hawke, to commemorate the 75th anniversary of the ANZAC landing. You will recall that the Australian journalists covering the event discovered to their horror that Turkish journalists were writing that the Australians had come to Turkey to apologise for their unprovoked invasion during the First World War.

The ANZAC landing at Gallipoli had become a cornerstone of Australian national identity and value; that is to say, it had been produced as an ideological narrative which had edited out numerous possible contexts of the landing. Gallipoli, for those Australian journalists, meant the bravery of Australian troops, and the mateship and selflessness of those involved; but they could only maintain that ideological position by conveniently forgetting the people the ANZACs were fighting against, and by forgetting that the ANZACs were invading another country which had its own version of events.

Doubtless there were Turkish versions of the Gallipoli story, and they probably bore little or no relation to the ANZAC legend. This was unthinkable to most Australian journalists, and presumably to most Australians. Ideology had succeeded in decontextualising Gallipoli to the extent that the only role for the Turks was as 'bit players' in an Australian narrative.

IDEOLOGY AND COMMUNICATION

What we have presented, up to this stage, is a very general conceptualisation of the notion of ideology and the way it functions. The characteristics we put forward as constituting or informing ideology do not by any stretch of the imagination enable us to appreciate the many different accounts of ideology that have been produced since Marx appropriated the term and deployed it as one of the central aspects of what has become known as Marxism. What we will do, at this point, is move to a brief but specific consideration of contributions to theories of ideology made by:

- Marx
- Volosinov
- Gramsci
- Althusser
- Laclau and
- Lefort

and suggest how these theorists have provided either the basis for our general theory of ideology, or critiques of that theory which challenge and extend it. From there, we will attempt to explain how the theories they provide tie in with the notion of communication practices, and examine how these various developments or critiques of ideology have anticipated and dealt with the way ideology functions in the mass media.

Marx

Marx did not coin the term ideology, but he was largely responsible for giving the term everyday currency. Marx did not have a single theory of ideology—his notion of ideology changed across his writings—but we will discuss the version that has come through as being representative. Consider this quotation from Marx:

> The mode of production of material life conditions the social, political and intellectual life processes in general. It is not the consciousness of men that determines their being, but, on the contrary, their social being that determines their consciousness.
>
> QUOTED IN O'SULLIVAN *ET AL.* 1991:108

Let us consider this statement and try to isolate some of the more obvious and important points that it makes about ideology.

The first point is that relations of production, and social being, determine consciousness. This means that social conditions and material contexts **(over)determine** our understanding of the world. To think otherwise is, for Marx, to see the world ideologically, or upside down.

Ideology is generally, for Marx, a pejorative term. Ideology is a kind of false consciousness, a duplicitous and abstracted version of the world put out by the ruling classes in order to maintain the

Karl Marx was a German political economist and philosopher who is usually considered, along with Freud, Darwin and Nietzsche, as one of the founders of modern western thought. Marx was the most influential of the group. His theories inspired the Bolsheviks in Russia, the communists in China, and countless revolutionary groups throughout the twentieth century. Marx's main works, all of which emphasise the importance of the economic sphere in human activity, include the three volumes of *Capital, Grundrisse, The Communist Manifesto, The Eighteenth Brumaire and* (with Engels), *The German Ideology.* All of the theorists we refer to in this chpater are responding, to a large extent, to Marx's work.

subordination of the lower classes. Ideology would include all those narratives and explanations of events, practices and activities which attempt to draw attention away from the material contexts and conditions in which people live, and the political and economic realities that define and determine people's existences.

For Marx, what was important in capitalist cultures was the relation between the owners of the means of production (capitalists) and those who sold their labour for wages (workers). Explanations about the realities of everyday life had to take this as their point of departure. Within this context, ideology could be understood as attempting to do two important things:

- to construct that relation as something other than exploitative and oppressive and historical; that is to say, ideology idealised and naturalised the relations between capitalists and workers ('capitalists and workers were part of a team or community helping to create wealth for everyone, and helping the nation to prosper')
- to draw attention away from the inequalities and oppressiveness of everyday life, and the politics of the material contexts which controlled people's lives.

With this second function, 'something else' is substituted so as to provide a false context or meaning for understanding life. This something else could be a love story, or a story about religion, patriotism, or the family. There is an excellent example of this practice in the Nicholas Roeg section of the film *Aria*, which is made up of a series of short films supposedly based on the music and themes of famous opera arias.

In Roeg's film, a group of obviously desperate and impoverished revolutionaries is going to attempt to assassinate a nobleman. A considerable part of the film is taken up with emphasising the desperation of the plotters, who are badly clothed, hungry and cold, and not really adequately equipped or prepared for the assassination attempt. The nobleman, on the other hand, is confident, well dressed, and undisturbed by material needs. He lives 'on a higher level' of existence. The pathetic assassination attempt fails, the plotters are killed, and the nobleman is united at the end of the film with his lover. The operatic aria, which comes on at this point, is rich, lush and romantic, and celebrates the highly romantic ending to the story.

Roeg's point, in this film, is that aspects of high culture, such as opera, produce stories of life that concentrate on, emphasise and value so-called high feelings and sensitivities, and promote these as being the most significant aspects of life. Moreover, these high feelings and values have generally been associated, in high culture, with the nobility or the upper classes. The idea of a (genuine) peasant or low-class worker being a high romantic figure is unthinkable in, say, a Shakespearean play or a Wagnerian opera.

Roeg's short film demonstrates how false consciousness works. The romantic love between the noble and his lover is produced as 'the' meaning of life. Everything else—the suffering of the workers, for instance—is edited out, unless it can be shown to fit in with this romantic narrative. In the film, the plotters are presented as a threat to the romance, and they are quickly edited out—killed—so that 'love can triumph'.

Conventional Marxist notions of ideology are characterised, then, by two points:

- the overdetermining role of the relations of production and the economic sphere as an explanation for the realities of life, and
- the use of stories, narratives and explanations to create a false consciousness which edits out those political and economic realities.

Ideology, in this sense, can be understood as the means by which the dominant class disguises the true nature of its relation with subordinate classes and thus helps perpetuate inequality and oppression.

Volosinov

Marx's pioneering work on ideology was developed by the Russian Marxist V.N. Volosinov, a philosopher and linguist who wrote a very influential text titled *Marxism and the Philosophy of Language* (1986) (see Chapter 2). We are not going to deal with this text in any broad way (it is largely concerned with critiquing various linguistic traditions from a Marxist perspective), but instead will concentrate on some ideas Volosinov posited about the connection between ideology and language, or signs.

For Volosinov, ideology is produced at the same time that signs are produced as meaningful. Without signs, he argues, there would be no ideology. All cultural meanings—which is to say all meanings, because there can be no meaning outside culture and language—are produced by signs such as words, clothes, posters, films and photographs.

Volosinov's text is particularly important because it alerts us to the point that since all meanings are produced within cultures, there can be no natural meanings, or pre-cultural meanings. Ideologies work, of course, to naturalise their meanings and perspectives; but if there are no natural meanings, then a culture can be understood as a kind of ideological battlefield in which various groups strive to impose their meanings at the expense of other groups.

A example of a culture as an ideological battlefield is the 1960s television comedy *Gilligan's Island*. In this series, a group of people are marooned on a previously uninhabited Pacific island. The group is composed of a selection of 'types' from American society: the skipper, the millionaire couple, the scientist, the country girl, the movie star/sex goddess and Gilligan, a sailor. All the characters act entirely in keeping with their type: for instance, the scientist (the 'professor') is technically minded but also often impractical and nerdy, and the millionaire male (Mr Howell) reduces everything to a matter of money.

The interesting thing about this series is that the island serves as a microcosm for (certain areas of) American culture, in that each type tries to explain every problem, address every crisis, and most importantly run the island in terms of their own 'world view'. The professor wants things to work in an orderly, sensible, intellectual, rational and scientific fashion; which means, of course, that as he is (in his opinion, and in terms of his cultural capital) the person most closely associated with those characteristics, he should be in charge. Every sign (the trace of a native presence, the material conditions which provide them with food and clothing) is ideologised by 'the professor'; that is to say, it is produced as meaningful in terms of the values of a particular field and ideology (in this case, scientific rationality).

For Ginger, the movie star, what overdetermines life on the island is the culture of Hollywood: she must be admired, she must be seen as sexy, she must be able to present herself as glamorous. Whereas the professor might see the island as a material context that had to be researched and catalogued, for Ginger it is an exotic setting perfect for a movie (with her as star). Whereas a sign of native life might be treated as an anthropological opportunity by the professor, Ginger would see it as the opportunity to meet somebody tall, dark and handsome (and presumably male). In Mr Howell's view, of course, they are both wrong: the island is a place to make money, every decision can be read in terms of financial considerations, and the indication of a native presence would be read as an opportunity to buy their canoe and get home to the stock exchange, or maybe trade with (that is, exploit) them for goods.

Does it really matter which ideology prevails here? The answer is yes, because a naturalising of one meaning at the expense of others has political ramifications. We have made the point that if an ideology of rationality, intellectualism and scientifism were to hold sway on Gilligan's island, then the professor would end up running things. There is obviously an important connection, then, between a group imposing its ideology on others, and the exercising of power.

Marx's version of ideology argues that consciousness is produced through an understanding of the reality of material contexts, in particular an understanding of economic contexts and relations (the relation between workers and capitalists, the importance of the ownership of the means of production). Volosinov turns this argument on its head to a certain extent—a remarkable thing for a Marxist (as Volosinov was) to do.

How does Volosinov overturn the notion of an overdetermining economic base to 'reality', to true consciousness? He does this by making the point that economic relations and activities do not 'naturally' mean by themselves. Rather, any relation or activity will come to have meaning through a process of ideological conflict fought out by different groups within a culture.

This is an extremely difficult point: is the meaning of a culture and its practices overdetermined by economic relations, or is that just one of a number of spheres we have to take into account? Perhaps if we go back to Gilligan's island and fantasise a little, we might be able to clarify things.

Let us presume that Mr Howell has set up a factory on the island. The factory produces coconut products (coconut milk, ice creams, shampoos). Work is overseen by the skipper, the professor runs the technical side of things, and Gilligan (a blunderer) and Maryanne (a simple country girl) do the labouring. Obviously ownership of the means of production is crucial here. Mr Howell is the wealthiest and most powerful person on the island. Moreover, he increases his wealth by creaming off the surplus value created by the labour of Gilligan and Maryanne.

Can we presume, then, that this economic power will automatically translate into an ability to control the meanings and practices on the island? The answer Volosinov—and Bourdieu—would give (if they were viewers of *Gilligan's Island*) is 'not necessarily'. Why? Remember the professor has a considerable amount of cultural capital: his intellectualism, his supposed rationality and problem solving skills, and his air of scientific detachment would all count for a great deal in certain circumstances.

Let us presume Mr Howell wants to cut down all the guava plants on the island because they compete with the coconut trees for space and nutrients. The professor, however, is extremely interested in doing research on guava trees. He tells the others that his research is extremely important because it will tell them more about the environment in which they live, and could help them to survive when they start running out of food. The professor has the cultural capital here that Mr Howell lacks. Mr Howell can talk about profits and higher wages, but the professor can ideologise this struggle in terms of long-term environmental damage, the pursuit of important knowledge, and his ability to decide—given his supposedly detached, objective background—what is in the best interests of the group.

At the same time, many Marxists might argue that the professor was still working under the auspices of, and for, the company, just as scientific institutions, workers and research are part of, help perpetuate, and are often controlled by, capitalist institutions. We just have to accept that there is strong disagreement, even among Marxists, on this particular point.

For both Marx and Volosinov, contexts constrain and produce meaning. However, classical Marxism presumes that economic relations overdetermine all other spheres of meaning, and that economic relations themselves are self-evident; that is to say, their (true) meaning can't be contested. For Volosinov, the economic sphere is only one (important) area in which meaning is contested and produced. Other areas (the media, for instance) are also important because they can influence or determine how people understand economic relations. So while for classical Marxism materiality produces consciousness, for Volosinov:

- materiality and consciousness are always interacting, and meaning is always disputed. Moreover, because of this constant ideological conflict, conducted, for instance, through television, newspapers, radio, school teaching and graffiti:
- meanings are always changing, and
- different meanings of the same event or sign are simultaneously available within a culture.

Why are there so many conflicting ideologies at work within a culture? Every meaning that is produced is tied up with, and informed by, the context or contexts associated with the individual or group that is making the meaning. Contexts associated with class, gender, race, sexual preference, age, marital status, educational qualifications and religious beliefs influence the kinds of meanings that an individual or group will produce. Remember the point we made in Chapter 7, that habitus—roughly translated as the set of dispositions an individual or group acquires according to its particular path through a culture—largely determines thoughts, practices and values.

The professor and Mr Howell, in our *Gilligan's Island* fantasy, are taking part in an ideological struggle involving different types of habitus, and therefore different values, goals and agendas. For Mr Howell the only important consideration is to make as much money in as short a time as possible; the professor's references to research, scientific value and long-term ecological damage are simply nonsense standing in the way of his profits. The professor, on the other hand, thinks Mr Howell's values crass and philistine; he cannot have some loud-mouthed, uneducated millionaire jeopardising the search for knowledge.

Mr Howell has an advantage over the professor in that he is a wealthy capitalist and can largely control the media on the island—he owns the newspaper that Ginger puts together once a week. The professor, on the other hand, has a considerable amount of cultural capital—associated with his profession—that is likely to influence people as much as Mr Howell's wealth. If Gilligan were to enter the conflict—suggesting, for instance, that the dispute could be resolved by getting rid of all the vegetation on the island—his position would have little or no chance of success because he has neither financial nor cultural capital.

What this demonstrates is that some groups within a culture—normally those with the greatest economic or cultural capital—have a greater opportunity to promote their ideologies to wider audiences, and to convince those audiences to accept their claim to power. The term we use to describe this process, developed by the Marxist theorist Antonio Gramsci (1986), is **hegemony**.

Gramsci and Althusser

The central point to Gramsci's notion of hegemony is that people are not usually forced to concede power or control to another group or groups; rather they are convinced that their interests are best served by that other group being in power, or that one group is 'naturally' superior. They become convinced that:

- the dominant group's interests are the same as their interests, or that
- it is in their interest for the dominant group to be in power, or that
- the dominant group deserves to rule (American capitalists of the 1890s supposedly dominated American politics because of Darwin's notion of 'natural selection', and European kings and queens supposedly ruled through the 'grace of God').

Ideology, and hence hegemony, is produced, according to Gramsci, through various cultural institutions, some of which are more powerful than others. This point was taken up by the French Marxist Louis Althusser (1977), who was interested in the way in which cultural institutions (such as the school system, religious groups and the family) help the spread of ideology, and the construction of hegemony, by producing 'cultural identities' for people. Althusser called this process **interpellation**.

Identity, for Althusser, and for many contemporary theorists of ideology, is bound up with the way institutions produce (interpellate) individuals and groups. These identities are characterised by certain supposedly natural values, goals, desires and affiliations.

How is interpellation tied up with ideology and hegemony? In the Brian de Palma film *The Untouchables*, the Elliot Ness character (played by Kevin Costner) chases and apprehends a member of the Mafia on the roof of a tall building. The gangster, who has just helped murder one of Ness's men, gives himself up, but taunts Ness by suggesting that the justice system won't convict him, and that he will go free or serve a short sentence.

At this moment the audience has been 'set up', if you like, to take on a particular identity. The audience has seen one of the good guys (a member of the Untouchables) murdered by a ruthless criminal (from the Mafia), who is about to get away with his crime (because the justice system doesn't work properly). At the same time the gangster is standing close to the edge of the roof, and Ness has him in his power.

Now, if you were to ask members of the film's audience—away from the film—if they were in favour of police officers executing criminals rather than turning them over to the courts, presumably most of them would answer in the negative; that is to say, they wouldn't be in favour of the police murdering people they suspected of committing a crime. However, in this film, at this moment, the audience is positioned, is interpellated, through the following questions being implied in the action of the film:

- Do you think the Untouchables are brave men doing a necessary and valuable job?
- Do you think the Mafia gangsters are despicable, ruthless killers not worthy of human status?
- Do you think it fair that this particular gangster should be able to murder a police officer and get away with it?

- Do you think justice would be done if Elliot Ness were to force him off the roof (which is what he does)?

The individual members of the film's audience are 'given' identities through this action, identities in keeping with the ideology of the film (which is that the justice system protects criminals, who should be disposed of).

At this point it is important to refer to Bourdieu's notion of habitus. Obviously not all members of the film's audience are going to be successfully interpellated. People who have a habitus similar to the Mafia character's, for instance, will simply refuse the identity that is offered to them. Many members of the audience will be successfully interpellated, however, even if it is not to their advantage (they may understand this the next time they are stuck on the roof of a high building with a highly emotional police officer who is convinced that justice can be done by murdering them). How we respond, and whether we take up the position texts offer to us, depends to a large extent on our own habitus.

Laclau

The connection between hegemony and the interpellation of identity has been explored by Ernesto Laclau (Laclau 1990), who argues that cultural identities or subject positions are perhaps the most important sites, within a culture, of ideological conflict. This means there are no essential identities or subjectivities; rather, subject positions (student, woman, feminist, worker) are:

- empty, and then filled up, or made to mean, as they are ideologised
- always undergoing changes of meaning, and
- able to carry a variety of meanings.

An example of subject positions being exchanged and then being filled up by different ideologies can be found in the film *Europa, Europa*, which is set in Germany at the beginning of the Second World War. The main character in the film is a male teenager who has a mixed identity: he is Jewish but lives in a part of Eastern Europe where German is spoken, along with a number of other languages. Because of the radically different contexts in which he finds himself, he is continually forced to (ex)change identities.

- When the Nazis start sending Jews to the concentration camps, he escapes and passes himself off as a German.
- Then he is captured by the Soviet communists, and becomes a good communist, fighting for the Soviet army.
- When his company is wiped out by the Germans, he starts talking German, and convinces the Nazis that he is a fellow German who has been separated from his people.
- In fact, he is so good at being a German and a Nazi that he becomes one of the leading lights in the Hitler Youth and is formally adopted by a high-ranking German officer.
- At the end of the war, he is captured by the Soviets, who prepare to execute him.
- Desperate, he changes identity once again, telling them that he is Jewish. The Soviets refuse to believe him: they point out that if he were Jewish, he would have ended up in a concentration camp.

The identity switching in this film exemplifies Laclau's point that subject positions are taken up and filled in, and change in meaning, rather than being essential or tied up with substances. The teenager was Jewish as long as that was the role required of him. Being Jewish was fine—in a Jewish community—but the Nazis brought a new series of meanings to that subjectivity: Jews were worthless, less than human, and had to be eliminated. The subject position of a German was fine—among Germans. For the Soviets, who were being invaded by Germany, a German had only negative meanings—negative enough to get you shot. A communist was a good subject position—among Soviet communists, but not among Nazis, who tended to kill communists without question. A Nazi was a good subject position—among Nazis, but not among Soviet troops at the end of the war, who were killing most German soldiers they came across, but were liberating Jews, which is why it became useful to be Jewish—again.

Lefort

Claude Lefort writes from a position very close to Laclau's. Where he makes a valuable contribution, for our purposes, is in the way he has theorised about changes to ideology in an age of mass media and globalisation (Lefort 1986).

Lefort distinguishes between what he calls 'bourgeois ideology' and 'new ideology'. Bourgeois ideology makes use of what he calls 'capitalised ideas'—the Family, Humanity, Nation, Science, Property—which are posited as being original and sacred truths. Dominant groups within a culture ideologise these terms just as subject positions are ideologised, so that the Family might be read, for instance, only as

• a certain type of family (father, mother, two children)
• operating in specific ways (the father is the breadwinner, the mother takes care of the domestic scene).

This sets an example, and operates as a model, which all other 'families' are measured against and have to copy.

Lefort argues, however, that bourgeois ideology is dying out and being replaced by what he calls 'new ideology'. New ideology, for Lefort, is a product of mass media, globalisation and general advances in communications technology. This new technology is able to reach mass audiences, and appears to be able to erase time and distance; after all, at any time satellite-based communication systems can 'bring together' people from all over the world.

New ideology uses this apparent erasure of time and space to pretend to have effected a general erasure of all differences. For Lefort, dominant groups within a culture **perform** communication by bringing every possible group—no matter how weird, exploited, disaffected, marginalised or fringe—into the communication network. The message is, 'If your group has a problem, come on a television current affairs show, along with a representative of business, someone from the government, a women's representative, a greenie, an ex-serial killer, and someone from the migrants' association, and we'll talk about it.'

Dominant groups take people's minds away from differences, oppression, exploitation and wrongdoings by making it seem as if everyone's views are taken into account and everyone is consulted. According to Lefort, this performance of communication doesn't actually change anything; what it does do is make it look as if things could change.

The new ideology, for Lefort, can be defined, quite simply, as the use of globalising and mass communication technology to talk away differences. You probably will have noticed that it ties in closely with Gramsci's notion of hegemony; after all, nothing naturalises one group's domination as much as the apparent erasure of all hierarchies. Are there racial problems in the US? Is the American police force full of racists? Do you want to do something to change things? Fine: go on *Donahue* or *Oprah* and have a debate/discussion with the mayor and a representative of the police force. Chances are you can have a perfectly reasonable discussion, get to know and appreciate and understand one another, and feel a whole lot better about things. Of course nothing will have changed, which is, Lefort argues, exactly the point.

Lefort's notion of new ideology is of considerable importance because it accommodates, very neatly, the two functions of ideology that all the theorists we have dealt with insist upon; that is to say, it functions to:

* conceal privilege, difference, oppression by
* appearing to unify a culture.

As Bourdieu suggests, and as all our theorists would accept to some extent, dominant groups produce ideologies and ideological effects by 'concealing the function of division beneath the function of communication' (Bourdieu 1991:167).

SUMMARY

In this chapter:

* We argued that ideology can be understood as the result of a particular kind of reading practice, a practice which naturalises the relationship between signs and meanings in an attempt to constrain and determine what can and can't be thought.
* We further argued that there are two major functions associated with ideology: to produce a notion of harmonious community, and to convince groups within a culture that the dominance of certain groups is just and natural.
* We described the Marxist arguments that social relations are based on economic relations, and that ideology works to conceal the economic overdetermination of social life and the class exploitation that accompanies it.
* We explained that Volosinov modified Marx's theories by suggesting that ideology is produced at the same time that signs are

read as meaningful, and that cultures are ideological 'battlefields' in which different groups compete in order to impose their meanings on others, a process Gramsci designated 'hegemony'.

• We described how Althusser and Laclau both emphasised the production or interpellation of identities as the most significant site of ideological conflict, and

• We finished with Lefort's suggestion that the advent of globalising communication technology has produced a new kind of ideology based on the continuous performance, in the media, of communication and community.

FURTHER READING

Thompson, J. 1990 *Ideology and Modern Culture* Polity Press, Cambridge
Zizek, S. 1992 *The Sublime Object of Ideology* Verso, London
Zizek, S. (ed.) 1994 *Mapping Ideology* Verso, New York

9

SUBJECTIVITY

In the chapter on ideology we examined how identities—what are usually referred to, in the field of cultural studies, as subjectivities—could be understood as sites of ideological conflict; that is to say, we followed the suggestions made by Althusser and Laclau in arguing that identities/subjectivities:

- are not essential or permanent, but
- are produced and made meaningful within a culture.

What we want to do in this chapter is to look more closely at the way the issue of subjectivity has been addressed and theorised within contemporary cultural theory, with particular reference to two questions:

- If subjectivity is produced within cultures, how does this process occur? In other words, how do subjectivities become ideological signifiers?
- What part does the body play in the production of subjectivity? What are the ramifications of treating human bodies as ideologised signs?

In our initial discussion of subjectivity and identity, we are going to deal with three main bodies of theory:

- psychoanalytical approaches,
- Foucault's theories of sexuality and the body, and
- theories of 'identity as performance' associated with the work of Judith Butler.

PSYCHOANALYTICAL APPROACHES

There have been numerous psychoanalytical contributions to the issue

Sigmund Freud was an Austrian physiologist who more or less 'invented' the discipline of psychoanalysis. During the first two decades of the twentieth century, Freud published a number of ground-breaking works dealing with such issues as the **unconscious, repression**, dreams, perversion and the central role of sexuality in human cultural life. His most influential texts include *The Interpretation of Dreams, The Psychopathology of Everyday Life, Civilisation and Its Discontents, Beyond the Pleasure Principle, The Ego and the Id, On Narcissism, Totem and Taboo, Moses and Monotheism*, and several famous 'case studies' ('The Rat Man', 'Schreber', 'The Wolf Man', 'Dora', 'Little Hans').

Jacques Lacan was a French psychoanalyst who is perhaps best known for his rather radical 'return' to Freud's theories, which he felt had been 'domesticated' by American ego psychology. Lacan's work has exerted a considerable influence on cultural theorists over the last 40 years, particularly in the areas of subjectivity, desire and the workings of the unconscious. Lacan's most influential works include his published seminars, Ecrits (a selection of his writings) and *The Four Fundamental Concepts of Psychoanalysis*. For a very accessible introduction to Lacan's theories, we suggest Elizabeth Grosz's *Jacques Lacan: A Feminist Introduction*.

of subjectivity, but we will limit ourselves to a consideration of the contributions made by Sigmund Freud and Jacques Lacan.

Freud

Freud's theories have been picked up and used in a variety of ways, and have passed into everyday culture in many popularised forms. What are the most significant features of Freud's work, and how do they relate to the issue of subjectivity?

It might be useful to provide some idea of the way subjectivity and identity were perceived in western culture before Freud. Notions of subjectivity had been dominated by the work of the philosopher René Descartes, who argued that the human subject was a rational, reasoned and (self)conscious entity whose identity was made certain, was proven, by his selfconsciousness: 'I think, therefore I am.' Descartes presumed that the 'I' that was spoken or written was the same as the entity that spoke the word, and that this 'I' was a stable and knowable entity. Humans, for Descartes, were reasonable and rational beings who were in full possession, at least potentially, of themselves; that is to say, their minds were masters of their (bodily) castles.

Marx, Nietzsche and Darwin, in their different ways, had already cast increasing doubt on Descartes' theory of subjectivity:

• Marx argued that, rather than being conscious subjects, people live in false consciousness under capitalism.
• For Nietzsche, consciousness was the result of a forgetting of the ways in which the body had been produced, formed and manipulated, and reason was simply an ideology (in other words, the notion of reason was not natural, but was produced historically).
• Darwin's notion of evolution tied this Cartesian godlike human subject rather too closely to amphibians, reptiles and monkeys.

These three theorists had already thrown enough bombs at Descartes's rational and self-knowing human subject to reduce it to scattered pieces: Freud simply blew away what was left. Generally speaking, Freud argued that the human subject was not in control of itself because its activities—its actions and practices—were all partly informed by desires that necessarily emanated from the subject's unconscious.

More specifically, Freud suggested that human subjectivity was produced in terms of a narrative that involved:

• sexual drives
• the **Oedipus complex**, and
• the unconscious.

How does this come about? For Freud, our biological drives—such as the desire for food—are 'taken over', in a sense, by sexual drives, which attach themselves to some part of the body that was the site of biologically driven pleasure, such as sucking milk from the mother's nipple(s). In early (pre-oedipal) childhood, these drives move across and around the body, attaching themselves to any biological drive, and (potentially) sexualising the whole body.

The second stage in this process of the production of (sexualised) subjectivity is the Oedipus complex. Broadly speaking, the child's first and in a sense only love object is the mother, but the child (who is, for Freud, more or less naturalised as a male) learns that it cannot desire its own mother (this is socially taboo), so these desires are repressed and rendered unconscious. The child is accepted into a culture and is given, and learns to take on, specific subjectivities, mainly through the process of transferring its previously unconstrained sexual drives into 'appropriate' activities (say, heterosexual activity).

The final stage of this narrative of subjectivisation is the production of the unconscious. Those repressed desires (repressed because they defy or scandalise conventional cultural notions of what is appropriate and natural) 'return' in a variety of ways: through slips of the tongue, in sublimation (where sexual desire is transferred onto 'higher' activities, such as writing a text book on communication and literacy), in fetishising certain objects (you can't have the person you desire, so you collect her/his clothes, and make do with those), and in dreams.

Dreams are the best known site of 'the return of the repressed', perhaps because Freud wrote a book on interpreting them (Freud 1986). Repressed desires attempt to be articulated within consciousness, but consciousness refuses to have anything to do with them. Those repressed desires may intrude into consciousness through dreams. Sometimes this may take place in an obvious way (I dream I want to have sex with X), but more often than not the repressed desire attaches itself in a less obvious way to the dream narrative. The point here is not so much that dreams can be read, but rather that the human subject is a split subject, split between conscious and unconscious desires, which means that we can never really know ourselves, simply because there is a part of us which can never be acknowledged, and can only appear in dreams.

Let's look at an example of these Freudian concepts as they are played out in popular culture. In David Lynch's film *Blue Velvet*, the narrative is concerned with two innocent teenagers (played by Kyle McLachlan and Laura Dern) who live in a sleepy, respectable American town. One day McLachlan finds a human ear in a field: his subsequent attempt to get to the bottom of the mystery pushes the couple into an underworld of violence and murder controlled by a psychopath named Frank (played by Dennis Hopper).

Now, dreams are often thought of in positive terms; the 'American dream', for instance, refers to the achievement of, among other things, an economically successful life. In pop songs, references to dreams and 'dreaming about you' are again usually highly positive; they suggest the achievement of some important part of our life and identity, the desire to have something or someone that will make our lives complete.

Blue Velvet is interested in exploring the other side of dreams, the side where what is repressed is given expression. The psychopath Frank is almost a walking 'return of the repressed': in one scene which is secretly watched by Kyle McLachlan, Dennis Hopper as Frank sexually abuses a woman called Dorothy (Isabella Rossellini) while openly playing out his desires for his mother. In one of the more ironic, and disturbing, scenes in the film, Hopper and his gang viciously beat up McLachlan while in the background Roy Orbison's 'In Dreams' is being played. The film is too complex to reduce to a few general points, but we can suggest that:

* Frank is more or less a representative of everybody's (or at least every male's) repressed desires, and the violence that accompanies those desires, and
* every dream (the American dream, romantic dreams) is informed by desire, and therefore by violence of some kind.

What the film makes clear, then, is the very Freudian point that:

* our cultural identities are dreamed up, if you like, and that
* any notion of rational and knowable identity is always a dream that has an unstable and violent side to it.

At the end of the film Kyle McLachlan and Laura Dern end up together, and everything seems fine . . . in dreams.

Lacan

Freud's theories of subjectivity were picked up and elaborated upon by the French psychoanalyst Jacques Lacan. Perhaps Lacan's most interesting contribution was the notion of the 'mirror stage' (Lacan 1977).

Lacan suggested that a child understands itself as a series of disconnected, atomised parts until the advent of what he called the

mirror stage. When the child sees its reflection (in a mirror, for instance), it recognises itself as a whole, a unity. This is the departure point for the child's assumption of subjectivity, but it is not without its problems. Although the child recognises itself, at the moment of recognition 'itself' is . . . 'over there'. In other words, at the moment subjectivity is given, it is also taken away: 'I am here, but I am also over there . . . am I here or there?'

As the child moves from a relationship based on its close connection with its mother (what Lacan calls the **imaginary**) to a full integration into society and culture, its identity will always be defined in terms of some other; something or someone is desired in order that the lack in the person's identity be filled in. Like Freud, Lacan identifies Oedipus as the crucial moment for the production of specific, subject identities, and like Freud he understands this process as being necessarily gendered (for instance, any identity in a culture is based on what Lacan calls the 'Law of the Father', which means that women are produced as non-male, as lack, as being castrated compared with men).

Our identity, for Lacan:

- is always changing and being transformed as we search for something or someone that will 'complete us', whether it be another person (love, romance), religion or the achievement of wealth or distinction.
- Further, this completion can never take place, of course, because our identity is caught up in a circle of desire that never meets itself.

Lacan's notion of subjectivity is often exemplified in Hollywood romance narratives where the (inevitable) male hero desires a particular woman who is usually described as being 'part of me', 'my fulfilment', 'my salvation' or 'the real meaning of my life'. A more Lacanian version of this narrative is to be found in the Hitchcock film *Vertigo*. The hero, played by Jimmy Stewart, falls in love with a woman, played by Kim Novak, who appears to commit suicide. Stewart is obsessed with the woman, and can't function once she has been removed from his life. In Lacanian terms, she was the 'other' who would have completed him, and her death seriously threatens to undermine the possibility of his social and cultural identity.

Stewart comes across another woman (who is actually the original woman, but she doesn't tell him that). He attempts to re-create what he thinks is a lookalike of the first woman, so he can recreate the 'original' woman. His obsessiveness eventually results in the woman being killed (for real this second time), but her death provides a liberation (for Stewart!), because he now knows that the woman who was his 'fulfilment' was a fake. Stewart becomes a normal, well-adjusted member of society because his desire is no longer attached too closely (too obsessively!) to one person, but can now move from one object to another without his ever having to face the truth that there is nothing to his desire (no woman can ever 'complete' his identity). Stewart almost loses his identity because he gambles that identity on, and commits his whole life and being to, an illusion . . . which he comes face to face with.

The fact that the woman ends up dead isn't a major issue in *Vertigo*, which, like most Hitchcock films, is primarily concerned with the ramifications of male desire and subjectivity. In other words, women are predominantly understood, in this and other Hitchcock films, as commodities to be exchanged by men.

Psychoanalytical theories of subjectivity are far more complex than we have suggested here, but perhaps we could sum up their contributions in the following, very generalised terms:

- Subjectivity is not essential or unchanging, but is tied up with the way cultures order and constrain our bodies and desires.
- Our identities are always based on something that is not conventionally understood as part of ourselves; for instance, repressed desires or an other who is both us and not us. ·
- Cultural identity is largely determined by the way bodies are gendered.
- Cultural identities are illusions which must be maintained if we are to continue to function within that culture.

FOUCAULT, SUBJECTIVITY AND DISCOURSE

One of the criticisms made of psychoanalytical theories is that they are too generalised, even universalist and ahistorical, and don't give any account of the specific ways in which different identities are produced within and across cultures. Michel Foucault is one theorist who more or less rejects psychoanalytical accounts and focuses instead

Michel Foucault was a French cultural theorist who between the 1960s and the early 1980s wrote a number of important texts which enquired into the relationship between cultural institutions (the prison, schools, hospitals, the family) and the production of subjectivities. Foucault's most influential contribution was to theorise about and describe the way bodies and identities are regulated through various mechanisms and discourses (medical, psychological, pedagogical, legal). His major works include *Madness and Civilization, The Birth of the Clinic, Discipline and Punish* and his three-part *The History of Sexuality*.

on the way in which cultures produce subject positions through institutionally sanctioned and legitimated discourses.

Perhaps Foucault's most useful and accessible analysis of the **discursive production** of subjectivity is to be found in *The History of Sexuality Volume One: An Introduction* (Foucault 1980) where he focuses on the ways in which the notion of sexuality came to be seen as the key issue in understanding and evaluating self and identity. Foucault starts by rejecting the conventional idea that during the nineteenth century, and particularly in the Victorian period, sexuality was repressed and censored, whereas in the twentieth century a kind of sexual liberation occurred. Foucault makes the point that, on the contrary, during the Victorian period an extraordinary amount of material was produced about sexuality. He writes:

> At the level of discourses and their domains . . . There was a steady proliferation of discourses concerned with sex-specific discourses . . . from the eighteenth century onward . . . [there was a] multiplication of discourses concerning sex in the field of exercise of power itself: an institutional incitement to speak about it, and to do so more and more; a determination on the part of the agencies of power to hear it spoken about, and to cause it to speak through explicit articulation and endlessly accumulated detail.
>
> FOUCAULT 1980:18

Foucault refers here to the disciplining of sexuality; that is to say, sexuality is taken as an object of study by various authorities and institutions and subjected to the gaze and analysis of medical and other sciences. Sexuality is identified, according to Foucault, as the site that would give up the truth about each person; and scientific instruments, theories and techniques were called on to help in this deliverance. The term Foucault uses to describe this process, whereby scientific knowledge of the subject is employed as a means of disciplining, evaluating, categorising, regulating, developing and reforming the subject, is bio-power.

The advent of bio-power replaced, for Foucault, old-fashioned exercising of power (by the king, for instance) as naked violence, punishment or threat, with the notion of scientific normality. From this time on, subjectivity was understood as a form of normality which had to be adhered to. People's subjectivities came to be regulated through being written about; that is to say, from the moment a child comes into contact with institutional authorities (which these days is the day of its birth), those institutions produce discourses which define normal identity and which carry the seal of scientific credibility and authority.

Sexuality is only one of the areas, of course, that have been targeted by discursive regulation, but it is an extremely important one. To quote Foucault again:

> sex . . . was at the pivot of the two axes along which developed the entire political technology of life. On the one hand it was tied to the disciplines of the body: the harnessing, intensification and distribution of forces, the adjustment and economy of energies. On the other hand, it was applied to the regulation of populations, through all the far-reaching effects of its activity. It fitted in both categories at once, giving rise to infinitesimal surveillances, permanent controls, extremely meticulous orderings of space, indeterminate medical or psychological examinations, to an entire micro-power concerned with the body. But it gave rise as well to comprehensive measures, statistical assessments, and intervention aimed at the entire social body or at groups taken as a whole. Sex was a means of access to the life of the body and the life of the species. It was employed as a standard for the disciplines and as a basis for regulations.

> FOUCAULT 1980:145

Let's look at the main points in this passage:

• sex is used to normalise and regulate individual behaviour and practices, and to create hierarchies of subjectivity based on the approximation to a sexual norm or set of norms. Heterosexuality, for instance, is normal and valuable, while homosexual activity is perverse and should be eliminated.

- Both the micro and macro processes of normalisation and regulation involve increased surveillance by the state and its institutions and practitioners (educational, medical, psychological, legal). Throughout our lives, institutional agents (teachers, doctors) direct us towards normal behaviour.

- There is a presumption that not only is sex the 'answer' to individual and mass identity, but that sex is to be found in every aspect and corner of existence. Foucault is particularly critical of psychoanalytical claims that sex informs all our actions.

- Sex becomes both the marker of individuality ('your sexuality is what you really are, and what distinguishes you from others') and the key to reshaping that individuality ('this is what we want you to become, and it is through the manipulation and regulation of your sexuality that you can be normalised').

- Finally, the institutional surveillances, descriptions and analyses of these 'sexualised' human bodies produce knowledge which underpins regulation and normalisation. What this means, for Foucault, is that scientific knowledge is closely linked to the exercising of power. In other words, the knowledge produced and used by institutions (by teachers and doctors, for instance) is not neutral or disinterested. There is a politics to it.

What kind of evidence is there for these claims? Think of the way in which western cultures and their institutions and discourses have made the notion of the **deviant** and deviance (as opposed to normality) so central to the notion of identity. For instance:

- we can refer to a whole series of so-called deviant subject positions—involving, for instance, 'male' homosexuality, lesbianism, nymphomania, frigidity, masturbation, paedophilia, exhibitionism, infertility, impotence, masochism, sadism, bondage—all of which have been 'identified' by scientific or quasi-scientific discourse and institutions and used to categorise and 'explain' people.

- Moreover, none of these categories 'existed' until the last 200 years or so; that is to say, there were homosexual practices (in ancient Greece, for instance, such practices probably constituted a relatively large proportion of all sexual practice), but there wasn't the subject category 'the homosexual', nor the 'illness' of homosexuality.

Another example of Foucault's thesis can be found in the way sexuality functions in popular institutions and discourses. Any reading of lifestyle magazines demonstrates that sexuality and sexual practices have become virtually the principal criterion for determining social normality, identity and value.

What these magazines simultaneously presume and reproduce is the notion that people understand themselves in terms of, and are completely dominated by, an interest in sexuality (theirs and everybody else's). Consider, for example, the contents lists, taken from an issue of *Dolly* magazine (see Figure 26).

Dolly is a magazine generally aimed at teenage girls, and its contents are divided into the following sections:

- Features
- Health and beauty
- Make-up manual
- It's special
- Rock
- Fashion
- Fiction
- Real Life, and
- a collection of columns listed under 'Every Month'.

In the first section, 'Features', only two articles are specifically about sexuality and identity ('Is it cool to lose your virginity?' and 'Why he thinks you're desperate'), but at least half of the other feature articles produce sexuality, or at the very least body image, as an important marker of identity and worth.

The 'Are you insecure?' quiz (81), for example, uses the following scenarios as the basis for its questions:

- 'Your boyfriend dumps you, without giving you a reason'
- 'You're in a cafe, and you see an absolutely beautiful guy with a killer smile sitting at the other end of the room'
- 'When you look in the mirror, you see . . .'

Moreover, a number of questions which don't appear to be connected with sexuality provide options/answers that work to

194 COMMUNICATION AND CULTURAL LITERACY

FIGURE 26 Contents page of *Dolly Magazine*, September 1993

FEATURES

62 Is It Cool To Lose Your Virginity? So you're scared about being the only virgin in your group. Does this mean you should have sex just for the sake of getting the first time over and done with?

70 The Daintree Is In Danger How we can save the Daintree Rainforest from being destroyed

72 The Price of Acting Dumb We take a look at which celebs have made stupid career decisions

78 The Mouth That Roared Billy Baldwin bags just about everyone in Hollywood, from Tom Cruise to Julia Roberts

80 Are You Insecure? Do our quiz to find out if your confidence rates

99 Daring To Make A Difference Check out why these six girls are the coolest in the country

108 Why He Thinks You're Desperate We find out why guys don't want the girls they think they can easily get

116 Read Poppy's Lips Lipstick queen Poppy King tells us why megastars want to wear her make-up

HEALTH & BEAUTY

46 Sport Report Snooker

48 Body Rap

126 Make Me Up

MAKE-UP MANUAL

83 The ultimate make-up manual

84 Two Weeks to Great Skin The amazing 14-day diet that will clear up your complexion

88 Colour Coded Find out which make-up shades suit your skin tone

92 A Bundle Of Beauty Tanya Arpadi lets you in on what life as a model is really like

96 Best Buys For Under $20 Forget the beauty hype and suss out these sensational bargains

IT'S SPECIAL

17 Win 1,000 Rock Books You can score the exclusive Michael Jackson photo album, and stacks of other must-reads

19 Win 200 Revlon Packs Get your hands on Cindy Crawford's favourite moisturisers

74 Subscribe To *Dolly* And Win The massive Pert Shampoo giveaway

76 Dolly Club Natural knits and the most awesome freebies

127 Fun Foto Win a wild Summertime bikini

ROCK

38 Spin Out Music reviews

60 Diesel Lobbies For A Different Direction Why Diesel has had enough of his old rock'n'roll routine

106 Lenny's Comin' Our Way As he prepares to tour Down Under, we try to find out what makes Lenny Kravitz so sexy

FASHION

24 Tropical Tie-dye Once you take a look at this hip gear, you'll be dyeing to get into the tropics

52 The Best On The Beach We've found the sexiest swimsuits that will suit every body

64 Look Out LA Why Alison Brahe is set to make her mark on Hollywood

110 Show Some Skin Baring your midriff is the coolest fashion focus around

125 Where It's At Where to buy

FICTION

50 Beverly Hillbillies, 0810 Find out what's made the libidos of the male ranchers go through the roof

125 Short Pieces

REAL LIFE

50 Boys & Girls On Breaking the law

118 Dolly Doctor

121 What Should I Do?

122 Sex and Your Body Taking control

128 What You Wrote Someone who cares

EVERY MONTH

6 Upfront

8 Letterbox

9 Who's Hot Jeremy Jordan

12 What Now

14 What Matters Stop blaming rape victims, Southern Cross Cultural Exchange

26 What's Cooking Boom Crash Opera's Dale Ryder whips up a gourmet extravaganza

35 Watch Out Movie reviews

36 Watch In Video reviews

40 Read It Book reviews

123 Stars

124 Pen Pals

128 Winners

129 Next Month

130 Girls' Talk Beating the boys at their own game

COURTESY OF DOLLY MAGAZINE

sexualise the question. For instance, one option regarding 'the biggest worry you might have in giving a speech in front of the whole school' is that 'All the boys in the front row will fall in love with you.' And in the article 'Which TV character do you most relate to?', one of the options is '*Melrose Place*'s Jo—she's dating the most gorgeous guy around.'

It's not just these specific articles that conflate sexuality with identity, interest and value; other sections, whether they refer to fashion, beauty hints, fiction, medical advice, rock or media stars, share this tendency:

- The fiction 'Beverly Hillbillies 0810' asks 'What's made the libidos of the male ranchers go through the roof?'
- The regular column 'What matters' (listed on the contents page under 'Every Month') is about not 'blaming rape victims'
- In Fashion, there are references to 'the sexiest swimsuits that will suit every body' and 'Baring your midriff'
- In Rock, the magazine asks 'what makes Lenny Kravitz so sexy?'

This preoccupation with sexualised identities is not confined to the written pieces; if anything it is more accentuated in the photographs used in the magazine, most of which define their subjects (both male and female) as sexually attractive, alluring, available or assertive. This goes for both the pin-up (of a semi-clad male hunk), and the fashion, celebrity and advertising shots. Most of these photos share the following characteristics:

- the emphasis is on bare flesh, or on clothes that accentuate curves, such as swimsuits or tight-fitting outfits
- shots are often centred on breasts, thighs or buttocks
- a large proportion of the photos of women have the woman staring, lips pursed, at the camera
- many of the photographs are sexualised through the choice of pose, with women coyly half covering themselves, or sticking out their breasts, or appearing to be undressing
- much of the clothing that is worn in these shots is 'tantalisingly' half-revealing (half open or partly see-through)
- the camera angles used in some of the shots again accentuate and work to help reveal conventionally sexualised areas (by being directed down a dress top, or up legs).

What we have been suggesting is that this magazine, which we think is not unrepresentative of magazines targeting the western youth market, strongly sexualises most of its written and visual material. How does this tie in with Foucault's notion that sexuality is used to produce, regulate, normalise and evaluate social identities? Let us consider the following extract from the article 'Why he thinks you're desperate' (Unreich 1993:109), and make use of Foucault's insights to analyse the way the article deals with the question of social identity (see Figure 27).

The first two paragraphs set up a romantic narrative which positions both subjects (Naomi and David) as potentially fulfilled and happy precisely because they had been integrated into 'normal' sexualised subject positions: 'they were perfect for each other . . . David spent the evening holding Naomi's hand (while) . . . she spent the night gazing into his eyes'. What we have here is a normalising narrative (they are more or less promised perfection through being perfect for the other) which is based on their both assuming gendered roles that are simultaneously valuing and valued:

• The man values the woman by holding her hand; and by letting him hold her hand she legitimates him as a desirable man.

• The woman values the man by gazing into his eyes, and by offering himself up as her temple, he transfers some of his value to her.

So far, so good: 'It was all going to work out fine'—but it didn't. Why not? What follows doesn't read like the kind of scientific or quasi-scientific discourses produced by a major social institution (psychology or medicine, for instance), but there are quite extraordinary similarities at work here. The article is scientific, to a certain extent, in that it:

• describes and analyses, in an almost anthropological way, Naomi's practices

• writes out of a position of presumed knowledge, which allows analysis and diagnosis to take place, and

• identifies the 'problem' (the deviance, if you like) in Naomi's behaviour.

Naomi's deviance is based on her inability to produce herself as a normal sexualised person; that is to say, her practices mark her out as 'desperate':

• She has produced herself 'as a commodity', as something that can

FIGURE 27 'Why he thinks you're desperate'

YOU WANT HIM BAD, AND YOU'RE SURE IF YOU FOLLOW HIM AROUND LONG ENOUGH, HE'LL WANT YOU TOO, RIGHT? WRONG. ACTING LIKE THIS WILL PROBABLY SCARE HIM AWAY. RACHELLE UNREICH LOOKS AT WHAT MAKES GUYS THINK YOU'RE DESPERATE FOR A DATE.

When I introduced Naomi to David, I was sure they were perfect for each other. They shared a weird sense of humour, and were the only people I knew who loved both Stephen King novels and country music.

Sure enough, they went out on a date and really hit it off. David spent the evening holding Naomi's hand and speaking about Dwight Yoakam; she spent the night gazing into his eyes. I told her it was all going to work out fine.

What I didn't anticipate was Naomi's determination to make David hers. The following Monday, she bought two tickets to the theatre, and sent them to him. That Wednesday, because he'd said that he loved Pearl Jam, she sent him all the CDs they'd ever recorded.

On Thursday, she called him for a chat, and on Friday she dropped over to his house, unannounced, after work, in a gorgeous black dress. His eyes lit up when he saw her, but, three hours of conversation later, they had a glazed look. After that, he didn't return her calls, and went out of his way to avoid her.

Naomi couldn't believe it. What had she done wrong? She'd laughed at his jokes, agreed with everything he said, and acted loving and sweet and good-humoured all the time. Couldn't he see that she'd make a perfect girlfriend?

But, the fact she didn't realise was that if you're the slightest bit desperate to be with a boy, he'll sense it. Most males have a commitment phobia, so you can imagine how turned off he gets if it's obvious you're trying to hook him.

You may think you're being subtle, but believe me, a guy knows when you're walking the long way between your science and maths classes just so you can bump into him.

COURTESY OF DOLLY MAGAZINE. UNREICH 1993:109

be exchanged (for male company, approval, sexual interest), but her commodity value is destroyed by her 'deviant' behaviour.

- The excesses of her behaviour (sending David the tickets and the CDs) are diagnosed as an abnormality which, at the very least, puts her into the 'uncool' category.

Not exactly scientific, you think? Not in any traditional sense, but this discourse has some functions in common with medical or psychological discourses. That is, this story is produced as a narrative of normality, as a description and diagnosis of deviancy, and as a warning about the consequences of that deviancy (a version of 'stop it, or you'll go blind!').

At this point it is useful to recap on our two main sets of theories of subjectivity, those associated with psychoanalysis and with Foucault.

How can Freudian and Lacanian theories help us to read this article?

• This article, and in fact the whole production of identity and sexuality in this magazine, brings into focus the contradiction of living with, and at the same time necessarily repressing, desire. Desire, in the 'Desperate' article, is a given: it is only right and proper and healthy to desire; desire provides Naomi with an identity (she is a valued, desirable woman).

• At the same time, desire is something that needs to be controlled; it is, potentially at least, a threat to identity. Why? Desire, for Freud, is something that has to be regulated by what he called the 'reality principle'. The desire for the mother is repressed precisely because of the intervention of the reality principle. Naomi's desire for David is, in a sense, potentially destructive because it is not subject to the reality principle.

• Lacan's notion of the subjectivity based on a desire that is an illusion, but has to be continually reproduced is of even more relevance here. Like Jimmy Stewart in *Vertigo*, Naomi has identified too closely with the object of her desire; the choices available to her are to step back from that object and modify her desire, or transfer her desire elsewhere.

We referred earlier to the psychoanalytical insight that desire both constitutes and threatens identity, and we made the point that *Dolly* exemplifies this. It does this by continually sexualising bodies and by producing bodies and identities as valuable and desirable, as commodities that can be exchanged (for positions in romance narratives, for instance) for profit. At the same time it counters and contradicts its own production of desire as having a life of its own, and as ranging about in a kind of 'free-market' economy.

For *Dolly*, sexuality gives both identity and value, to the extent that most of the magazine could be summed up by imperatives such as 'enjoy!' and 'indulge your desire'. And yet there are sections of the magazine that counsel moderation and regulation in the most morally conservative way. The article 'Is it cool to lose your virginity?', for instance, suggests that you take the plunge only after fulfilling a list of criteria which, if followed by the general population, would put sexual contact on the 'endangered species' list.

We have already made numerous references to Foucault's theories of the relationship between institutions, discourses and knowledge, on the one hand, and the production and regulation of normalised subjectivities, on the other. If there is one major shortcoming with Foucault's theories, however, it is his disinclination to theorise about these moves at the level of practice. In other words, Foucault's work helps us to understand what happens, but he is less helpful with how it happens. To address this extremely important point, we want to stay with the 'Desperate' article but to consider it in terms of the theories of gender and subjectivity offered by Judith Butler.

BUTLER AND PERFORMANCE

Butler specifically addresses this question of the relationship between discourse, bodies, identities, commoditisation and practice in her book *Bodies that Matter* (1993). She writes:

> What I would propose . . . is a return to the notion of matter, not as a site or surface, but as a process of materialization that stabilizes over time to produce the effect of boundary, fixity, and surface we call matter . . . the question is no longer, How is gender constituted as and through a certain interpretation of sex? . . . but rather, Through what regulatory norm is sex itself materialized? (10)

Butler answers her own question by suggesting that the sexualising of the body, and as a result the production of identity, occurs through what she calls 'the reiteration of norms' (10). This means:

- Bodies don't come to mean naturally; rather they are produced as meaningful by discourses which divide them up and evaluate them (female breasts are sexualised in a particular way, as are men's stomach muscles, for instance).
- At the same time, people respond to these discourses by

'performing' their bodies 'in time' with these discourses. The effect of the combination of discursive evaluations and imperatives ('this is what bodies mean, therefore do this') produces what we might call performances of subjectivity.

Let's return to Naomi and David. Naomi is performing 'appropriately' as a young woman at the beginning of the narrative: remember, she does all the right things, such as allowing her hand to be held and gazing into David's eyes. What we have here is a romance genre, and in this genre, at least according to *Dolly*, the appropriate performances involve:

- David being in control ('holding her hand'), and
- Naomi doing the worshipping ('gazing into his eyes').

Everything was 'going to work out fine' as long as they remembered their lines and moves and didn't 'misperform'.

As *Dolly* makes clear, Naomi's performance fell to pieces. It is interesting that the *Dolly* article, which seemingly deals with supposedly deep and meaningful feelings and topics like romance and love, should so unashamedly and unambiguously diagnose the failure of the relationship in terms of misperformance. Naomi fails to perform like a young woman. She gives up her passivity in favour of a performance which is much too close to what is expected of the man.

This doesn't mean that Foucault is wrong when he suggests that identity is sexualised in terms of notions of normality, and that deviance is treated as a kind of medical or psychological disorder. All it means is that we have to extend Foucault's ideas about normality and regulation to include Butler's insight that repeated and appropriate performance is the means by which normality is reproduced—as a practice.

Let's recap:

- for Foucault, sexual categories, roles and attributes are discursively produced, and
- as Butler elaborates, this means that the 'truth' of sexuality is perhaps better understood as the 'performance' of gender; in other words,
- the repetition of 'appropriate' performances provides models for the practice of subjectivity.

Judith Butler is an American feminist and gender theorist who very usefully employs and combines both psychoanalytical theories and the work of Foucault to address issues of the production and reproduction of subjectivities. Her ability to move across and combine complex and seemingly antithetical theoretical positions makes her one of the most interesting and important cultural theorists writing today. Her most recent books are *Gender Trouble* and *Bodies that Matter*.

Moreover, Butler points out that certain gender genres, and the successful performance of those genres, have been used to construct hierarchies within cultures. The broad genre of 'male' has generally been valued over that of 'female', for instance. Similarly, a successful male performance—this will vary from one context to another—will be valued over unsuccessful male performances.

If we accept that masculinity and femininity are performed, we need to consider such questions as:

- What kinds of performances are normally legitimated?, and
- What constitutes a successful performance?

The answer to these questions will of course vary from culture to culture, and even within cultures. However, we can identify and describe some of the more obvious rationales used to legitimate and define gender categories in western cultures. These rationales, most of which function as gendered binaries, include:

- public/private
- subject/object
- desiring/desired
- reasonable/emotional
- active/passive.

These binaries do not in themselves constitute any straightforward recipe for gender genres. All binaries can be—and are—turned around at different times, so that in some contexts the conventional identification of, say, women with emotion and men with reason can be reversed. Generally, however, these binaries are used to construct gender genres and the performances, narratives and desires that go with them. A successful male performance, for instance, might involve a man demonstrating that he is:

- active
- dominating
- reasonable
- sexually potent (with a woman), and
- literate in the public sphere.

A woman might be expected to perform as:

- passive
- supportive
- emotional
- sexually desirable, and
- literate in the private or domestic sphere.

Keep in mind that we are not offering these binaries as prescriptive, or suggesting there is such a thing as an objective notion of what is reasonable, for instance. They often function, however, as a group of generic characteristics that help shape and determine gender performances.

What kinds of narratives are tied to and produced by these characteristics, and how do they help to legitimate each other? The public/private binary has an accompanying narrative which can be traced back to the social-contract theorists in the eighteenth century. These theorists used the public/private binary to get over the problem of how all people could be understood to be free and equal if large numbers of people in a culture were treated as inferior.

For various social-contract theorists (such as Rousseau and Locke), women, for instance, were 'by nature' unsuited for the duties and responsibilities associated with the public sphere; that is to say, they were unsuited for government or administration. Woman were only suited to the private—that is to say, the domestic—sphere, where they could look after children, prepare food, maintain the home, and ensure the continuation of the male line.

How was this division of duties and responsibilities rationalised? Precisely in terms of the various masculine/feminine binaries we referred to previously. If women were by nature emotional, selfish, untrustworthy, unintelligent, unreasonable and promiscuous, then it would make no sense to have them participate in the governing of

the state. And if women were incapable of improving themselves—
and nature had decreed that this was the case—then there was no
point in wasting resources on, say, attempting to educate them.

Despite the strong influence these genres, narratives and performances undoubtedly exercise over people, they don't entirely control
practices associated with gender. One reason for this is that while
each performance must be like previous performances, no two performances are ever exactly alike—if only because no two contexts are
exactly alike. Time and repetition produce normality and regulation,
but they also produce deviation and change. That there are so many
gender genres and performances testifies to Freud's point that deviance is more or less the norm in western culture.

Cultures counter this tendency towards deviance by ensuring that
there are very serious political, social and economic consequences
involved in the non-performance or misperformance of gender genres.
We will now provide three examples of what we might call the
'politics of gender misperformance': the first involves the misperformance of masculinity, the second the misperformance of femininity, and
the third the 'overperformance' of masculinity.

Example 1: A misperformance of masculinity

When the then US president, George Bush, went to Tokyo in 1992,
he did so with the express purpose of convincing the Japanese to
further open their domestic markets to American goods and services,
thereby cutting the huge trade surplus Japan was running with the
US.

Before Bush left the US the discourses he and his advisers used
could be described as aggressive and masculinist: the US was sick of
being fobbed off by the Japanese, the US was the superpower, and
the Japanese would listen and act accordingly, or else.

Unfortunately, at a state dinner in Tokyo Bush became ill, threw
up on the trousers of then Japanese prime minister Kiichi Miyazawa,
and fell under the table. Finally he was assisted to his feet, and needed
help to leave the room.

Nothing was ever officially made of the incident (the Japanese
expressed sympathy, and Bush said he was fine), but American
newspapers lambasted Bush as a 'wimp'—a charge that had been
made on other occasions. Indeed, to a certain extent, the subsequent
US invasion of Panama, and the war with Iraq, could be understood

in terms of the United States's—and particularly Bush's—attempts to successfully perform its much-questioned 'masculinity'.

Example 2: A misperformance of femininity

In the Professor Anita Hill/Judge Clarence Thomas affair, Hill accused Thomas, who had been nominated to the US Supreme Court, of sexual harassment (for a different discussion of this event, see Chapter 1). During the Senate questioning of Hill, she remained cool and in control, and did not offer anything like the kind of performance the all-male inquiry panel expected.

After Thomas's appointment was confirmed, a number of senators said they didn't believe Hill because she hadn't responded to questions in an emotional manner, and it was also suggested in the press that Hill's performances weren't 'warm enough'.

Now, nobody would have complained if a male general or diplomat or lawyer had performed in a calm and composed manner in this settting—in fact, it would have been expected. Anita Hill, on the other hand, was expected (by men) to perform as a woman who had been sexually harassed: that is to say, emotionally.

Example 3: An 'overperformance' of masculinity

In 1991 the then world heavyweight boxing champion, Mike Tyson, was convicted of raping 17-year-old Desiree Washington. At his trial, Tyson made no attempt to play down his 'masculinity'. He boasted that he found it difficult to keep his hands off attractive women, and usually tried to have sex with them as soon as possible.

Tyson's performance was an excellent example of how a normally acceptable masculine performance could become illegitimate (Judge Thomas recognised this and played down his masculinity). Tyson's performance became illegitimate because it clashed too obviously with, or devalued, aspects of other legitimate gender performances: the victim was a woman, but she was also a seventeen-year-old girl and another man's daughter.

These examples all demonstrate that gender performances are at the same time political performances, with serious consequences. The reasons for this can be read as follows:

- Gender categories, and the performances that accompany them, are more or less ambiguous. Masculinity is normally valued in western (masculinist) cultures, but at the same time performances of masculinity that ignore, threaten or devalue romantic or domestic genres and narratives can have negative ramifications for the performer (though not all judges would seem to agree with this point).

• Gender genres change: the recent furore over comments made by British and Australian judges during rape trials—comments that would have been made with impunity a few years ago—gives a good indication of how the legitimacy of certain genres has been questioned in recent times.

SUMMARY

In this chapter we have argued that subjectivities are culturally produced, and that the identities we take on and use are closely connected to our communication practices. We addressed the question of subjectivity in terms of three major approaches:

• We described various psychoanalytical theories, associated with Freud and Lacan, which argue that subjects are always split because they are partly constituted out of repressed or unconscious desires.

• We looked at Foucault's notion that subjects are produced, regulated and normalised through the mechanisms and discourses of cultural institutions.

• We used Judith Butler's work to explain how subjectivities are connected to communication practices through the notion of appropriate gender (and other generic) performances.

FURTHER READING

Butler, J. 1993 *Bodies that Matter* Routledge, New York
Grosz, E. 1990 *Jacques Lacan: A Feminist Introduction* Allen & Unwin, Sydney
Grosz, E. 1994 *Volatile Bodies* Allen & Unwin, Sydney
Patton, P. (ed.) 1993 *Nietzsche, Feminism and Political Theory* Allen & Unwin, Sydney
Zizek, S. 1991 *Looking Awry* MIT Press, Cambridge, Mass.

10
VISUAL MEDIUMS

The main focus of this chapter is on visual mediums and genres, and the ways they function in western cultures. More specifically, we suggest that western cultures are becoming predominantly 'visual cultures', and that any consideration of **cultural literacy** needs to take this development into account.

LITERACY REVISITED

When the term literacy is used in, say, the media, the reference is usually to reading and writing skills. We made the point earlier in this book, however, that the notion of literacy need not be confined to this narrow meaning but could be understood in a more general sense. We have used the concept to refer to a working familiarity with:

- the rules, both official and unofficial, by which various **cultural fields** operate
- the **genres** and **discourses** that characterise different cultural fields, and
- the relationship, within a culture, between economic and cultural capital.

Even more important, this general notion of literacy refers to an ability to make use of this familiarity with cultural fields, genres, discourses and capital as a practice.

An example of this more general notion of literacy can be seen in the Japanese film *Tampopo*. Some Japanese businessmen are having a meal at an exclusive French restaurant in Tokyo. In keeping with the 'rules' of Japanese business culture, group behaviour is strictly hierarchical. The exact nature of the pecking order is quite easy to read because each person waits for his superior to speak or act first.

Things change once the group members have to 'perform' in the French restaurant; that is, as soon as they are required to be literate in the cultural field of French food and wine. The leader of the group is obviously illiterate in this area: he can't make any sense of the food menu and doesn't know which wines go with different meals. All of his colleagues, except for the last and lowliest, are also illiterate—they order what their boss ordered.

The last to order, a young businessman who has been treated with disdain by the rest of the group, turns out to be extremely literate in French food and wine. He recognises, reads and analyses the menu and, most important, employs this skill and information in his practices. He chats confidently and intelligently with the head waiter, asks knowledgeable questions, and makes extremely 'tasteful' decisions. All his colleagues are very impressed, and this obviously augurs well for his promotion up the corporate pecking order.

The point made by the film is that he has displayed two forms of literacy:

- first, he has demonstrated that he is literate inside a French restaurant, and
- second, and equally important, he is literate inside his own business culture, since he has understood how to use this first literacy to impress his colleagues.

There are two aspects of this kind of literacy that set it apart from the more conventional version, which relates to reading and writing skills:

- Literacy is understood as potentially referring to all fields, genres, discourses and mediums within a culture, and even across cultures.
- Literacy is not simply understood as a kind of retrieval of rules (for instance, the grammatical rules of a language). Instead, it refers to a connection between the recognition, production and retrieval of what is constituted as information, on the one hand, and its use or deployment as a communication practice, on the other.

THE POLITICS OF LITERACY

There is, of course, a politics, and considerable cultural capital, tied up with defining what constitutes literacy. Even when definitions of literacy are broadened to take into account wider fields, they usually confine themselves to the reproduction of what we can call 'high' cultural material or information. Think of the newspaper articles that appear every few months complaining that eighteen-year-olds don't know:

- who won the Second World War, or
- what Shakespeare is famous for, or
- the fruit that prompted Newton to work out his theory of gravity.

There are, of course, very few articles complaining that 50-year-olds don't know anything about Pearl Jam, or how to play a computer game.

The point we are making here is that speech and writing genres are involved in only a small proportion of communication practices in contemporary western cultures. Communication in western cultures is dominated by visual genres and mediums: photographs, television, film, video, cartoons, posters, t-shirts, comics and computer simulations, to name just a few. Increasingly, an argument can be mounted that a literate person in contemporary western cultures is, first and foremost, someone who is able to recognise, read, analyse and deploy a variety of visual genres and mediums.

THE VISUAL AS REAL

Perhaps the first thing we can say about a number of contemporary visual mediums—photographs or film, for instance—is that they have gained a high level of credibility as means of communication precisely because they seem to be able to reproduce reality in an apparently objective way. Visual texts do not appear to be mediated; that is, there appears to be no obvious difference between the image the text provides and the 'reality' it stands in for.

Unlike visual mediums, speech and writing are quite obviously mediated; that is to say, there is an obvious difference between their own materiality (sounds, words on a page) and the materiality they stand in for or deliver up (people, events).

The same argument could be made, of course, for older visual communication mediums, such as drawing and painting. The images to be found in paintings—at least in 'realist' paintings—seem very close to the 'original' image that is being represented. But are such images any more real than words or sounds?

The French painter René Magritte produced a picture which consisted of a remarkably realistic-looking smoking pipe; the painting's title, which appeared on the image, was (as it translates into English) *This is not a Pipe*. What was the point of giving that title to an extremely realistic painting of a pipe? Magritte's title draws attention to the constructed and mediated nature of any kind of representation, whether it is 'realistic' or otherwise. *This is not a Pipe* is exactly what it claims to be—it is *not* the object it represents. Just like sounds and words, however—just like any medium of communication—it presents itself as being a genuine or faithful substitute for 'the real thing'.

There are two other issues related to the 'reality' of visual representations which we need to address before we move on to a more detailed consideration of visual communication mediums and genres:

- What do we mean when we describe a representation as realistic?
- Paintings, drawings and other less technologically sophisticated and advanced forms of visual representations may be no more real than speech or words, but what about those mediums (such as photographs or film) which seem to directly reproduce reality? And is there any form of visual representation or reproduction that is completely unmediated and objective?

When discussing the 'realistic' aspects of some visual mediums and genres, it is worth bearing in mind that the notion of realism is not something that we can take for granted, nor do all cultures agree on what is realistic. To give an example, in ancient Egyptian culture, people and things were usually drawn using hard, straight lines which made their features look rigid and geometric. Moreover, those representations did not make use of the same notion of perspective or balance that characterises most contemporary western visual representations. People in a drawing were not represented according to their relative physical size, nor could people be positioned just anywhere within the drawing. The pharaoh was generally represented as being much larger than her or his subjects, and was also usually positioned above them (see Figure 28).

This might seem rather strange and unrealistic to us, but it would probably not have appeared that way to most ancient Egyptians. How can we account for this?

We need to understand that different cultures have different ideas of what is realistic, because what is accepted as real depends very much on specific cultural contexts, literacies and ideologies. In Chapter 8, we made the point that ideologies were produced by groups within a culture in order to make it appear as if their world view was the only possible and natural, the only real, world view.

Claude Lefort suggests that in pre-capitalist cultures, ideologies were presented as if they came directly from, and were sanctioned by, God or the supernatural world (Lefort 1986). For most ordinary people living in ancient Egypt, the world and all its activities were seen and understood in terms of the ideology of the rule of the god-pharaoh. This meant that the pharaoh was far more powerful and important than mere mortals, and therefore it was only realistic to represent her or him as bigger—that is to say, greater—than anyone else except some gods.

What about the geometric and rigid faces and bodies? Again, it is worth recalling Volosinov's argument, also discussed in Chapter 8, that every representation is a sign that has been ideologised, and Laclau's suggestion that this process also applies to those signs that are subjects/identities.

In ancient Egypt, the ruling ideologies would have produced a series of identities that grouped people within the culture according to their function in relation to the pharoah. That is, the identity of each person referred, in some way, to the identity of the pharoah.

In visual texts, these identities corresponded to different styles of representation; different angles, geometric shapes, sizes and the inclusion or exclusion of different material details all had significance within the culture. A high priest, for instance, had a very different identity from, a peasant or a soldier, and so it was only natural—and realistic—that they be represented differently.

In other words, in ancient Egypt, as in every culture, materiality or reality and the cultural production of that reality could not be divided from one another. Put simply, ancient Egyptians saw reality—both literally and metaphorically—differently from us, precisely because the ideological meanings available to them were different. As

FIGURE 28 Akh-en-Aton and family worshipping the Sun-Disk

ILLUSTRATION BY PAT GOON

a result, their pictures and drawings were probably realistic to them, but seem stylised and unrealistic to contemporary viewers.

OBJECTIVITY

Our argument about the relativity of representations might apply to Egyptians who lived and communicated 4000 years ago, but they never had access to photographs, television, film or computers. Can we make the same argument in an age when technology enables us to reproduce reality quickly, and in remarkable detail? In other words, have advances in communication technology enabled us to reproduce objective reality?

It has been argued, ever since photographs first appeared, that at last a medium of representation was available which produced only the truth or reality; that is, what was really there. The first objection

to this proposition is a simple one: photographs can be 'doctored'—
that is, they can be tampered with.

During the late 1960s, when long hair was fashionable but often
frowned upon by school principals, a school magazine editor at an
Australian high school took the liberty of trimming the hair of male
students in class photographs! Perhaps a little more serious and
sinister was the 'editing' of photographs and films that took place in
Eastern European countries in the 1950s and '60s. A powerful politician would appear in official photographs until she or he fell from
grace; after they had been disposed of, those same official photographs
were edited to remove any sign of the now-disgraced politician. In
other words, according to the official photographic record, they had
never existed: 'So you say comrade Chekhov was at the opening of
the sports stadium in 1956? Look, here is the photograph of the
opening, and he isn't in it.'

That is one argument against the objectivity of the new visual
mediums. But surely those doctored photographs were objective and
faithful before they were tampered with?

'EDITING' THE VISUAL

The answer is that visual mediums, like other communication mediums, are produced through processes of selection and omission.
Anyone taking a photograph always makes decisions, sometimes quite
unconsciously, about:

* what to include and what to leave out
* how close to get to the material being photographed
* the angle from which the photograph is to be taken, and
* when to take the shot.

Moreover, how is the photograph going to be used? Is it to be
placed in an album or pinned on a wall? Will it accompany an article
in a newspaper, or be used to blackmail a politician? These, and the
almost infinite number of other possibilities we haven't mentioned,
constitute the contexts that will produce and constrain possible
readings of the photographs.

Let's address this question of the 'editing' of the visual through
reference to some examples. First, what is included in and excluded

from any photograph or film shot is significant because it constrains how the text can be read. This was demonstrated in a commercial for an Australian television news show screened in the early 1990s.

The channel was not attracting viewers to its news, so it ran a commercial with a voice-over which said, 'Some news services only show you part of the picture.' Accompanying this voice-over was film of a woman, getting out of a car, who is startled and frightened when she sees a man running towards her.

From what we saw in this particular version ('not the complete picture'), it looked as if the woman was about to be assaulted or robbed by the man. However, the so-called 'complete picture' showed details, not included in the first version, which changed our reading of what was happening; there was an object about to fall onto the woman, and the man had seen it and was attempting to push her to safety.

The 'real' and complete picture, then, was to be seen on Channel X; but its commercial was as guilty of giving us an incomplete picture as its rivals' ads. Why? Because if the commercial had widened its perspective even further, it would have shown us television cameras filming the commercial. In other words, in order to claim to be giving us the complete picture ('here is a man saving a woman from an accident'), the TV station's commercial had to edit out its own involvement in the activity ('here is a television company shooting a commercial about a man saving a woman from an accident—which didn't really happen').

The distances and angles involved in taking photographs and shooting film also work to produce the end product. This is all reasonably straightforward: a shot from above or below, or from near or far, can influence how people read the 'captured' material, precisely because:

• those aspects determine what other material is included in the shot
• angles and distances change the place from where we see the material (viewing position), and
• different angles and distances often have specific cultural meanings.

In many films it is customary to open with a long shot which gives the viewer the 'macro-picture', and then to zoom in to a close-up of the more specific action or scene (the 'micro-picture'). In *Blade Runner*, for instance, the opening shots are of a huge metropolis dominated by skyscrapers and electronic billboards; these are followed, however, by closer shots of crowds of people (made up of mixed races) going about their business in a market area. The first shots can be read as producing a sense of the inhuman character of the city (all buildings and billboards), while the next shots seem to reverse that notion, providing plenty of evidence of humanity, although the shots of the crowd tend to reinforce the earlier sense of depersonalisation.

The position from which we view is equally important in determining what we view. There is a famous scene in the Alfred Hitchcock film *Lifeboat* where a German survivor of a battle between a U-boat and an Allied ship is pulled onto the lifeboat by people he has just finished attacking. This is how the cultural theorist Slavoj Zizek describes the scene, and the importance of viewing position in film analysis:

> Let's take a small detail from *Lifeboat*, from the scene where the group of Allied castaways welcome on board their boat a German sailor from the destroyed submarine: their surprise when they find out that the person saved is an enemy. The traditional way of filming this scene would be to let us hear the screams for help, to show the hands of an unknown person gripping the side of the boat, and then not to show the German sailor, but to move the camera to the shipwrecked survivors: it would then be the perplexed expression on their faces that would indicate to us that they had pulled something unexpected out of the water. What? When the suspense was finally built up, the camera would finally reveal the German sailor. But Hitchcock's procedure is the exact contrary of this: what he does not show, precisely, is the shipwrecked survivors. He shows the German sailor climbing on board and saying, with a friendly smile, '*Danke schön!*' Then he does not show the surprised faces of the survivors; the camera remains on the German. If his apparition provoked a terrifying effect, one can only detect it by his reaction to the survivors' reaction: his smile dies out, his look becomes perplexed.
>
> ZIZEK 1991:144

By showing the German's reaction to the other survivors' reactions, Hitchcock changes things around, as Zizek suggests. Normally, the subjects in such a scene, and the people we (that is, English-speaking audiences) would be expected to identify with, would be the survivors. The German would be the object we gazed at—in fear, hatred and horror. Hitchcock makes the German the subject, however, which works to personalise and humanise him—particularly when we are able to see, as Zizek points out, the very human emotions displayed across his face.

Angles and distances are also important because they have specific cultural meanings which change from one context to another. In an introduction to a program on Australian television which replays American football games, one of the opening shots is of a group of football players shot close up and from waist height. The shot gives you the impression that the players are huge (which they are) and towering threateningly above you. In other words, the idea is to suggest that American football is a frightening and intimidating physical contest.

A second example is a commercial about an insurance company screened a few years ago on Australian television. The company featuring in the commercial wanted to give the impression that it treated policy holders in a courteous, friendly and personalised way. It did this by showing a smiling employee standing side by side with another man making a claim, then offering him a seat and sitting a comfortable distance from the claimant (about two metres, which was politely close but not intrusively so; the claimant still had plenty of personal space). This was juxtaposed with a scene of what other insurance companies supposedly do. The employee remained seated when the claimant entered, but when he (the claimant) sat down the employee stood over him and stuck his face next to and above his head, interrogating him.

The meanings that are associated with angles and distances within a culture are used by photographers and film makers to add to the meanings that can be read into their shots: we have seen examples of this with the football show and the insurance commercial. However, it is important to remember two points about angles, distances and meanings. First, there are always a variety of ways of reading angles and distances. Extreme closeness need not suggest intimacy; it might simply mean that there isn't much space available (for example, a scene in a lift). And second, angles and distances can always be re-contextualised, which can change their meanings.

There is a famous poster of James Dean, shot full length in the foreground, walking alone along a street, while in the background crowds of people are milling around, seemingly inhabiting the same space. One reading of this deployment of space is that Dean is a loner but also somebody different and special who stands out from the everyday, ordinary crowd.

If that shot had been taken from a different angle and distance, however, it could be read differently. A shot from within the crowd (full of happy faces and personalised interactions), for instance, which only picked up Dean as a tiny figure on his own in the background, could produce him negatively, as being excluded from human company and activities. In other words, the meaning of the relation of the two groups (Dean and the crowd) would depend to a large extent on how those two groups, and the distance between them, were positioned by the camera.

VISUAL CONTEXTS AND INTERTEXUALITY

The last point we want to address in this discussion of the supposed objectivity of visual mediums and genres is the issue of context. We have already covered this issue to a large extent in our references to, and examples of, the editing processes that produce final shots. What we need to add here is a reference to the notion of intertext as context.

How does **intertextuality** inform the debate about the objective status of visual mediums? Intertextuality refers, broadly, to the different cultural literacies we bring to any reading of a text. When we watch a film, for instance, we usually make sense of it in terms of other films we have watched. Audiences watching John Carpenter's 1980s remake of *The Thing* could have had at least three intertexts available to them as they watched the film:

- they could have been familiar with previous Carpenter films, and/or
- they could be highly literate in Hollywood science fiction films, and/or
- they could have seen the earlier 1950s version of the film.

Any or all of these intertexts—and lot more we could have mentioned—will predispose us to pick up on some features of scenes from Carpenter's film, and to miss or ignore others. Intertexts provide us with reading patterns and dispositions which we don't have to adhere to, but which do influence our view of 'what is there'.

VISUAL LITERACIES AND PRACTICES

We have been arguing that visual mediums are similar to other communication mediums mainly because the meanings and realities we produce and read into them are connected to, and based upon, different cultural literacies and contexts. Visual mediums are different from other communication mediums, however, mainly because their materiality produces a different kind of relationship between the medium and its audiences.

Different visual mediums constitute a cultural context of their own, a context that has to be taken into account when reading and analysing communication practices involving visual texts. For instance, telephone conversations will become quite different communication practices when the technology for accompanying voice with visuals becomes commonly available.

Similarly, watching a film or television is not the same kind of experience as reading a book. They are different kinds of experiences, not because you have to do more work or be more imaginative reading a book (this is the usual story put out by those who privilege written literacies), but because different mediums require different reading practices and literacies. While reading a book is usually a private experience, watching a film is often a more communal activity: you travel to a theatre, buy a ticket, and sit with a group of people who may be reacting to the film (say, if it is a comedy) in a very audible way. In other words, whereas reading a book is usually a self-contained exercise, watching a film is often done together with other people whose reactions become part of the experience.

Moreover, there is a huge time difference or commitment that differentiates the two activities. Reading a book can take several hours, days or months, while watching a film takes a couple of hours. That is, books and films are characterised by different **economies of pleasure**. This is not to say that one activity is better than the other; what it does mean is that people may take this factor into account when they choose between the two.

It could be argued, for instance, that films deliver a quicker, more intense and 'economical' pleasure fix than, say, conventional novels. After all, in a film you can be kidnapped, fight off a vampire, escape, fall in love, have sex, break up, become rich, save someone's life and expose crooked politicians with Winona Ryder or Jeff Bridges, all within two hours of committed time. The same commitment to *Anna Karenina* might leave you with the impression that all happy families are very similar to each other, while all unhappy families are unhappy in their own way.

If more happens in a shorter time in a film, and if the pleasure fix is more intense, why do people read books? Simply because there are different kinds of pleasure that can't be quantified. As Bourdieu argues, what counts as pleasure, or as legitimate pleasure, depends very much on **habitus**. People who share a particular habitus can spend days reading a book because they are disposed to experience, appreciate and legitimise the pleasures associated with reading. The same people might dismiss the pleasures associated with film watching as superficial, trivial or worthless.

In contemporary western cultures, however, and particularly in youth cultures, visual mediums and genres are becoming increasingly popular at the expense of other mediums. The move to more inter-active visual mediums (such as video games, virtual reality) will only increase this popularity, simply because of the lure of greater access to 'reality', and the greater involvement that interactive systems offer ('don't just read about it or see it: do it').

VISUAL NARRATIVES, IDEOLOGY AND CULTURAL LITERACY

It is important to emphasise that all visual texts, from photographic stills to film shots, constitute, and are usually read as, narratives. That is, the choice and arrangement of objects and the use of space in a visual text are all potentially meaningful, and when those meanings are brought together or integrated (either through reference to a single image or multiple images) we have a narrative.

There are three important points we want to consider here:

* the details of a visual text are usually read in terms of different cultural meanings, even in something as 'meaningless' as an abstract painting, or a succession of apparently random images in a music video
* the narratives of visual texts are just as susceptible to ideologising as those of written texts, and

- visual texts are always read in terms of a particular habitus and cultural literacy.

If materiality has no natural meaning, but is produced as meaningful within cultures, then the same must be true of the material in visual texts—even apparently neutral material such as colours and space. Consider the following passage about the paintings of the American abstract artist Mark Rothko:

> All late Rothko paintings are manifestations of a struggle to save the barrier separating the real from reality, that is, to prevent the real (the central black square) from overflowing the entire field . . . Rothko pictures this struggle as a tension between a gray background and the central black spot that spreads menacingly from one painting to another (in the late 1960s, the vivacity of red and yellow in Rothko's canvases is increasingly replaced by the minimal opposition between black and gray) . . . In the canvases immediately preceding his death, the minimal tension between black and gray changes for the last time into the burning conflict between voracious reds and yellows, witnessing the last desperate attempt at redemption and at the same time confirming unmistakably that the end is imminent.
>
> ZIZEK 1991:190

This is an excellent example of the cultural narrativising of materiality: the colours are read as being involved in a struggle (the blacks and grays, for instance, seem to spend their time menacing or being menaced by each other), and that struggle is made more specifically meaningful if (as Zizek does) we read those colours in terms of certain cultural codes (black equals death or insanity, red equals passion). The deployment, by Rothko, of paint on canvases becomes a story about life and death and hope and despair informed by the intertextuality of Rothko's suicide.

Our second point was that visual texts are just as easily ideologised as written texts. This refers as much to the way visual texts are put together (the paint on the canvas, the decision to cast all the non-whites in a film as criminals, or female business executives as sexually threatening) as it does to the way those details are read by an audience. We defined ideology (in Chapter 8) as the process whereby a particular perspective is naturalised and other possibilities excluded or dismissed. Consider, in this light, another extract from Zizek's analysis of the work and life of Mark Rothko:

If we look at these paintings in a 'cinematic' way, i.e., if we put the reproductions one above the other and then turn them quickly to get the impression of continuous movement, we can almost draw a line to the inevitable end—as if Rothko were driven by some unavoidable fatal necessity . . . Rothko was one day found dead in his New York loft, in a pool of blood, with his wrists cut. He preferred death to being swallowed by the Thing, i.e., precisely by that 'gray and formless mist . . .' (1991:19)

How is this formulation ideological? First, the relationship between the materiality (the colours, the spaces) and what they mean is produced as being beyond contention (black, for instance, *is* the Lacanian **Real**). Second, the narrative Zizek uses to make sense of the deployment of colours (black menacing gray) is transposed onto another, quite familiar narrative, that of the sensitive artist unable to cope with life who chooses, finally, to forestall madness or ugliness by ending it all (van Gogh has a lot to answer for in this regard). This produces Rothko's life (and death) in abstract philosophical terms rather than, say, as being overdetermined by an inability to pay his gas bill, or in terms of suffering induced by terminal acne. Marx's original notion of ideology was based, you will recall, on precisely this distorted privileging of the abstract idea over the reality of material (particularly economic) conditions.

Zizek also introduces a teleological dimension to the paintings, the narrative he uses to make sense of them, and Rothko's life, so that not only is there no possibility of another set of meanings here, but there never was that possibility. By equating the narrative of Rothko's paintings with his life story, Zizek reduces the paintings and their potential meanings to 'an inevitable end—as if Rothko were driven by some unavoidable fatal necessity' (19). This, of course, is simply a case of reading inevitability and necessity after the event. After all, Rothko's death was contingent: he might have killed himself on the spur of the moment when the New York Knicks missed nine consecutive free throws and lost a play-off game in overtime. Contingency is completely ruled out of this account, however, because the meanings and narratives of Rothko's paintings are naturalised and read as a (necessary and inevitable) explanation of his life and death.

Finally, we made the point that any reading of a visual text is closely tied up with the notions of habitus and cultural literacy. People wandering through the New York Metropolitan Museum of Art might

FIGURE 29 'After Rothko'

ILLUSTRATION BY PAT GOON

all be confronted (as Zizek obviously was) by a series of canvases painted by Mark Rothko (or so we presume—we can't really know if Rothko painted all of them, or if his cat added something to one of them when Rothko was asleep). Now Zizek is, among other things, a Lacanian who reads most cultural practices in terms of Lacanian ideas, and writes about them using Lacanian discourse ('reality . . . obtains its consistency . . . by the exclusion of the real, by the change of the status of the real into that of a central lack' (19)). A person from a different background and with a different habitus would not frame those blacks and grays in Lacanian terms; indeed, as Bourdieu points out, groups with less formal education often display considerable hostility towards abstract painting because it is removed from their own idea of what constitutes art, which is, Bourdieu argues (1989), closely tied up with 'realism'. Zizek's ideologising of Rothko's paintings will only appear convincing to an audience which either shares his habitus and cultural literacy or acknowledges that his literacy and cultural capital are superior to their own (this relationship between ideology and cultural capital is addressed in some detail in Pierre Bourdieu's *Distinction*).

VISUAL TEXTS AND SUBJECTIVITY

As we mentioned in Chapters 8 and 9, ideologies are closely connected to, and tend to work through, the notion of subjectivity. And if, as we suggested earlier in this chapter, contemporary western cultures are predominantly visual cultures, then it is reasonable to presume that contemporary western subjectivities are increasingly being produced in and negotiated through visual texts.

In Chapter 9 we referred to three different theories of the production of subjectivity:

* the psychoanalytical theory of subjectivity based on a lack
* the Foucauldian notion of the institutional regulation of subjects based on discipline-based knowledge, and
* the notion, developed by Judith Butler, that subjectivity is based on repeated performances of bodily genres.

We will now analyse the following series of photographs taken from a sunscreen lotion advertisement in order to observe how the connection between ideology and subjectivity is negotiated and produced in visual texts (see Figure 30).

These photographs have written texts that help contextualise them, the most explicit of which reads as follows:

> Smart people don't even think about stepping outside without protection. Lucky Ambre Solaire has got you covered. Whether you're shopping, socialising or working up a sweat at tennis, we've got the product to suit you!

Let's consider these photographs, and this written text, as an ideologised narrative. people who use this sunscreen lotion are 'smart' both in the sense that they are intelligent (they won't get sunburnt), and in the sense that, because they are intelligent, they will (naturally enough) wear attractive clothes and do trendy things (smart here refers to them being fashionable). What we are dealing with here is a very straightforward example of interpellation: the advertisement is suggesting that smartness is connected to the use of sunscreen lotion, and in particular to the use of the advertiser's product. The reader is not so much being given advice about how to become smart—that the readers are smart is already presumed and communicated in the written text through the implied connection between 'Smart people' and 'Whether you're shopping . . . we've got the product to suit you'.

What kind of subjectivity is being called up here, and how is it produced visually? Let's return to our three theories of subjectivity and see how they can be used to analyse these photographs.

In psychoanalytical terms, the notion of subjectivity based on the need to fill in a lack works in all three photographs through what is called the fetishising of objects. The fetish, in psychoanalytical terms, stands in for the lack that defines subjectivity. In the top photograph the fetishised object could be read as the tennis racket (and perhaps the sports clothes that go with it), while in the photograph on the left it might be the baby or the clothes the woman is considering buying (there is a certain truth to the saying 'I shop, therefore I am'). These objects are used to fill up the lack or complete the person because they stand in, metonymically, for generic identities. In other words, the tennis racket, clothes and/or the child function as proof of your (rightful) place in an ideologised narrative of subjectivity: here is a healthy sportswoman, successful, sexually attractive, stylish and vital, and a loving, caring mother who has kept her figure; both narratives produce the woman as attractive and valuable.

If you think this is a little far-fetched, consider the following story: in the late 1980s in France a couple of men robbed a bank in the middle of the city and drove to an outlying suburb, pursued by the police. The robbers quickly dressed in tennis gear, tipped the money into their tennis bags, and walked straight past the cordon of police, who warned them to be careful because there were robbers about! The robbers understood that the possession of tennis gear guaranteed their identity as respectable citizens.

In Foucauldian terms, this advertisement is an excellent example of the regulation of subjectivity through deployment of the (visual) discourses of health and sexuality. The written and visual texts specifically prescribe a regime of activities (shopping, socialising, tennis) which a normal, healthy person would follow. Moreover, that emphasis on a varied, active and healthy lifestyle ties in with the notion of sexual normality. The woman in the photographs obviously exercises and eats well, and as a result she has a classically attractive

FIGURE 30 Visual construction of subjectivity

COURTESY OF AMBRE SOLAIRE

figure. This suggests that she recognises the necessity of producing herself as sexually attractive and desirable (presumably for men or, more specifically, for her husband or partner).

Finally, for Butler subjectivity is culturally inscribed on the materiality of the body through the repeated performance of bodily genres, so that the body literally comes into being (that is to say, comes to mean) by learning to (successfully) perform itself! All three photographs provide examples of this. In the top photograph we recognise a sportswoman because of the way her body is configured: the leg stretched across her body, the left arm extended for balance, head held steady and eyes on the ball. Of course, in practical terms, this is only a performance of tennis, and a bad one at that—try actually hitting a proper tennis shot in this obviously staged position! The point, however, is not that she is a tennis player—she wouldn't want to be, since actually playing tennis would get in the way of the performance of subjectivity. Why? The written text may refer to 'working up a sweat at tennis', but there isn't any sweat evident in this photograph; sweat is messy, unstylish and unfashionable, and would spoil the effect!

Much the same process is at work in the photograph on the right. Here we have a controlled and very deliberate simulation of casual, stylish attractiveness. The sunglasses lowered to connote visual attentiveness, the raised eyes, the half smile, the wine glass held ready, but not so close it gets in the way, the left arm carefully balancing the body: the marvellous integration of these bodily gestures testifies to a successful performance of the 'real' of subjectivity.

The photographs we have referred to here are obviously staged, and do not convincingly pass themselves off as unmediated, objective reproductions of reality. At the same time, this staging (and the ideologising and subjectivising that go with it) is not just characteristic of the genres of visual advertising, but is to be found, to some extent, in all visual texts. To demonstrate this point, we will move from advertisements to an analysis of the supposedly more objective visual genre of news photographs.

VISUAL GENRES: THE NEWSPAPER PHOTOGRAPH

What we want to do now is to examine, in some detail, a news photography genre. We have chosen the medium of photography rather than moving visual mediums for two reasons—convenience of analysis and reproduction. Static pictures are easier to write about because the details that constitute them, and the contexts they are involved in, are easier to identify and reproduce.

There are specific differences and difficulties associated with reading moving visual mediums. However, the kinds of questions we can ask about static visual mediums—what has been included and excluded, how has the subject material been 'edited', what features have been privileged—pertain equally to moving visual mediums.

The photographs we are analysing were published in the same edition of the Central Queensland newspaper the *Morning Bulletin* on Friday, December 16, 1994. The photographs are part of the news genre, but that generic categorisation doesn't get us very far, since there are considerable generic differences within that very broad term. We will therefore pitch our descriptions/analyses at a more specific generic level—at the 'soft' news photography genre.

'Soft' news usually refers to stories that:

• are 'positive'
• are of local rather than international importance
• are not characterised by violence, antagonism or conflict, and
• are meant to act as a balance to more sensationalised, serious and 'negative' stories.

All the articles and photographs we make use of fit neatly into this genre, which is not unexpected considering that the *Morning Bulletin* is a 'local' (rather than state or national) paper, which usually identifies its main function or rationale as being a form of community service. Part of that function would be to provide stories (and photographs) which reflect positively on the community.

Let's look at the four photographs from the *Morning Bulletin*, (see Figures 31–34). We can label them according to their accompanying headlines:

(A) 'Firefighters get funds' (1994:2) (Figure 31)
(B) 'Exchange student off to Germany' (1994:3) (Figure 32)
(C) 'Mobile screening unit near' (1994:4) (Figure 33)
(D) 'Week's leave, 50 years service' (1994:5) (Figure 34)

The first point to make is that every photograph functions as little more than an adjunct to an article. All the pertinent details are in the written text, which means that these photographs are deployed primarily as evidence or support for ('yes, it did happen, here is a picture to prove it), and as a means of personalising ('here are some smiling faces'), the article. These photographs do not make wide demands on our cultural literacy, mainly because there is an expectation that the audience will recognise and share the paper's strong communal values.

FIGURE 31 'Firefighters get funds'

FIGURE 32 'Exchange student off to Germany'

FIGURE 33 'Mobile screening unit'

FIGURE 34 'Week's leave, 50 years service'

We can be more specific. In photograph B, three people are arranged close together, smiling. They are part of the same 'community' (Rotarians) and share a common purpose (the young girl's trip to Germany as an exchange student is supported by Rotary, which values this kind of activity). There is no obvious conflict, ambiguity or unintegrated meaning in this photograph.

Much the same is true of photograph A (again, three people working together, a worthy cause, smiles all round), C (the narrative is almost a perfect copy of A's) and D (which features a couple celebrating their wedding anniversary). With D, we move away from the public sphere (the other photographs involve community work) to the private (a long-married couple still in love), but the reporting of the story gives it a public dimension (it functions as an example of communal values at work).

Why do these photographs seem unambiguous? The answer to a certain extent can be found in the way each photograph has been edited—more specifically, in the way details (the subject matter) within the shot have been arranged. First, notice that all four photographs are carefully 'staged': in each there is a narrative theme represented by a physical object which is placed in the foreground or the centre of the photograph:

- In A, the narrative relates to the generosity of community groups in raising money for the fire brigade. The physical object is the cheque which is located in the middle of the photograph.
- In B, the Rotarians' trip and the values associated with it are represented by the blazer held in the foreground.
- In C, the theme of bringing resources to outlying parts of the community is represented by the breast-cancer screening unit, which is again centrally located.
- In D, the foregrounded photograph of the couple's wedding testifies to, and provides evidence of, their successful 50 year old marriage.

What we wrote previously about these photographs functioning as adjuncts testifying to the reality and humanity of the articles they accompany can be applied to the 'special' objects within the photographs. The written pieces require a 'little piece of the real'—a photograph—to provide them with credibility. However, these photographs are themselves arranged as narratives (handing over the cheque or blazer, delivering resources to the outback, celebrating an anniversary). They give the article credibility, but require another 'piece of the real' (the cheque, the blazer, the equipment, the photograph in the photograph) to 'ground' their own, photographic, narratives.

The mirroring of narratives between articles and photographs requires very close and careful editing—hence the lack of ambiguity or spontaneity in the photographs. In A, the written narrative is about members of a caring community pitching in to help others, and every detail in the photograph works to reinforce this:

• The national flag—an obvious marker of community—is located in the background.
• The three people are situated below the flag, and all are smiling broadly.
• They are grouped quite close together: the two donors are active (holding up the cheque, playing the guitar), while the recipient looks appreciative (or just plain deliriously happy). There are few other details to detract from this careful production of communal cooperation and goodwill.

The tendency to keep the space between subjects to a minium functions as another marker of community:

• In B, for instance, the angle from which the photograph has been taken means that the three figures seem to overlap with one other as they share what looks like a small park bench.
• C is more generous in its deployment of space, but this is largely because the article's focus is on machinery. Consequently, the three subjects couldn't be in each other's pockets without getting in the way of the focal point of the story. Moreover, the subject matter of C is slightly more formal than that of the other narratives (this is a government delivery of a resource, not a community inspired effort), and the subjects have professional status (a politician and two health management professionals). Hence a certain distance (literal and metaphorical) is evident in this photograph.
• The use of space in D is, of course, the most intimate: the couple are touching and take up nearly all the space in the photograph. The reproduction of this private moment projects the intimacy

UNIVERSITY OF
WOLVERHAMPTON
HARRISON LEARNING CENTRE

28/03/03

04:20 pm

Item:Km7 - see!
22826300
Due Date: 02/05/2003 23:59

Item:Communication andcultural literacy :
an introduction
20971362
Due Date: 02/05/2003 23:59

Thank You for using
Self Service Issue

Please return or renew by date quoted
above. (Telephone renewals: 01902

of the couple's personal life into the community as a public spectacle, testifying to the practical, everyday human reality of the community and its values.

Let's recap:

• Reading these photographs does not require a wide cultural literacy.
• There is an expectation that the audience will identify closely and unambivalently with the values that inform the articles.
• The subject matter is predominantly concerned with highly 'positive' representations of the community.
• The photographs are all staged.
• The photographs function as 'pieces of the real' which testify to the truthfulness of the written articles.
• Within those photographs some object is foregrounded as a 'piece of the real' which testifies to the truthfulness of the photographic narrative.
• The photographs tend to erase or minimise the distance between subjects, reinforcing the communal theme of the articles.

Why this commitment to the notion of community? People will be inclined to buy a local newspaper only if they identify, to a certain extent, with the community it promotes. People who think of their identity in terms of a wider sense of community—say at a state or national level—are unlikely to be particularly interested in, or read, the local newspaper.

Most local newspapers can only survive as viable businesses if there is a market for them. In a sense, any local paper needs to promote a notion of local identity and community in order to make a place, if you like, for . . . a community newspaper. This explains why, in the *Morning Bulletin*, articles and photographs are carefully arranged so as to mirror one another, and also explains the need for those 'little bits of the real' of the community to be held up for our inspection. A community comes into being, in a sense, when newspaper articles and photographs 'call it up'; and as we have seen, the soft news genre and its accompanying photographs are ideally suited for this purpose.

232 COMMUNICATION AND CULTURAL LITERACY

SUMMARY

In this chapter we have argued that:

- Conventional notions of literacy have tended to emphasise and value verbal and written, rather than visual, mediums of communication and representation.
- At the same time contemporary western cultures, and the communication practices that characterise them, are making increasing use of visual mediums and genres.
- Visual mediums—such as photography and film—are sometimes privileged over other mediums because they seem to be able to represent reality in an unmediated way.
- Visual mediums, however, selectively reproduce, rather than faithfully mirror, reality.

FURTHER READING

Bourdieu, P. with L. Boltanski, R. Castel, J-C. Chamboredon and D. Schnapper, 1990 *Photography* trans. S. Whiteside, Polity Press, Cambridge
Kress, G. and T. van Leeuwen 1990 *Reading Images* Deakin University Press, Geelong
Silverstone, R. 1994 *Television and Everyday Life* Routledge, London
Turner, G. 1988 *Film as Social Practice*, Routledge London

AFTERWORD

In the General Introduction to his 1988 book *The Practice of Everyday Life*, Michel de Certeau describes his work as

> a continuing investigation of the ways in which users—commonly assumed to be passive and guided by established rules—operate. The point is not so much to discuss this elusive yet fundamental subject as to make such a discussion possible; that is, by means of inquiries and hypotheses, to indicate pathways for further research. This goal will be achieved if everyday practices, 'ways of operating' or doing things, no longer appear as merely the obscure background of social activity, and if a body of theoretical questions, methods, categories and perspectives, by penetrating this obscurity, make it possible to articulate them. (xi)

De Certeau makes two explicit points here:

- People's practices cannot be explained in terms of the overt rules and regulations of a culture. In other words, people do not simply lead passive, consumption-oriented lives.
- While practices cannot be fully explained in terms of cultural rules and regulations, at the same time research needs to be conducted in order to devise ways ('theoretical questions, methods, categories and perspectives') of understanding and describing those practices.

This book has attempted to follow de Certeau's lead by approaching the notion of communication as a practice. At no stage do we suggest that individual communication practices are objectively reducible to any one theoretical explanation or perspective. What we have attempted to do is to describe and work through a variety of different ideas or positions associated with contemporary cultural theory in order to analyse communication as a practice.

It is probably fair to say that this book has introduced and made use of a very wide variety of cultural theories. The reason for this was that no one body of theory struck us as being adequate to the task of satisfactorily addressing or assimilating all the issues we felt we needed to cover. One theorist, the French sociologist Pierre Bourdieu, is represented extensively, but his work, comprehensive and admirable as it is, does not deal in any detailed way with certain concepts (subjectivity, ideology, genre theory) that we felt were important. Moreover, neither Bourdieu's work nor any of the other bodies of theory we have referred to are without their weaknesses—something we have attempted to address through our 'mix and match' approach.

Bourdieu's work has provided us with a particularly important set of theoretical categories—habitus, cultural capital, distinction, dispositions, cultural field—which we have condensed into a general notion of cultural literacy. Literacy, as we understand it, enables us to make sense of how and why certain types of communication practices occur and not others—which in itself is a significant step. But the notion of literacy—at least the version derived from Bourdieu—enables us to go even further and analyse the 'politics' of communication; that is, it helps us understand the relationship between communication practices, on the one hand, and the uses and evaluations made of those practices, on the other.

It is perhaps appropriate to explain our extensive use of popular cultural texts as examples of communication practices, literacies and politics. Analysing Marxist notions of ideology through reference to *Gilligan's Island*, or habitus through *The Flintstones*, might be convenient (after all, these and other popular cultural texts are likely to be familiar to many of the readers of this text), but is it justifiable? In other words, how can we translate from specific cultural products (a television series, films) and the practices they represent to 'real life'? The answer we would put forward is that there is no essential difference between the two. There are, of course, specific generic and material differences between, say, a film about a romance between two people, and a 'real' romance, but the point is that both romances are 'framed' in terms of the same cultural values, rituals, rules and regulations. Indeed, the old saying that 'life imitates art' might be modified to read 'people's practices are often influenced or determined by the literacies they acquire from popular cultural texts'.

Finally, we wish to make the point that this text is itself a cultural product and an example of a communication practice; one which, like all communication practices, is informed by notions such as habitus and cultural politics—a cultural politics which has, we hope, been 'openly and without embarrassment' presented as our 'politics, not someone else's' (Frow 1995:169).

■
NOTES

1   Process school communication theories have incorporated this perspective up to a point by using a model which talked about sender and receiver. However, this was a mechanistic and decontextualised model. Alternatively, structuralist and semiotic theories of language and communication have generally not given emphasis to the social dimension of communication, focusing on what Saussure called *langue* rather than on *parole*.

2   For a fascinating and readable account of what can go wrong with language and thought when the brain is damaged, read Oliver Sacks's book *The Man Who Mistook His Wife for a Hat*.

3   The discipline of pragmatics is an exception to this. It attempts to explain language use, although still within the framework of a mentalist approach, suggesting speakers/writers possess 'pragmatic competence'.

4   There are exceptions to this, notably the work done in sociolinguistics, and more recently discourse analysis, ethnomethodology and pragmatics.

5   Steiner (1992) provides a readable account of the gendering of the journalistic profession over the last century.

GLOSSARY

affect: A term used in the analysis of tenor relations to refer to the attitudes, emotions and values which are produced or expressed as part of the textual interaction. See *tenor*.

agency: The ability to exercise control over social processes and events. Agency is generally regarded as a human attribute, but may be attributed to non-human entities through the operation of discourses. An unqualified belief in individual human agency is part of the doctrine of subjectivism. See *discourse, subjectivism*.

binary: Binary oppositions, or binaries, are pairs of terms whose meaning is produced in opposition to one another. The meaning of one term is produced through what that term is not (its opposing binary term). Binaries are always hierarchical, that is, one term is considered good (or natural, valuable, strong) while the other is considered bad (or artificial, insignificant, weak).

bio-power: A term from Foucault used to describe the process whereby scientific knowledge of the subject is used as a means of categorising, evaluating, disciplining, regulating and reforming the subject.

capital, cultural: A set of resources which have cultural value within a specific cultural field. Like economic capital (wealth, material assets) cultural capital can be distributed and exchanged. What constitutes cultural capital and how it is to be valued are determined within and by specific cultural fields.

citation: The speaker's or writer's introduction of another's speech into a text, either by quoting their words directly ('direct speech') or reporting their meanings (paraphrase, 'indirect speech').

code: A system of signs organised according to a set of rules or conventions. The term can also be used to refer to these organising rules or principles.

commodity, commoditisation: A commodity is anything which is 'packaged' to be bought, sold or otherwise exchanged. Commoditisation is the process of producing an object in terms of its 'exchangeability'. Signs and texts become commoditised when their most socially relevant feature is their exchangeability.

context: A set of circumstances in which communication practices (texts) are produced and read. The particular environments in which communication, texts and meaning making occur, and in which they function as meaningful.

contact: A term used in the analysis of tenor relations to refer to the degree of social distance or level of intimacy constructed as an aspect of the tenor relation between the participants. See *tenor*.

cultural capital see *capital, cultural*

cultural field see *field, cultural*

cultural literacy see *literacy, cultural*

cultural practice see *practice, cultural*

cultural trajectories see *trajectories, cultural*

dialogism, dialogic: The principle that all language, whether spoken or written, indeed all communication, is structured as dialogue. That is, all texts (or utterances, in Bakhtin's terms) function to respond to a prior text and to anticipate a response; they do not mean in isolation from other texts or utterances.

discourse: One meaning of discourse is simply as an alternative term for text, regarded as a social process. The sense in which we generally use the term discourse in this book, however, is as a type of language or way of speaking/meaning associated with a particular institution. Such discourse types are not merely sets of texts but groups of ideas, statements and ways of thinking which express particular institutional values.

dispositions: Dispositions are the tendencies we have to hold certain attitudes and values, and to act in specific ways, because of the influence of 'where we've been' in the culture. See *habitus*.

economies of pleasure: The relationship between the time and energy consumers/readers expend in reading texts as against the pleasure they gain from this. Different mediums (e.g. watching a film or listening to a CD compared to reading a book) provide different economies of pleasure.

field, cultural: A cultural field is both a set of institutions and rules which constitute an objective hierarchy, and the interaction between these institutions and rules, on the one hand, and cultural practices, on the other. Cultural fields produce and authorise specific practices, and attempt to determine what constitutes cultural capital within specific fields, and how that capital is to be distributed. See *capital, cultural*.

field (of discourse): A semiotic dimension of context which concerns the relation between a text and the social action which it is performing or participating in. Analysis of field pays attention to the subject matter of the text and also to the discourse/s involved.

genre: Genres are ways of making sense of texts as particular types. Genres are text types which structure meanings in certain ways, through their association with a particular social purpose and social context. In social semiotic terms, genres can be analysed as culturally defined and expected combinations of field, tenor and mode.

habitus: Can be understood as a 'feel for the game' that is everyday life. More technically, habitus is a set of dispositions gained from our cultural history that stays with us across contexts. See *dispositions*.

hegemony: A dominant group's rule by ideological consent. Hegemony is achieved by an ideological process whereby the dominant group achieves power and control over other groups by representing to them that this state of affairs is in their best interests.

ideology: A practice whereby a particular group within a culture attempt to naturalise their own meanings, or pass them off as universally accepted and as commonsense.

imaginary, the: In psychoanalytic terms, the imaginary is the stage in a child's formation as a social identity when it still identifies closely with the mother.

intentionality: This refers to the concept that the intention of the producer/sender of the message/text is crucial or intrinsic to its meaning. Intentionality is assumed to be essential by various models of communication, particularly process school models, and is very prevalent in 'commonsense' notions of communication. This assumption has been critiqued by semiotics as the 'intentional fallacy'.

interpellation: The hailing or calling up of a person as a particular cultural identity so that the person accepts that identity as given. The term comes from Althusser, who strongly linked interpellation to the workings of cultural institutions. See also *subjectivity*.

intertextuality: The meaning relations which exist between texts, and the process of making sense of texts in reference to their relations with other texts. Intertextuality may involve one text making direct reference to another text, or may refer more generally to the ways in which texts embody meanings that have already been made, in one form or another, in other texts. See also *dialogism*.

literacy, cultural: A knowledge of meaning systems combined with an ability to negotiate those systems within different cultural contexts.

materiality: This refers to the physical (as opposed to purely conceptual) aspect of communication practices. Materiality or material conditions affect or constrain communication practices in three ways: the physical nature of the medium involved and its possibilities and limitations, the participation of bodies in communication, and the material dimension of all social and cultural contexts.

meaning potential: The possibilities for meaning provided by sign systems such as language. Meaning potential is a way of viewing sign systems as constituted by the set of actual options for meaning making (what the speaker can mean). The term comes from Halliday.

medium: A general term referring to the means of communication. Communication media or mediums (we take either form of the plural as acceptable) are generally identified in either physical (oral, aural, visual, spoken, written) or technical categories (print, radio, film, television, compact disc, the Internet, etc.).

mirror stage, the: In psychoanalytic terms, the point at which the child recognises itself as a coherent identity (for example, by seeing its reflection in a mirror) but at the same time realises that it is also separate from itself (it is not its reflection) and separate from everything around it, including the mother.

mode (of discourse): A semiotic dimension of context which concerns the formation of the communication as a text. Analysis of texts and contexts in terms of mode pays attention to the ways in which the code and the medium constrain the meanings which can be made. See *code, medium*.

move: A unit of speech communication which can be equated with the utterance in speech and the sentence in written language. The move is an utterance viewed as a communicative act. Moves perform various speech functions. See *performative, speech function*.

myth see *narrative*

narrative: A way of structuring meanings in the form of a story. Narratives relate a sequence of events, implying a temporal order and often causal relations between events. Narratives work to structure cultural meanings in specific ways, and can come to constitute culturally ratified stories about social experiences (for example, the romance narrative, the capitalist success story, the ANZAC myth). Such widely accepted narratives are also known as *myths*.

Oedipus complex, the: In psychoanalytic terms, the Oedipus complex refers to the child's (necessarily repressed) desire for the mother and hatred of the father as a rival for the mother's affections.

objectivism see *subjectivism*

objectivity: The concept that a stable reality or truth exists independently of the means used to signify or represent that reality or the producer or reader of the representation/text. The notion of objectivity (the 'mirror model' of representation) is often invoked by the media when they claim to be reporting events objectively or providing 'faithful' visual images.

paradigm/syntagm: A paradigm is a set of possible meanings which could be selected in a particular context. A syntagm is the linking of signs together, their combination to form (part of) a text.

paralanguage: The vocal resources available to speakers in addition to spoken words. Paralanguage includes the tone, pitch, pace, rhythm and volume of the voice.

performative: A term from speech act theory used to refer to a class of utterances which function to perform the action they name (e.g. christening, warning, naming, blessing). See *speech function*.

phatic communion: Communication whose primary function is to make and maintain social contact, and which therefore relies mainly on the 'exchange' of already shared meanings or common information.

power: A general term in semiotic and cultural analysis which refers to unequal relations between individuals and groups. Power relations are arguably part of every communicative event or practice, and every social relation, whether or not they are explicitly or overtly at stake. More specifically, the analysis of power in tenor relations refers to the extent to which participants are positioned as equal or unequal. Power can be seen to relate directly to the possession of cultural and economic capital. See *tenor, capital*.

practice, cultural: The activities performed in everyday life and their relationship with cultural rules, conventions and structures. Cultural practice can be considered as the performance of cultural literacy. See *literacy, cultural*.

semiology/semiotics: The 'science of signs' or study of sign systems. Semiotics is used to refer to theoretical approaches to the production of meaning which argue that meaning is produced through the interrelation of signs within a socially produced system.

sign, signifier, signified: In semiotic theory, according to Saussure, the basic unit of meaning is the sign. The sign is composed of the relation between the signifier and the signified. The signifier is the material or physical form of the sign (a sound, visual image or written word). The signified is the mental concept which it invokes.

speech function: A term used to refer to the concept of the function or act performed by an utterance or move. The speech function of a move may be classified broadly as statement, question, offer or command. See *move, performative*.

subjectivism/objectivism: Subjectivism is the theoretical doctrine that human behaviour and the decisions people make at particular moments are largely the result of the individual's exercise of his/her free will. Objectivism describes the opposing position; that is, that what people do (their practice) is basically determined by 'objective' structures such as institutions, laws and systems of relationships.

subjectivity, subject positions: Subjectivity is a concept derived from psychoanalytic theory and used in cultural studies to replace commonsense notions of the self/individual. Subjectivities are the cultural identities produced through discourses and ideologies. These are also referred to as subject positions. See also *interpellation*.

tenor (of discourse): A semiotic dimension of context which concerns the interaction the text is constructing or taking part in. Tenor concerns the relations between participants, and the positions which they are taking up or being assigned. The analysis of tenor involves paying attention to the coding of power relations, social distance, and attitudes, values and emotions. See *power, contact, affect*.

trajectories, cultural: The paths through a culture that a person has taken, which can be understood as a map of that person's cultural history.

unconscious, the: In psychoanalytic terms, the unconscious is the site of repressed desires, desires which the split subject cannot consciously admit and which must therefore be censored (e.g. the child's desire for the mother).

utterance see *move*

BIBLIOGRAPHY

Adams, D. 1980 *The Restaurant at the End of the Universe* Pan Books, London

Adas, M. 1992 *Machines as the Measure of Men* Cornell University Press, Ithaca

Althusser, L. 1977 *Lenin and Philosophy and Other Essays* trans. B. Brewster, New Left Books, London

Appadurai, A., (ed.) 1988 *The Social Life of Things* Cambridge University Press, New York

Austin, J.L. 1962 *How to Do Things With Words* Clarendon Press, Oxford

Australian 1995 March 10, News Limited, Sydney

Australian Magazine 1994 May 28–29, News Limited, Sydney

Bakhtin, M.M. 1981 'Discourse in the novel' in *The Dialogic Imagination* University of Texas Press, Austin, pp. 259–422

——1986 'The problem of speech genres' in *Speech Genres and Other Late Essays* trans. V. W. McGee, ed. C. Emerson and M. Holquist, University of Texas Press, Austin, pp. 60–102

Ballaster, R., M. Beetham, E. Frazer & S. Hebron, 1991 *Women's Worlds: Ideology, Femininity and the Woman's Magazine* Macmillan, London

Barthes, R. 1977 *Image-Music-Text* trans. S. Heath, Fontana, Glasgow

Baudrillard, J. 1975 *The Mirror of Production* trans. M. Poster, Telos Press, St Louis

——1981 *For a Critique of the Political Economy of the Sign* trans. C. Levin, Telos Press, St. Louis

——1983 *Simulations* trans. P. Foss, P. Patton and P. Beitchman, Semiotext(e), New York

——1995 'The Gulf War did not take place', trans. P. Patton, Power Publications, Sydney

Bernstein, B. 1971 *Class, Codes and Control* vol.1, Routledge & Kegan Paul, London

Birch, D. 1991 *The Language of Drama: Critical Theory and Practice* Macmillan, London

Bourdieu, P. 1962 *The Algerians* Beacon Press, Boston

——1986 *Distinction* trans. R. Nice, Routledge, London

——1990a *In Other Words* trans. M. Adamson, Polity Press, Cambridge

——1990b *The Logic of Practice* trans. R. Nice, Polity Press, Cambridge

———1991a *Language and Symbolic Power* ed. and introduced by J. B. Thompson, trans. G. Raymond and M. Adamson, Polity Press, Cambridge

———1991b *Outline of a Theory of Practice* trans. R. Nice, Cambridge University Press, Cambridge

———1993 *The Field of Cultural Production* trans. R. Johnson, Polity Press, Cambridge

Bourdieu, P. with L. Boltanski, R. Castel, J-C. Chamboredon and D. Schnapper 1990 *Photography* trans. S. Whiteside, Polity Press, Cambridge

Bourdieu, P and J-C. Passeron 1990 *Reproduction in Education, Society and Culture* trans. R. Nice, Sage, London

Bowe, Claudia 1992 'The office politics of pregnancy', *New Woman* Murdoch Magazines, Sydney, July, p. 3

Burton, D. 1980 *Dialogue and Discourse: A Sociolinguistic Approach to Modern Drama Dialogue and Naturally Occurring Conversation* Routledge & Kegan Paul, London

Butler, J. 1990 *Gender Trouble* Routledge, New York

———1993 *Bodies that Matter* Routledge, New York

Candlin, C.N. 1987 'Explaining moments of conflict in discourse' in *Language Topics: Essays in Honour of M.A.K. Halliday* vol. 2, ed. R. Steele and T. Threadgold, Benjamins, Amsterdam

Certeau, M. de 1986 *Heterologies* trans. B. Massumi, University of Minnesota Press, Minneapolis

———1988 *The Practice of Everyday Life* trans. S. Rendell, University of California Press, Berkeley

Chomsky, N. 1968 *Language and Mind* Harcourt Brace, New York & London

Coulthard, M. (ed.) 1985 *An Introduction to Discourse Analysis* 2nd edn, Longman, London

Davies, B. and R. Harre 1990 'Positioning: the discursive production of selves', *Journal for the Theory of Social Behaviour* 20:1

Derrida, J. 1988 *Limited Inc* trans. S. Weber and J. Mehlman, Northwestern University Press, Evanston, Ill.

Dolly 1993 September, Australian Consolidated Press, Sydney

Eco, U. 1979 *A Theory of Semiotics* Indiana University Press, Bloomington

Fairclough, N. 1989 *Language and Power* Longman, London

Fairclough, N. 1992 *Discourse and Social Change* Polity Press, Cambridge

Fiske, J. 1990 *Introduction to Communication Studies* 2nd edn, Routledge, London & New York

Foucault, M. 1971 *Madness and Civilisation* trans. R. Howard, Tavistock, London

———1972 *The Archaeology of Knowledge and the Discourse on Language* trans. A.M. Sheridan Smith, Pantheon, New York

———1973 *The Order of Things* Vintage Books, London

———1975 *The Birth of the Clinic* trans. A. Sheridan Smith, Vintage Books, New York

——1977 *Language, Counter-Memory, Practice* ed. and trans. D. F. Bouchard and S. Simon, Cornell University Press, Ithaca, NY

——1980 *The History of Sexuality Volume 1: An Introduction* trans. R. Hurley, Vintage, New York

——1986 *The Use of Pleasure: The History of Sexuality Volume 2* trans. R. Hurley, Vintage Books, New York

——1988 *The Care of the Self: The History of Sexuality Volume 3* trans. R. Hurley, Vintage Books, New York

Fox, Andrew 1994 'Push for jobs', *Morning Bulletin* 29 July 1994, p. 1

Freud, S. 1977 *Case Histories 1* ed. and trans. J Strachey, Penguin, Harmondsworth

——1986a *On Sexuality* ed. and trans. J. Strachey, Penguin, Harmondsworth

——1986b *The Interpretation of Dreams* ed. and trans. J. Strachey, Penguin, Harmondsworth

——1986c *The Origins of Religion* ed. and trans. J. Strachey, Penguin, Harmondsworth

——1987a *Case Histories 2* ed. and trans. J. Strachey, Penguin, Harmondsworth

——1987b *Civilization, Society and Religion* ed. and trans. J. Strachey, Penguin, Harmondsworth

——1987c *On Metapsychology* ed. and trans. J. Strachey, Penguin, Harmondsworth

——1987d *The Psychopathology of Everyday Life* ed. and trans. J. Strachey, Penguin, Harmondsworth

Frow, J. 1988 *Marxism and Literary History* Basil Blackwell, Oxford

——1995 *Cultural Studies and Cultural Value* Clarendon Press, Oxford

Gatens, M. 1991 *Feminism and Philosophy: Perspectives on Difference and Equality* Polity Press, Cambridge

Gilbert, P. and S. Taylor 1991 *Fashioning the Feminine: Girls, Popular Culture and Schooling* Allen & Unwin, Sydney

Goodall, H. 1993 'Constructing a riot: television news and Aborigines', *Media Information Australia* no.68, pp. 70–7

Gramsci, A. 1986 *Selections from Prison Notebooks*, ed. and trans. Q. Hoare and G. Smith, New Left Books, London

Grosz, E. 1989 *Sexual Subversions* Allen & Unwin, Sydney

——1990 *Jacques Lacan: A Feminist Introduction* Allen & Unwin, Sydney

——1994 *Volatile Bodies* Allen & Unwin, Sydney

Halliday, M.A.K. 1978 *Language as Social Semiotic*, Edward Arnold, London

——1984 'Language as code and language as behaviour', *The Semiotics of Culture and Language* vol.1, ed. R.P. Fawcett *et al*, Frances Pinter, London

——1985a *An Introduction to Functional Grammar* Edward Arnold, London

——1985b *Spoken and Written Language* Deakin University Press, Geelong

Halliday, M.A.K. and R. Hasan 1976 *Cohesion in English* Longman, London

——1985 *Language, Context and Text: Aspects of Language in a Social-semiotic Perspective*, Deakin University Press, Geelong

Harker, R., C. Mahar and C. Wilkes 1990 *An Introduction to the Work of Pierre Bourdieu* MacMillan, London

Harris, S. 1984 'Questions as a mode of control in magistrates' courts', *International Journal of the Sociology of Language* 49, pp. 5–27

Hasan, R. 1986 'The ontogenesis of ideology: an interpretation of mother child talk' in *Semiotics Ideology Language* Sydney Studies in Society and Culture no.3, Sydney Association for Studies in Society and Culture, Sydney, pp. 125–46

Hawkes, T. 1977 *Structuralism and Semiotics* Methuen, London

Hodge, R. and G. Kress 1988 *Social Semiotics* Polity Press, Cambridge

hooks, bell 1990 'Feminism: a transformational politic', in *Theoretical Perspectives on Sexual Difference* ed. Deborah L. Rhode, Yale U.P., New Haven

Johnston, E. 1992 'Evonne goes back to the beginning' *Australian Women's Weekly*, July, Australian Consolidated Press, Sydney, pp. 12–13

Kress, G. 1985 *Linguistic Processes in Sociocultural Practice* Deakin University Press, Geelong

——(ed.) 1988a *Communication and Culture: An Introduction* University of New South Wales Press, Kensington

——1988b 'Language as social practice', in Kress (ed.) 1988a, pp. 79–129

Kress, G. and T. van Leeuwen 1990 *Reading Images* Deakin University Press, Geelong

Kress, G. and T. Threadgold 1988 'Toward a social theory of genre', *Southern Review* vol.21, no.3, pp. 215–43

Lacan, J. 1977 *Ecrits: A Selection* trans. A Sheridan, Norton, London

Laclau, E. 1990 *New Reflections on the Revolution of our Time* Verso, London

Laclau, E. and C. Mouffe 1990 *Hegemony and Socialist Strategy* Verso, London

Lefort, C. 1986 *The Political Forms of Modern Society* trans. J. Thompson *et al*, MIT Press, Cambridge, Mass.

Legge, K. 1993 'In the case of Pat O'Shane', *The Australian Magazine* July 31–August 1, News Limited, Sydney pp. 8–12

Lemke, Jay L. 1990 *Talking Science: Language, Learning and Values* Ablex, Norwood N.J.

Martin, J.R. 1985 'Process and text: two aspects of semiosis' in J.D. Benson and W.S. Greaves (eds) *Systemic Perspectives on Discourse* vol.1, Ablex, Norwood, N.J.

——1986 'Grammaticalising ecology: the politics of baby seals and kangaroos' in T. Threadgold *et al* (eds) *Semiotics Ideology Language* Sydney Studies in Society and Culture no.3, Sydney Association for Studies in Society and Culture, Sydney, pp. 225–68

——1992 *English Text: System and Structure* Benjamins, Amsterdam

Marx, K. 1976 *Capital: A Critique of Political Economy,* 1 trans. B. Fowkes, Penguin, Harmondsworth
——1981 *Surveys from Exile* ed. D. Fernbach, Penguin, Harmondsworth
——1984 *Grundrisse* ed. D. Fernbach, Penguin, Harmondsworth
Marx, K. and F. Engels 1988 *The Communist Manifesto* Penguin, Harmondsworth
Mattelart, A. 1991 *Advertising International: The Privatisation of Public Space* trans. Michael Chanan, Routledge, London
——1994 *Mapping World Communication: War, Progress, Culture* trans. S. Emanuel and J. Cohen, University of Minnesota Press, Minneapolis
Mattelart, A. and M. Mattelart 1992 *Rethinking Media Theory: Signposts and New Directions* trans. J. Cohen and M. Urquidi, Media and Society 5, University of Minnesota Press, Minneapolis
McGregor, W. 1991 'Photographs of Aborigines and police', *Social Semiotics,* vol.1, no.2, pp. 123–58
McGuinness, P. 1994 'History of invasion ignores more balanced school of thought', *The Australian* June 15, News Limited, Sydney, p. 15
Melrose, S. 1994 *A Semiotics of the Dramatic Text* Macmillan, London
Morning Bulletin 1994, December 16, Capricornia Newspapers, Rockhampton
Muller, V. 1991 'Packaging the "New Woman": a look at some new women's magazines', *Australian Cultural Studies Conference 1990* ed. D. Chambers and H. Cohen, Faculty of H&SS, UWS Nepean, pp. 79–90
Nietzsche, F. 1956 *The Genealogy of Morals* trans. F. Golffing, Doubleday Anchor, New York
Nightingale, V. 1992 'Contesting domestic territory: watching rugby league on television' in *Stay Tuned: An Australian Broadcasting Reader* ed. A. Moran, Allen & Unwin, Sydney
O'Sullivan, T., J. Hartley, D. Saunders, M. Montgomery, J. Fiske 1994 *Key Concepts in Communication and Cultural Studies* 2nd edn, Routledge, London
O'Toole, M. 1992 'Institutional sculpture and the social semiotic', *Social Semiotics* vol.2, no.1
Pateman, C. 1989 'Feminist critiques of the public/private dichotomy' in *The Disorder of Women* Polity, Cambridge, pp. 118–40
Patton, P. (ed.) 1993 *Nietzsche, Feminism and Political Theory* Allen & Unwin, Sydney
Pattow, D. and W. Wresch 1993 *Communicating Technical Information* Prentice Hall, New Jersey
Pinter, H. 1961 'Last to go' in *A Slight Ache and Other Plays* Methuen, London
Poynton, C. 1985 *Language and Gender: Making the Difference* Deakin University Press, Geelong
——1993 'Grammar, language and the social: post-structuralism and systemic linguistics' *Social Semiotics* 3:1
Pratt, M.L. 1987 'Linguistic utopias' in *The Linguistics of Writing: Arguments*

between Language and Literature ed. N. Fabb, D. Attridge, A. Durant and C. MacCabe, Manchester University Press, Manchester, pp. 48–66

Robbins, M. 1994 'Philosopher's art escapes the duty of reality', *The Australian*, April 22, News Limited, Sydney, p. 6

Sanders, N. 1993 'Azaria Chamberlain and popular culture' in *Nation, Culture, Text: Australian Cultural and Media Studies* ed. G. Turner, Routledge, London

Saussure, F. de 1989 *Course in General Linguistics* trans. R. Harris, Open Court, London

Shea, V. 1995 *Netiquette*, Albion Books

Shnukal, A. 1983 'Blaikman Tok: changing attitudes to Torres Strait creole', *Australian Aboriginal Studies* 2, pp. 25–33

Silverstone, R. 1994 *Television and Everyday Life* Routledge, London

Steiner, L. 1992 'Construction of gender in newsreporting textbooks 1890–1990', *Journalism Monographs* no.135

Tannen, D. 1989 *Talking Voices: Repetition, Dialogue and Imagery in Conversational Discourse* Cambridge University Press, Cambridge

Thibault, P. J. 1988 'Knowing what you're told by the Agony Aunts: language function, gender difference and the structure of knowledge and belief in the personal columns' in D. Birch and L.M. O'Toole (eds) *Functions of Style* Pinter, London

Thompson, J. 1990 *Ideology and Modern Culture* Polity Press, Cambridge

Threadgold, T. 1986 'Semiotics-Ideology-Language', Introduction to *Semiotics Ideology Language* ed. T. Threadgold *et al*, Sydney Studies in Society and Culture no.3, Sydney Association for Studies in Society and Culture, Sydney, pp. 15–60

——1988a 'Language and gender', *Australian Feminist Studies* vol.3, pp. 41–70

——1988b 'Stories of race and gender: an unbounded discourse' in D. Birch and L.M. O'Toole (eds) *The Functions of Style* Frances Pinter, London

——1989 'Talking about genre: ideologies and incompatible discourses', *Cultural Studies* vol.1, no.3, Jan. 1989, pp. 101–27

Thwaites, T., L. Davis and W. Mules 1994 *Tools for Cultural Studies: An Introduction* Macmillan, Melbourne

Todorov, T. 1984 *Mikhail Bakhtin: The Dialogical Principle* trans. W. Godzich, University of Minnesota Press, Minneapolis

Turner, G. 1988 *Film as Social Practice* Routledge, London

——1990 *British Cultural Studies: An Introduction* Unwin Hyman, Sydney

Unreich, R. 1993 'Why he thinks you're desperate', *Dolly*, Australian Consolidated Press, Sydney, September p. 109

van Leeuwen, T. 1986 'The consumer, the producer and the state: analysis of a television news item' in *Semiotics Ideology Language* Sydney Studies in Society and Culture no.3, Sydney Association for Studies in Society and Culture, Sydney, pp. 203–24

——1991 'The sociosemiotics of easy listening music', *Social Semiotics* vol.1, no.1, pp. 67–80

Virilio, P. 1991 *The Lost Dimension* trans. D. Moshenberg, Semiotext(e), New York

Volosinov, V. 1986 *Marxism and the Philosophy of Language* trans. L. Matejka and I. Titunik, Harvard University Press, Cambridge, Mass.

Williams, R. 1983 *Keywords* Fontana, London

——1990 *Television, Technology and Cultural Form* Routledge, London

Windschuttle, K. 1990 *The Media*, 3rd edn, Penguin, Ringwood

Winship, J. 1987 *Inside Women's Magazines* Pandora, London

——1991 'The impossibility of *Best*: enterprise meets domesticity in the practical women's magazines of the 1980s', *Cultural Studies* vol.5, no.2, May, pp. 131–56

Wright, J. 1991 'Gracefulness and strength: sexuality in the Seoul Olympics', *Social Semiotics*, vol.1, no.1, pp. 49–66

Zizek, S. 1991 *Looking Awry* MIT Press, Cambridge, Mass.

——1992 *The Sublime Object of Ideology* Verso, London

——(ed.), 1994 *Mapping Ideology* Verso, New York

INDEX

OTHER TITLES IN THE SERIES

Australian Television
Programs, pleasures and politics
Edited by John Tulloch and Graeme Turner

Australian Television Culture
Tom O'Regan

Dark Side of the Dream
Australian literature and the postcolonial mind
Bob Hodge and Vijay Mishra

Fashioning the Feminine
Girls, popular culture and schooling
Pam Gilbert and Sandra Taylor

Featuring Australia
The cinema of Charles Chauvel
Stuart Cunningham

Framing Culture
Criticism and policy in Australia
Stuart Cunningham

From Nimbin to Mardi Gras
Constructing community arts
Gay Hawkins

From Pop to Punk to Postmodernism
Popular music and Australian culture from the 1960s to the 1990s
Edited by Philip Hayward

High Culture, Popular Culture
The long debate
Peter Goodall

Making it National
Nationalism and Australian popular culture
Graeme Turner

Myths of Oz
Reading Australian popular culture
John Fiske, Bob Hodge, Graeme Turner

National Fictions
Literature, film and the construction of Australian narrative
Graeme Turner

Out West
Perceptions of Sydney's western suburbs
Diane Powell

Public Voices, Private Interests
Australia's media policy
Jennifer Craik, Julie James Bailey and Albert Moran

Racism, Ethnicity and the Media
Edited by Andrew Jakubowicz

Resorting to Tourism
Cultural policies for tourist development in Australia
Jennifer Craik

Stay Tuned
The Australian broadcasting reader
Edited by Albert Moran

Temptations
Sex, selling and the department store
Gail Reekie